INSIGHTS AND ESSAYS ON THE MUSIC PERFORMANCE LIBRARY

Edited by
RUSS GIRSBERGER & LAURIE LAKE

Published by
Meredith Music Publications
a division of G.W. Music, Inc.
4899 Lerch Creek Ct., Galesville, MD 20765
http://www.meredithmusic.com

MEREDITH MUSIC PUBLICATIONS and its stylized double M logo are trademarks of
MEREDITH MUSIC PUBLICATIONS, a division of G.W. Music, Inc.

Reproducing or transmitting in any form or by any means, electronic or mechanical,
including photocopying, recording, or by any informational storage or retrieval system
without permission in writing from the publisher is forbidden.

While every effort has been made to trace copyright holders and obtain permission,
this has not been possible in all cases; any omissions brought to our attention will be
remedied in future editions.

Copyright © 2012 MEREDITH MUSIC PUBLICATIONS
International Copyright Secured • All Rights Reserved
First Edition
June 2012

Cover photo and design: Russ and Shawn Girsberger

International Standard Book Number: 978-1-57463-176-0
Cataloging-in-Publication Data is on file with the Library of Congress.
Library of Congress Control Number: 2012935573
Printed and bound in U.S.A.

CONTENTS

Preface vi

About the Authors vii

Chapter 1 **The Variety of Performance Librarians** 1

Band Librarian
BY SARAH ANDERSON 2

Opera Librarian
BY PAUL J. BECK. 6

Music Festival Librarian
BY ELIZABETH CUSATO 10

Music Publisher Rental Librarian
BY AMY DIANE DICKINSON 13

College and Conservatory Librarian
BY ERIKA KIRSCH 16

How to Run a Choral Library
BY SALLY MILLAR 19

Ballet Music Librarian
BY MATTHEW NAUGHTIN. 23

Jazz at Lincoln Center
BY KAY NIEWOOD AND CHRISTIANNA ENGLISH 32

Does the High School Music Department Need a Librarian?
BY WALTER O'KEEFE. 37

Film and Studio Librarian: Music Preparation for Film Soundtrack Recording Sessions
BY ERIC SWANSON. 40

Chapter 2 **The Librarian and the . . .** 42

. . . Orchestra Conductor
BY JAMES DEPREIST. 43

. . . Wind Band Conductor
BY MICHAEL J. COLBURN. 44

... Composer
    BY ELLEN TAAFFE ZWILICH 47

... Music Dealer
    BY CARLA BOYER 48

... Music Publisher
    BY RACHEL PETERS 52

Chapter 3 **Aspects of the Profession** **56**

So, You Think You Might Want to Be an Orchestra Librarian?
    BY LAWRENCE TARLOW 57

Auditioning and Interviewing for the Performance Librarian
    BY SARA GRIFFIN 61

Teach Our Own
    BY PAUL GUNTHER 65

The Librarian as Mentor — Hand to Hand
    BY ELENA LENCE TALLEY 69

Communication: Say What?!
    BY MARCIA FARABEE 72

Strength-Based Organization, Communication Pattern and Work Values
    BY KAZUE MCGREGOR 76

The "One Man" Show
    BY PATRICK MCGINN 81

Beyond the Library
    BY KAREN SCHNACKENBERG 84

Chapter 4 **The Nuts and Bolts** **87**

Advance Planning
    BY ROBERT SUTHERLAND 88

Where are Those Orchestra Parts?
    BY CLINTON F. NIEWEG AND JENNIFER A. JOHNSON 95

Choosing Editions
    BY RONALD WHITAKER 103

Proofreading
    BY BILL HOLAB 107

Orchestral "Pops" Music: Take Nothing For Granted
    BY ELLA M. FREDRICKSON 113

Music Information Centres
    BY JARI ESKOLA 118

Small Rights, and Print, Mechanical, and Synchronization Licensing
    BY JANE CROSS 120

Grand Rights
    BY ROBERT SUTHERLAND 129

Important Features to Look for in a Performance Library Copier
    BY COURTNEY SECOY COHEN 131

Using a Database
    BY MICHAEL K. RUNYAN 133

Chapter 5 **Additional Responsibilities** **139**

Working With a Composer: The Process of Music Editing
    BY CHARLIE HARMON 140

Orchestra Tours
    BY JOHN G. VAN WINKLE 144

Preservation in the Performance Library
    BY D. MICHAEL RESSLER 150

Using Technology and Community Partnerships to Archive Your Orchestral Collection
    BY ROBERT OLIVIA 154

Input on Your Output: Thoughts from a Professional Music Copyist
    BY DOUGLAS RICHARD 161

The Art of the *Retouche* (Does Beethoven know what we're doing?)
    BY MARSHALL BURLINGAME 166

Index 187

PREFACE

This is the book that I always wanted to read when I first became a performance librarian. I wanted a book that would tell me how to do this unusual job more efficiently and more professionally. I wanted the secrets from the pros, the people at the top of their fields, and now I finally have it.

These are original essays, commissioned for this publication, many on topics that are being addressed in print for the first time. They provide an insight to this career that comes only with years of training and experience.

The response to this project from our contributors and colleagues was overwhelming. Laurie and I have been humbled by the willingness of these busy people to share their time and vast knowledge. Thank you all for your generosity.

Thanks also to our publisher and friend, Garwood Whaley of Meredith Music Publications, for supporting this project and making it available in print. The royalties from this book will go directly to the Major Orchestra Librarians' Association (MOLA) to increase the opportunities for further education and outreach in this field.

We hope you will enjoy this book and benefit from it as we have.

Russ Girsberger
Virginia Beach, Virginia

Laurie Lake
Cleveland, Ohio

ABOUT THE AUTHORS

Sarah Anderson toured for six years with the Soldiers' Chorus of The United States Army Field Band, giving free public concerts in forty-nine states. She served as the chorus librarian and later the assistant unit librarian while performing with the ensemble, before becoming the full-time librarian in 2003. Prior to joining the Field Band, she performed with the Lutheran Choir of Chicago and the University Singers of The George Washington University, as well as GW's vocal jazz ensemble, the Troubadours. Sergeant First Class Anderson earned a BA degree at The George Washington University and received her Master of Library Science from the University of Maryland-College Park.

Paul J. Beck is Principal Orchestra Librarian of The Juilliard School and Principal Librarian for the Mostly Mozart Festival at Lincoln Center in New York City. He is active in New York City as an orchestral librarian and music preparation professional, having current and past affiliations with the Metropolitan Opera, New York Philharmonic, The Juilliard School, Aspen Music Festival and School, Brooklyn Philharmonic, and the YouTube Symphony. Well-versed in opera music preparation, Paul is also the concert librarian for Renee Fleming. Mr. Beck is a 1998 graduate of the Manhattan School of Music.

Carla Boyer graduated with bachelor's degrees in music and Spanish and a master's degree in Spanish from the University of Arkansas, Fayetteville. She also began studies toward a second master's degree in library science. She taught stringed instruments in the Springdale, Arkansas public school for three years and Little Rock, Arkansas public schools for six years, also playing in the cello section of the Arkansas Symphony for six years. She worked as Assistant Librarian with the Saint Louis Symphony with John Tafoya for three years. She began working at Educational Music Service in 1981 where she serves as Sales Manager.

Marshall Burlingame is the Principal Librarian of the Boston Symphony. He graduated from the Eastman School of Music as a double major in Clarinet and Music History, receiving the Performer's Certificate in Clarinet. Following service in the U.S. Air Force Concert Band, in Washington D.C., he became a Reference Librarian at the Library of Congress Music Division. He entered the orchestra library field as Principal Librarian of the Cincinnati Symphony, leaving after twelve seasons, to initiate OLIS, the Orchestra Library Information Service, (a component of the current OPAS database), for the League of American Orchestras on a three-year grant from the National Endowment for the Arts. Mr. Burlingame supervises the three libraries at Tanglewood, mentors the Tanglewood Music Center's Library Fellow, and gives seminars for the Composer and Conductor Fellows.

Courtney Secoy Cohen is the Principal Librarian for the San Diego Symphony and the San Diego Opera. She previously worked as the Assistant Librarian for the Kansas City Symphony and the Florida West Coast Symphony (now the Sarasota Orchestra). Prior to these positions, she served as the Performance Librarian for the Boston Conservatory. She is active in the Major Orchestra Librarians' Association (MOLA), serving as the Managing Editor of *Marcato*, working on the Errata Committee, writing the "Transitions" article for *Marcato*, and acting as the Pops Resources Database Coordinator. She also maintains her music engraving and copyist business, Piperlass Music Engraving.

Michael J. Colburn, a native of St. Albans, Vermont, earned a bachelor's degree in euphonium performance at Arizona State University and a master's degree in conducting from George Mason University. In 1987, Colburn won a position playing euphonium with "The President's Own" United States Marine Band, and was designated principal euphonium in 1991. In 1996 he was appointed Assistant Director, and since 2004 he has served as the 27th Director of the U.S. Marine Band. Colburn is an active guest conductor and clinician. He has twice led the All-New England Festival Band, the All-Eastern Band, and in December 2009 he served as the "Arnold D. Gabriel Resident Wind Conductor" on the campus of Ithaca University. Colburn serves as music director of Washington, D.C.'s prestigious Gridiron Club, a position first held by John Philip Sousa, and is a member of the Alfalfa Club, the American Bandmaster's Association, and is a board member of the Sousa Foundation.

Jane Cross joined "The President's Own" United States Marine Band in May 1997 and was appointed Chief Librarian in 2008. She earned her bachelor's degrees in music (clarinet) and English (technical writing) from the University of Tennessee at Chattanooga in 1997. In 2003, she earned a master's degree in library science from the University of Maryland at College Park. Prior to joining "The President's Own," Master Sergeant Cross was a Senior Airman with the 572nd Air National Guard Band in Knoxville, Tennessee. She has been active in serving both the Major Orchestra Librarians' Association (MOLA) and the Music Library Association (MLA), and has presented sessions on copyright at their annual conferences. Outside of work, she is a slow triathlete and an avid gardener.

Elizabeth Cusato is the Associate Librarian at The National Symphony and has been Orchestra Librarian for The Glimmerglass Festival since 2004. Prior to moving to Washington, D.C., Elizabeth was Associate Principal Librarian at the Utah Symphony and Utah Opera, and Interim Associate Principal Librarian at the Detroit Symphony Orchestra. In her spare time, Elizabeth enjoys knitting, cooking, and running.

James DePreist, widely esteemed as one of America's finest conductors, is Director Emeritus of Conducting and Orchestral Studies at The Juilliard School and Laureate Music Director of the Oregon Symphony. He served as Permanent Conductor of the

Tokyo Metropolitan Symphony Orchestra from 2005 until 2008. As a guest conductor he has appeared with every major North American orchestra and has also conducted widely with international orchestras. Maestro DePreist has appeared at the Aspen Music Festival, with the Boston Symphony at Tanglewood, the Philadelphia Orchestra at the Mann Music Center, and the Juilliard orchestras at Lincoln Center and Carnegie Hall. He has been awarded fourteen honorary doctorates and is the author of two books of poetry. Among his many awards is the National Medal of Arts, the nation's highest honor for artistic excellence, awarded in 2005.

Amy D. Dickinson is the Head of Rental Services for Schott Music Corporation and European American Music Distributors LLC. She has degrees in both music performance and business administration and currently resides in New York City with her two cats.

Christianna English is an Associate of Music Administration at Jazz at Lincoln Center in New York City. She holds graduate degrees in library and information science from the University of North Texas, and in clarinet performance from Oklahoma City University. She is a member of the Major Orchestra Librarians' Association (MOLA).

Jari Eskola, a former principal librarian of the Royal Stockholm Philharmonic (2007–2010), the Gothenburg Symphony (2001–2007), the Helsinki Philharmonic (1999–2000) and the Tapiola Sinfonietta (1998–1999), currently works as manager of services and development at the Finnish Music Information Center (Fimic) in his native Helsinki. He is a musicologist and saxophonist, an arranger and orchestrator, and an editor and copyist in demand by the leading publishers and ensembles. Eskola is an honorary member of the Major Orchestra Librarians' Association (MOLA), a recognition to his active service for the organization.

Marcia Farabee, Principal Librarian of the National Symphony Orchestra, is a graduate of the Capital University Conservatory of Music with a BM in violin performance and music education. Prior to her work with the National Symphony Orchestra, she taught strings for the Fairfax County Public School System (VA), toured with the National Ballet, and performed with the Richmond Symphony, the NSO, the Kennedy Center Opera House Orchestra, the Filene Center Orchestra (Wolf Trap), and the National Theater. Marcia began her work with the NSO Library in the fall of 1983. She is active in the Major Orchestra Librarians' Association (MOLA), having served as President three times, as well as chairing a number of committees. She is particularly interested in education and publisher relations.

Ella M. Fredrickson is Principal Librarian for The Florida Orchestra. Ms. Fredrickson is an active advocate for new music and has served as music librarian for the Cabrillo Festival of Contemporary Music in Santa Cruz, California since 2002. She is an alumna of the University of Miami School of Music (Coral Gables, Florida) and has a keen interest in electronic music and performing theremin and violoncello. She is a free-lance music copyist and editor and is the personal librarian for conductor Marin Alsop, music director of the Baltimore Symphony Orchestra. Ms. Fredrickson also acts as the fellowship coordinator of the Taki Concordia Conducting Fellowship, a non-profit organization whose mission is to promote, present, and encourage talented women conductors at the beginning of their professional careers.

Russ Girsberger is the Librarian at the School of Music for the United States Navy and Marine Corps in Virginia Beach, Virginia. He has worked as a performance librarian with The Juilliard School, the New England Conservatory, the Boston Symphony and Boston Pops, the New York Philharmonic, and the United States Marine Band. Girsberger holds degrees in music education, music history, and library and information science. He is the author of A *Manual for the Performance Library*, *Percussion Assignments for Band & Wind Ensemble*, and A *Practical Guide to Percussion Terminology*.

Sara Griffin holds a bachelor of music and a doctorate of musical arts degree from the University of Missouri-Kansas City Conservatory of Music and a master of music degree from the University of Illinois at Urbana-Champaign; all in oboe performance. Ms. Griffin began her career as a performance librarian with the Kansas City Symphony in 2004 and in 2006 became the Associate Librarian of the National Symphony Orchestra in Washington, D.C. In 2009, she became a member of the New York Philharmonic as Assistant Principal Librarian and currently resides in Manhattan.

Paul Gunther is Principal Librarian of the Minnesota Orchestra. He trained as a percussionist and has played in the U.S. Army Band, the Milwaukee Symphony, and the Minnesota Orchestra. As a longtime member of the American Federation of Musicians, he is an active union musician, serving on the Governing Board of ICSOM, the International Conference of Symphony and Opera Musicians. He is a pescatarian chocoholic Scorpio who enjoys exercise, TV dramas, and exercising while watching TV dramas. He is a Past President of the Major Orchestra Librarians' Association (MOLA).

Charlie Harmon is a freelance editor, working with Christopher Rouse, John Adams, Lorin Maazel, and Stephen Sondheim, among others. As an editor, Mr. Harmon corresponded directly and extensively with these composers, with orchestra librarians, publishers, conductors, and performers. Mr. Harmon was music editor for the Estate of Leonard Bernstein, having worked with Bernstein as his personal assistant from 1982 through 1985. Some of the works Mr. Harmon was responsible for include the first publication of the full scores of *West Side Story*, *Candide*, and *Mass*, and the first complete piano vocal scores for *On the Town* and *Wonderful Town*. Mr. Harmon holds a degree in music composition from Carnegie-Mellon University, where he studied with Nikolai Lopatnikoff, Roland Leich, and Leonardo Balada.

Bill Holab is the owner of Bill Holab Music, a firm that provides essential services to composers and publishers including high-end typesetting, design, music engraving, and publishing representation. Holab has served as Director of Publications for G. Schirmer/Associated Music Publishers, Director of Production for Universal Edition, Editor for C.F. Peters Corporation, and Director of Publishing for Schott Music Corporation. As a consultant, Holab has worked with Avid (Sibelius), MakeMusic (Finale), San Andreas Press (Score) and wrote the technical documentation for Score. He is a composer and studied at the University of Michigan and The Juilliard School.

Jennifer A. Johnson is a music librarian at the Metropolitan Opera. Before arriving in New York, she was assistant librarian with the Houston Symphony and staff librarian with the Philadelphia Orchestra. Her writings have appeared in *Notes*, the quarterly journal of the Music Library Association, *Journal of the Conductors Guild*, Polyphonic.org, and various publications of the Major Orchestra Librarians' Association (MOLA). She trained as a trombonist at the Peabody Conservatory and also earned a bachelor's degree with honors in political science and philosophy from Bryn Mawr College.

Erika Kirsch is a senior specialized cataloguing editor and acquisitions assistant for the Schulich School of Music at McGill University in Montreal, Quebec, Canada. Originally a bassoonist, she began working in ensemble libraries while studying at the Eastman School of Music, later working at the American Symphony Orchestra (New York City), Houston Grand Opera, Aspen Music Festival, and Sewanee Summer Music Festival. She is currently studying for a master's degree in library and information science at McGill University.

Laurie Lake holds a BM in music performance from Northwestern University and an MLS from Indiana University. She served as Associate Principal Flute in the Honolulu Symphony for ten years where she was also the orchestra's librarian. She has managed the libraries for the Aspen Music Festival and School for six summers, as well as run the ensemble libraries at Indiana University and the Interlochen Center for the Arts. Ms Lake served the Major Orchestra Librarians' Association (MOLA) as their first president from an educational institution. She is currently active in the Music Library Association and works as the Reference and Electronic Resources Librarian at the Cleveland Institute of Music's Robinson Music Library.

Patrick McGinn has been a professional librarian since 1980 and currently serves as the Principal Librarian of the Milwaukee Symphony Orchestra, a position he has held since 1986. Prior to this he was the Assistant Librarian of the Milwaukee Symphony Orchestra under the guidance of Paul Gunther. Patrick has been active in the Major Orchestra Librarians' Association (MOLA) for many years serving in a number of positions including president, vice-president, past-president, secretary, and administrator. Patrick graduated with a bachelor of music degree in percussion performance from the University of Michigan in 1979 where he studied with Charles Owen. Additional percussion instructors included Vic Firth and Frank Epstein of the Boston Symphony, Barry Jekowsky of the San Francisco Symphony, and Norman Fickett of the Detroit Symphony. When time allows Patrick performs with the Milwaukee Symphony as their principal extra percussionist.

Kazue Asawa McGregor is a librarian with the Los Angeles Philharmonic. During her twenty-seven year tenure, she has collaborated closely with conductors and artists, performed frequently as a musician in the Philharmonic, and worked as a consultant in the designing of performance libraries. Other pursuits include certificate work in college and career guidance counseling, volunteer service on school boards and committees, and spending time with her family. She is a Past President of the Major Orchestra Librarians' Association.

Sally Millar is the Administrative Assistant for Choruses at the New England Conservatory, a job title that also includes manager and librarian duties. She has worked as NEC Chorus Librarian for eighteen years and sung in choruses for over forty-five years (and still loves it). A native of the Boston area, she has an undergraduate degree in art history. She loves to bake, read, admire her cats, and make Ukrainian Easter eggs.

Matthew Naughtin is a composer, violinist, violist, program annotator, and music librarian who started writing music at the same time he began violin lessons at age 11. He left Omaha for Northwestern University in Evanston, Illinois where he studied violin performance, theory, and composition and was awarded a bachelor's degree in music performance in 1970. He taught and performed in the Chicago area for several years before returning to Omaha to play in the Omaha Symphony Orchestra from 1977–1997 and serve as the Symphony's Music Librarian, Program Annotator, Resident Composer, and Musical Arranger. Matt's original orchestral compositions and arrangements have gained wide recognition and are played all across America on Christmas, Pops, Youth and Family concerts, and his music written especially for children has been used extensively on family concerts and concerts for grade school and preschool children. He was appointed Music Librarian of the San Francisco Ballet in 1997 and now lives and works in San Francisco.

Clinton F. Nieweg, retired Principal Librarian of The Philadelphia Orchestra, is the owner/manager of ~Proof Purr-fect Research~ for conductors, librarians, and players. He is co-founder and Past President of the Major Orchestra Librarians' Association (MOLA), and has founded a Yahoo! Group—OLI (Orchestra Library Information). Eighty corrected editions have been prepared under his direction in the *Nieweg Performance Editions* series, which are published by Edwin F. Kalmus & Co., LC. In 2009 Nieweg was the first performance librarian to be a recipient of the Conductors Guild Award for Distinguished Service in recognition of his long-standing service to the Art and Profession of Conducting.

Kay Niewood is the Assistant Director of Music Administration at Jazz at Lincoln Center in New York, New York. She holds a master of music degree in jazz studies, jazz arranging and composition from William Paterson University and a bachelor of music in music education from the University of Minnesota. She has taught K-12 vocal and general music, and served as adjunct faculty at the college level. She is a member of the Major Orchestra Librarians' Association (MOLA).

Walter "Randy" O'Keefe holds a BA in music education from Ohio University and an MM in trumpet performance from the University of Notre Dame. He has been the Music Department Head and Director of Bands for the Masconomet Regional School District in Topsfield, Massachusetts, since 1990. In addition to his teaching and conducting responsibilities at Masconomet, Randy also finds time to conduct the Northshore Youth Symphony as well as perform with several regional orchestras in the greater Boston area.

Robert Olivia is the Associate Principal Orchestra Librarian of the Seattle Symphony Orchestra. Previously he served as librarian for the Oregon, Naples, Detroit, New York Philharmonic, and Boston Symphony orchestras. In addition to his symphonic work, Olivia has worked in Hollywood on more than one hundred motion pictures, television shows, and popular artist recording sessions. As an arranger Olivia has written for many artists including Doc Severinsen, Frederica von Stade, Samuel Ramey, and Marvin Hamlisch. He has also collaborated with publishers on several critical editions including Universal Edition on their new printing of Schubert/Webern *Deutsche Tänze* and with Janen Music for the restoration of Henry Mancini arrangements. In 2006, Olivia was chosen as a "mentor and supervisor" as part of the University of Washington Information School Directed Fieldwork Program and is very involved with the UW library school.

Rachel Peters has worked at Boosey and Hawkes since 2005 and has managed the Rental Library from 2007–2012. Former library work includes an apprenticeship with City Center Encores! and the New School of Music, where she was also on the musical theatre faculty. Rachel holds a double BA *summa cum laude* from Brandeis University and an MFA from New York University's Tisch School of the Arts. Her work as a music theatre composer is regularly seen Off-Off Broadway, in cabarets and with small opera companies throughout New York City. She is a member of ASCAP and the Dramatists Guild.

D. Michael Ressler has worked as a music librarian for a number of performing ensembles for over thirty years and is a former member of the Major Orchestra Librarians' Association. He has managed a large collection of historic materials for "The President's Own" United States Marine Band in Washington, D.C., and currently serves as the band's historian.

Douglas A. Richard is currently the music arranger for the United States Military Academy Band. He is also a professional music copyist whose clients include major American composers, arrangers, and conductors. He has presented numerous clinics on the values of working with a professional music copyist as well as how to improve the quality of the finished product when using computer software for notation.

Michael Runyan received a BM in music composition from Brigham Young University and a MM and DMA in music composition from the University of Cincinnati College Conservatory of Music. He has worked as a music copyist (pen-and-ink, then computer) since the mid-1970s, and as a teacher and performer. Since 1986, Runyan has been Principal Librarian of the Indianapolis Symphony, where on an Apple II computer he programmed his first database.

Karen Schnackenberg is Principal Librarian of the Dallas Symphony Orchestra. She was previously orchestra librarian and violinist with the New Orleans Symphony, Santa Fe Opera, Oklahoma Symphony, and Chamber Orchestra of Oklahoma City. A two-time Past President of the Major Orchestra Librarians' Association (MOLA), Karen is active throughout the field as a writer, speaker, mentor, and consultant. She is a contributing writer on the orchestral musician website Polyphonic.org and has her own blog "From the Orchestra Library." From 1987–1999 Karen was classical music columnist for the International Musician, the industry's trade paper for professional musicians. She is Vice President of the Dallas/Fort Worth local executive board of the American Federation of Musicians and is a freelance violinist in the DFW metropolitan area.

Robert Sutherland currently holds the position of Chief Librarian at the Metropolitan Opera. He began his career as Assistant, later Principal, Librarian of the National Arts Centre Orchestra in Ottawa, Ontario. After three seasons with the NACO he moved to the Canadian Opera Company as Principal Trumpet, swearing never to do library work again. He was wrong. At the Canadian Opera Company during a problematic production of Don Carlo he was overheard muttering, "I can do better than this." He was taken at his word and after serving as Principal Librarian for seventeen years, joined the Metropolitan Opera where he is in his eighteenth season. In addition to his library work, Mr. Sutherland has been active as a music editor, copyist and engraver, managed the Brassworks Music rental library, co-founded the Hannaford Street Silver Band (Toronto), and has served three terms as President of the Major Orchestra Librarians' Association (MOLA). His re-orchestrations of four of Berlioz's *Nuits d'été* for mezzo-soprano are published by Edwin F. Kalmus.

Eric Swanson attended the University of Miami, where he studied jazz bass and recording technology. He transferred to Fairleigh Dickinson University in New Jersey where he studied philosophy. After graduating, Eric worked for five years at the Boosey & Hawkes Rental Library in New York City. He also worked as a music librarian at the Aspen Music Festival in the summer of 2004. Currently he works at JoAnn Kane Music Service in Culver City, California, a company that provides music copying, printing, and audio transcription for film, television, recording artists, and concert tours.

Elena Lence Talley has been Principal Music Librarian of the Kansas City Symphony since 1992. She is also an active member of the Major Orchestra Librarians' Association (MOLA), serving on the policy committee and as President in 2011–12. She was a panelist at MOLA conferences in Washington, D.C. and Omaha. Talley is also active as a clarinetist, performing throughout the Midwest with the Lyric Arts Trio. She was Membership Coordinator of the International Clarinet Association for ten years, and has had numerous articles published in *The Clarinet* journal.

Lawrence Tarlow has been Principal Librarian of the New York Philharmonic since August, 1985. Before joining the Philharmonic, he had been librarian for the Atlanta and Oklahoma Symphony Orchestras. He also was librarian of the Berkshire (now Tanglewood) Music Center Orchestra and worked in the orchestra department of the music publishers C.F. Peters Corporation and G. Schirmer, Inc. His library career began when he took charge of distributing the music at rehearsals of his high school band and orchestra. A tuba player, Mr. Tarlow attended The Juilliard School and graduated from the Curtis Institute of Music. Lawrence Tarlow is an active member and former three-term President of the Major Orchestra Librarians' Association (MOLA).

Ronald Whitaker was the head librarian of The Cleveland Orchestra from 1975 until his retirement in 2008. He was assistant librarian for the Minnesota Orchestra for three years prior to his appointment in Cleveland. He is a Past President of the Major Orchestra Librarians' Association (MOLA).

In September of 2011, **John G. Van Winkle** retired as the Principal Librarian of the San Francisco Symphony. He joined the SF Symphony in the 1970–71 season as Librarian after earning his Masters in Music Performance (bassoon) from San Francisco State University. He has toured with the orchestra throughout the United States, Europe and Asia. John is one of the original members of the Major Orchestra Librarians' Association (MOLA), has served on several committees, and is active in their mentoring activities. John is also an avid photographer of Yosemite, Mono Lake, and the Pacific Coast, as well as Symphony tour destinations. His photographs are in private collections on at least three continents.

Ellen Taaffe Zwilich is the recipient of numerous composition prizes and honors, including the 1983 Pulitzer Prize in Music (for her Symphony No. 1), a Guggenheim Fellowship, and four Grammy nominations. She has been elected to the American

Academy of Arts and Sciences and the American Academy of Arts and Letters and was named to the first Composer's Chair in the history of Carnegie Hall. Ms. Zwilich, who holds a doctorate from The Juilliard School, has received honorary doctorates from Oberlin College, Manhattanville College, Marymount Manhattan College, Mannes College/The New School, Converse College, and Michigan State University. She currently holds the Francis Eppes Distinguished Professorship at Florida State University.

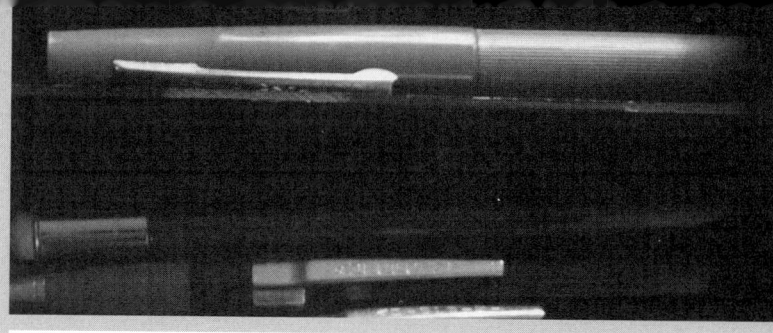

CHAPTER 1

The Variety of Performance Librarians

Band Librarian

by Sarah Anderson

Personal background and work experience

Although many music librarians come to the position via performing, my career included several additional layers of being in the right place at the right time. Despite years of violin and viola lessons, I wasn't dedicated enough to play professionally, and I knew enough about myself not to go into teaching. Since I assumed those were the only two jobs in music, I went to college intending to become a radio producer. Job-hunting with the impressive-sounding "special interdisciplinary degree in audial arts," but with my only hands-on experience on outdated equipment, I half-heartedly went to cattle calls for opera choruses and eventually ended up at an Army recruiting office looking at jobs in telecommunications. While I was working through the enlistment process, The U.S. Army Field Band and Soldiers' Chorus came to my hometown on tour, and there were chorus vacancies listed in the program. I auditioned the following month, and went to basic training two months later. Once at the band, I tended to spend my free time in the library because that's where the Mac computer users were. I became the assistant chorus librarian, then the chorus librarian, then the assistant librarian, all while performing. When the full-time librarian retired and her position was opened to internal auditions, I was the only candidate who, when asked to distribute a march to the concert band, asked, "Which edition?" Thus, I became the librarian.

My role and duties

Like any performance library, the Field Band library is an information hub for the organization, collecting, synthesizing, and distributing information to and from various levels inside and outside the band. Its ultimate goal is the same, as well: to get the right music in the right place at the right time. It's similar to a conservatory library in that it serves a variety of ensembles: a sixty-five-piece concert band, a mixed chorus, a jazz big band, a rock band, fourteen small ensembles, and ad hoc ensembles for a chamber series. We have the luxury of three staff arrangers, so a significant amount of time is spent securing licensing clearances for new arrangements and assembling the resulting scores and sets of parts. In the first hour of work today, I explained to a conductor why the requested new arrangement will not be available for rehearsal next week, advised a chorus member on what to prepare for a conducting audition, and talked with an intellectual property attorney about whether auditions via YouTube would be legal.

A typical day in the library

A year in the life of the Army Field Band generally revolves around three tours: five to six weeks each in the spring and fall, and two to three weeks around the Fourth of

July. Concentrating on tour areas defined by the Department of Defense, we cover the continental United States every two and a half years. The Concert Band and Soldiers' Chorus travel together, rotating through four complete shows and carrying additional music for use with video, guest conductors, student players, and "just in case." The Jazz Ambassadors big band also tours with at least four complete concerts of music, while the rock band, The Volunteers, is more fluid in their programming, changing the set at any moment based on the audience, the hall, the day's *Billboard* charts, or their general mood. Including tours, local concerts, recitals, and clinics, the band logs about 600 commitments a year, more than all four teams of Budweiser Clydesdales combined.

Any arts organization experiences a more or less cyclic workload for performers and support staff alike leading up to, during, and following a performance, and looking ahead to the next one. The Field Band's unique touring mission means we experience the same cycles on a grander scale, with periods of mounting activity leading up to each tour, culminating at load-out and followed by periods of relative calm for those few left behind. In the library, this leads to multiple to-do lists: before the band leaves, while the band is gone, when the band gets back, etc.

A few months prior to each tour, we receive proposed set lists for the four programs, distribute scores and parts to conductors and players, and coordinate with the production staff to supply information for the printed programs. Following that is a few weeks of normal rehearsal, perhaps interrupted by a performance with a guest conductor, a runout concert, or a recording session. In the last days before a major tour, we collect the podium scores for each piece and transfer each conductor's markings into his study score. When the band loads out, the individual players are responsible for putting their folders into the trunks, and the library liaison packs the four score cases. Members of the chorus hand-carry any music that is not memorized and the director of the jazz band hand-carries his scores as well. The librarians do not tour with the ensembles, but each ensemble has at least one library liaison to deal with emergencies on the road.

During tours, those remaining behind revert to their "while the band is gone" to-do lists, which for the library generally means licensing and purchasing new music, as well as filing and maintaining the music already on hand. Although supplying music to the musicians would appear to be the single most important library task, recovery and maintenance of music is equally vital: music that is not properly stored will not be useful in the future.

The greatest challenges

Because much commercially-available concert band music is marketed toward school band programs, rentals are far less common in the band world than for orchestras. Where an orchestra may have hundreds of scores but far fewer sets of parts, bands purchase both scores and parts for permanent addition to the collection.

Storing materials. Storage quickly becomes an issue not only because of the amount of music on hand, but because proper storage procedures mean even more space is needed. For example, parts and scores are properly separated by size. An octavo march score can no more be stored with its pouch-size parts than it could be interfiled with oversized scores. Interfiling increases the likelihood that smaller items will be lost or squished, and puts uneven pressure on larger materials which may cause curling or warping. Even the simple word "score" in the band world can mean anything from a full score to a piano or cornet part. Choosing between storing materials on shelves and drawers (or even in envelopes and boxes) might be based on space, budget, or any number of considerations, but storing like-sized paper together will dramatically increase the longevity of your collection at negligible expense.

Arrangement and shelving. Arrangement of the materials in the band library is often influenced by how they are shelved. An orchestra library may have performance and study scores alphabetized by composer and music sets arranged by title and/or genre. A band library divides music by size and ensemble (marches, march scores, concert parts, concert scores, and octavo parts and scores) to meet long-term paper preservation needs. Yet users must also be able to easily find and match scores to parts. This generally leads to filing by accession number rather than alphabetizing or arranging thematically, which in turn demands some kind of numbering and cataloging system even in a relatively small collection. Where a computerized catalog might be considered a luxury for a moderately-sized orchestra, it is essential for a comparably-sized band.

Scoring and instrumentation. Band and orchestra libraries also deal with similar challenges, not the least of which is the wide range of scoring available. Each ensemble has a "normal" setup but, of course, music is written (and subsequently sets are produced) with a particular sound in mind. For a concert band this may include upper or lower auxiliary clarinets, any number of double reeds, different trumpets or cornets, and certainly a vast assortment of percussion, from harp to sandpaper. European band music may include three kinds of tuba in its extensive brass scoring, and some American publishers include "world" parts to support this instrumentation, meaning what appears at first glance to be fifteen different low brass parts is just four in various transpositions. Even the "jazz big band" isn't a set instrumentation — are there four trumpets? Five? Do the saxophones double on any other wind instruments?

Reference materials and record keeping. While orchestras have a single reference book covering a vast number of works (David Daniels's *Orchestral Music*[1]), bands have no such resources. Standard references such as the *Heritage Encyclopedia*[2] and the books of Norman Smith[3] may make mention of extreme examples of orchestration,

---

1   David Daniels, *Orchestral Music: A Handbook* (4th ed. Lanham, Md.: Scarecrow Press, 2005). Online version available by subscription at http://www.orchestralmusic.com.

2   William H. Rehrig, *The Heritage Encyclopedia of Band Music*, ed. Paul E. Bierley (2 vols. Westerville, Ohio: Integrity Press, 1991. Vol. 3, Supplement, 1997).

3   Norman E. Smith, *Program Notes for Band* (Chicago: GIA Publications, 2002), *March Music Notes* (Lake Charles, La.: Program Note Press, 1986), and *March Music Melodies* (Lake Charles, La.: Program Note Press, 1983).

but do not list instrumentation. Consequently, it's equally as important for a band library as for an orchestra library to keep track of special instrumentation requirements of various pieces.

Errata. Another challenge in common is dealing with errata. Although as John Corigliano points out in the program notes for his massive band work, *Circus Maximus*, bands do tend to devote a lot more rehearsal time to any given piece, it's still annoying to waste that time finding and correcting errata, particularly when it could have been avoided. Music production is in a curious state in which newer works seem to be less likely to include errors, and so it is the warhorses that have the most pitfalls; however, it is also the warhorses for which thoughtful errata lists have been compiled. Frederick Fennell's articles in *The Instrumentalist* and *BD Guide*[4] magazines concentrate on problems in the most commonly-played works, and Timothy Topolewski's series of "Errata Studies"[5] address dozens of other band standards.

What would you tell a person interested in this field?

Band librarianship is a fairly specialized field, so it isn't necessarily required to specialize further within it. It helps to have a solid grasp of whatever repertoire the conductor is most interested in, but the rest of the ensemble will appreciate it if the librarian has a broader base of knowledge to draw from. That being said, an expert on a topic is always valuable, so if you are particularly interested in a style, period, composer, or instrument, there's no reason to stop researching it. Many librarians have special areas of focus and developing relationships with colleagues may give you ideas of who to ask first when you have a question in a subject that you're less familiar with. Knowing the specialties of certain vendors can assist your ordering process, as well.

What kinds of job opportunities are available in this career field?

Band librarianship is a curious career. To the best of my knowledge, there are fewer than two dozen full-time band librarian positions in the country, all at military bands, meaning there are fewer professional band librarians than professional euphonium players.

Sergeant First Class Sarah Anderson is the Chief Librarian of The United States Army Field Band, Fort George Meade, Maryland.

(The information presented in this publication has been prepared solely by the author and neither The U.S. Army Field Band, the U.S. Army, nor any other component of the Department of Defense of the U.S. Government has endorsed this material.)

---

4   *The Instrumentalist* (Northfield, Ill.: The Instrumentalist Publishing Co., 1946–. ISSN 0020-4331). *BD Guide* (Traverse City, Mich.: Village Communications Group, 1984–1996. ISSN 1072-9526).

5   Timothy Topolewski, "Errata Studies for the Wind Band Conductor" (N.p., 1990–2000).

Opera Librarian

by Paul J. Beck

Personal background and work experience

I started in music by studying the bassoon as a fifth grader in the South Milwaukee (Wisconsin) public school system. By the time I was part-way through high school, I was certain that a career in music would be the only possible path for me. All orchestra librarians have a similar tale to tell—whether the instrument was an oboe or a tuba, the story is the same—about a young person who finds their "calling" through performing the classics in a high school ensemble, perhaps supplemented by weekly youth symphony rehearsals and the occasional all-state competition. These early magical experiences certainly galvanized my determination to succeed in a career in classical music, in one form or another.

After high school I enrolled in the University of Wisconsin-Milwaukee. However, after two years I felt the tug of the big city's bright lights and won a full scholarship to the Manhattan School of Music to study bassoon performance with Dr. Frank Morelli.

While studying for my bachelor's degree at the Manhattan School of Music, I did some good work as a work-study student in the MSM performance library and had begun to really like the tasks. This resulted in the opportunity to join the New World Symphony in their library fellowship program.

Working as the New World Symphony library fellow lasted only eight months, but I learned so much there. I missed New York and took a job with the Little Orchestra Society in Manhattan and spent eight months or so working with them. Then it was off to an opening at The Juilliard School to run their orchestra library. The Metropolitan Opera announced an opening for assistant librarian and I went through the Met's rigorous process to join their three-person department, which had been running with two full-time librarians and temporary help for about a year.

When it was my time to complete my "trial week" in the Metropolitan Opera music library, I found the work demanding. The phone rang frequently and people were talking about operas and aria titles with which I was not familiar. I found myself pausing and telling people I would "check on that and get back with them" quite frequently, which is a much better policy than pretending to know something that in fact you don't know.

In the end I was one of those lucky people in the right place at the right time. I was offered the position and have been with the company for eight years. My colleagues in the library, orchestra, and staff positions are some of the most brilliant and creative people I have ever met. The Met is an internationally known company for a very good reason—the people who keep the machine going are simply amazing.

A typical day in the library

An average day in our library starts at 9:30 a.m. with a little chat around a cup of coffee or tea. By 10:00 a.m. the rehearsal space must be set up for our 11:00 a.m. rehearsal, which takes place most days of the week. We refer to this as the "day shift." Among our four full-time librarians, two usually work the day shift and two work the "night shift."

My role and duties

The organization depends on its librarians not only to prepare and manage the printed music, but also to supervise the setups of the orchestra's chairs and stands. So, after we set out our heavy opera books, you will often see us tweaking the setup by slightly adjusting the placement of chairs and stands so the players will have enough room to play comfortably, or asking a stage-hand to bring another chair, or to accommodate a special request for an artist or performer.

The night shift librarians arrive two hours prior to the curtain, which usually means 6:00 p.m. for an 8:00 p.m show. Once again, we set out the corpulent books in the pit and then tweak the setup as needed. We also adjust the conductor's podium according to each conductor's preferences, which we've recorded on a chart.

Another very important duty is to take care of offstage music, as well as to oversee the setup for such events that can occur at any point during the opera. (We refer to any non-pit musical events as "stage bands," even if it's played by just one harp). Generally, we know the operas well enough to anticipate when these will occur, though there is also an announcement over the loudspeaker by our stage managers to assemble the musicians. The location of these stage band calls occur literally all over the opera house, including in the dome eight stories above the pit. They add an opulence and drama, which can be very stirring, to the operas.

The greatest challenges

One of the challenges of this profession is simply the volume of activity. We are responsible for the preparation of twenty-eight to thirty-two operas, three Carnegie Hall symphonic concerts, concerts for the Carnegie Hall Chamber Ensemble series, as well as the occasional Farewell or Anniversary Gala.

An important part of our job that is challenging, especially to a novice, is preparing a concert of opera excerpts, better known as an Opera Gala. It takes practice and experience to know that you need to ask about the "Vienna Version" or the "Paris Version" of an opera excerpt; or that certain works can be identified by two or three titles, depending on if the recitative is sung; or to know that certain pieces might need rewrites to eliminate one vocal line that isn't there; or that the offstage music is to be played by the pit orchestra. There is no reference book for such details. Knowing these finer points is a matter of experience—and of paying attention and remembering.

What part of the job do you enjoy?

Day to day, I find that I very much enjoy the interpersonal aspects of my job. The orchestra library is the clearinghouse for information and this brings us in contact with a large number of people, all with diverse needs. I enjoy this interdepartmental contact quite a bit and find it a pleasurable part of orchestra librarianship.

Something else that I personally enjoy is the opportunity to improve on a daily basis. I find myself asking if there is a better way I could have accomplished that task. Is there some new technology that we can employ to our advantage? Could the insert I created by hand have been more seamless? These are the questions I ask myself, not on a daily, but really an hourly basis.

What did you wish you'd known before taking this job?

If there is one skill that I wish I could have focused on before working at the Met, it would have to be computer music engraving. This is very useful when preparing materials for operas. Often an insert will be needed or an offstage part will be missing. On the job, with diligence and hard work, I have acquired the skills necessary so that I now find the engraving program to be a handy tool on an almost daily basis.

Another very important skill to acquire is a natural feel for languages. In opera, we deal with English, German, Italian, Russian, Czech, and French. So often an indication in one of these languages might be just the puzzle piece you need when solving a problem. Develop a curiosity when you encounter a foreign phrase and keep your dictionaries handy.

It is also important to develop a keen eye for mistakes. For example, when marking bowings in a part, use your entire musical self to scan the page to identify missing dots, wrong rhythms, and other oddities. You make yourself more valuable to your organization and eventually to the music if you are constantly aware of such things.

What would you tell a person interested in this field?

A working knowledge of opera repertoire is a must for any aspiring opera librarian. It could help somewhat if you grew up as an opera buff, but it is also essential to know about oddities of instrumentation. (Can you name two or three operas with an alto saxophone?) It is also useful to pay attention to available editions/reprints of opera materials, including piano/vocal scores, conductor's scores, and orchestral parts. Each time you encounter such materials, make a mental note or keep a card file on what you encounter, indicating whether there were difficulties and, if so, how they were overcome. I guarantee it will help you in the future.

Are you familiar with the terms "grand rights" and "small rights?" Any organization that stages performances of copyrighted works will need to negotiate grand rights agreements with the copyright owners or their agents. A thorough knowledge of copyright laws and when to apply them is essential. "The Music We Perform," written by Robert Sutherland and Lawrence Tarlow,[6] is an excellent resource. Also of interest might be *The Art of Music Licensing*, by Al Kohn and Bob Kohn.[7]

---

6   Lawrence Tarlow and Robert Sutherland, "The Music We Perform: An Overview of Royalties, Rentals and Rights" (Rev. ed. N.p.: Major Orchestra Librarians' Association, 2004). Available online at http://www.mola-inc.org/pdf/MusicWePerform.pdf.

7   Al Kohn and Bob Kohn, *The Art of Music Licensing* (Englewood Cliffs, N.J.: Prentice Hall Law and Business, 1992).

Another important skill to develop is a neat hand for marking parts. Every stroke you etch on a part should be in the service of improving what is already there so that someone performing from that part can easily see what is intended. All will benefit from and appreciate nice-looking, clear handwriting.

What resources are valuable in this job?

Some websites that are useful to an opera librarian:

- www.aria-database.com — a collection of information about opera arias
- www.imslp.org — a resource for free public domain sheet music (the Petrucci Music Library)
- Various publishers websites will usually list instrumentations of their operas

In summary, opera librarianship is an interesting and rewarding profession. Long hours and hard work are required, but the payoffs are many. The thrill of hearing the orchestra seamlessly play the complicated cut you marked is unbeatable.

Paul J. Beck is the Orchestra Librarian at The Juilliard School in New York City.

Music Festival Librarian

by Elizabeth Cusato

Personal background and work experience

As have so many other librarians, I tripped into orchestra librarianship. After several years of teaching school (fourth to twelfth grade band and orchestra, and yes, I liked it), I took what I thought was going to be a one-year hiatus from the classroom and began an internship with Clint Nieweg at The Philadelphia Orchestra.

It soon became clear that the orchestra library is a different kind of classroom. Between the ever-increasing volume of information and the constant need to educate our colleagues and audiences about what we do, there is enough in the library to keep me busily growing and learning for the rest of my life.

When I tripped into orchestra librarianship, I tripped at the right time and in the right place. In my first two years as a librarian I experienced nearly every kind of library work: I was an intern at one of the best orchestras in the United States; I worked as an assistant at an opera company, at a ballet company, with a chamber orchestra, and a choir; and I was solely responsible for two orchestras, a youth orchestra, and a training orchestra for young professionals. On this foundation, I experienced my first summer at The Glimmerglass Festival. That first summer was fascinating, amazing, and exciting. I was hooked.

Beyond the thrill of watching opera come to life, I fell in love with festival work. I love learning and exploring great music as much as the process of creating and maintaining procedures to accommodate the preparation of so much music off-site.

My role and duties

Festival library work involves all of the same components as any other library job—gathering information about programming and using that information to procure music, proof, edit, format, and mark music to the specifications of the performance, then making the music (and information about the music) available to musicians and staff.

Because festival librarians tend to work off-site, music preparation must be done without regular office hours or face-to-face conversations with artistic, personnel, and musical staff. A festival librarian must be able to work independently.

The Glimmerglass orchestra contract stipulates that musicians receive music four weeks ahead of the first rehearsal. Allowing for shipping time, music for four operas must be performance-ready six weeks ahead of the first rehearsal. This means that my preparation actually starts in January or February so that I have time to proof, edit, circulate string parts to principal players, and transfer bowings. The process of preparing music in advance on the basis of phone calls and e-mails, and only months later hearing the results of that work is a strange and wonderful challenge.

The reality is that in all libraries, and especially festival libraries, library work must happen well in advance of the first rehearsal. Success requires organization, attention to detail, a willingness to self-evaluate, and the ability to be self-motivated and focused over a long period of time.

What would you tell a person interested in this field?

Ultimately, because every festival is unique and so much festival work happens off campus and away from staff and musician colleagues, it is very important to have a clear idea of expectations, yours and theirs. If you are thinking about whether you want to apply for a job at a festival, here are a few things to consider:

What is the job description? What must the librarian provide? Are there any other duties beyond part preparation and rehearsal/concert duty?

What is the timeline? When will programming be confirmed? When will music arrive? What is the deadline for cuts and edits? When must music be distributed to the orchestra?

What resources are available? Who manages the budget and orders music and supplies? Is there a library space? If so, is this a storage space, a workspace, or both? Is the space accessible year-round or only during the festival? Assuming there is a copy machine (even if shared) and possibly a binding machine, is it possible to use these in the off-season or will that library work need to be done elsewhere for reimbursement? Will the festival commit to the expense of a trackable shipping service (such as FedEx) if music must be shipped to the orchestra? Is there an assistant or intern?

From whom do you get information and when? Do you have the contact information you need (e-mails and phone numbers) to stay in the loop? With whom will you have direct contact and are there some questions that must be handled by the artistic department?

What are the in-house processes and protocols? Do these systems complement or conflict with your own processes and protocols? Can differences be resolved before the work begins and before problems arise?

What are your personal procedures for tracking outstanding questions on multiple programs? Do you use to-do lists or checklists? Do you write everything down? Do you carry it all in your head? Even more than in a full-time or resident library job, you will need systems for tracking information. As you are likely preparing multiple programs, you must be aware of what you need when, and who else needs what from you and when.

Does the festival run in repertory or is it a series of individual concerts? For the latter, library prep will likely be ongoing through the festival season. For the former, consider that all (or nearly all) of the music for the entire festival will need to be prepared at once and in advance.

If this still sounds interesting to you, there are many summer festivals all around the world. Several advertise for librarians on the MOLA website, some are sponsored by schools or universities, and others are run by major orchestras or arts institutions. Keep your ears open, watch for advertisements, and ask a lot of questions.

Personally, and perhaps largely because of the challenges, I have found festival work to be incredibly rewarding. I hope you will, too!

Elizabeth Cusato is the Associate Librarian at The National Symphony and has been Orchestra Librarian for The Glimmerglass Festival since 2004.

Music Publisher Rental Librarian

by Amy Diane Dickinson

Personal background and work experience

I was born and raised in Florida and originally trained as a classical musician on the cello. I have a bachelor's in music performance with an emphasis in business from Stetson University, a master's in music performance from Florida International University, and a master's in business administration from Baruch College, City University of New York. Upon graduating with my first master's degree, I came to work for this company and have remained in their employment ever since.

How I got the job

I found the job via the Internet while working as a temp at another agency. I was called in for an interview roughly a month after submitting a résumé and was hired shortly thereafter.

My role and duties

My main job is to assist our customers in contracting and acquiring music available on a rental basis. Beyond that, I assist in royalty and performance rights reporting for our composers and those publishing houses we represent, monitor the warehouse where we outsource for our pick/pack/ship operations, and do various other operational duties.

A typical day in the library

An average day for our offices starts at 9:00 a.m. The rental staff sits down and reviews the evening's e-mails, faxes, and phone messages and prioritizes those items based on their urgency. Signed rental agreements returned to us via fax are generally the first items to be updated in our system and the agreements are then put on a pick list used by our off-site warehouse. We then go through our rental in box where orders are received from our website and issue contracts/quotes/perusals accordingly. Throughout this process we also answer phone calls, providing rental information ranging from the ordering process to quotes to redirecting customers who have approached us for a work held by another agency, but we never issue agreements from those conversations until orders have been received in writing. The majority of our customers are community-based organizations not very familiar with the rental process. For example, an order with a major orchestra may only take us minutes, however working with individuals unfamiliar with the rental process can take a much longer amount of time. We occasionally have to deal with shipping errors or acquire further information on works not available through the standard outlets (Internet resources, David Daniels's book, etc.). We also have a great deal of communication with our off-site pick/pack/

ship facility in checking stock and shipment status. If materials are not available for an order on the pick list, we then make the arrangements with the appropriate parties to provide them, whether it is via importation or printing (when available). The day also includes a great deal of filing and issuing of invoices. Depending upon the day, we may have some composers visit or have staff meetings, but the majority of the day is spent in communication with our customers. Our offices close at 5:00 p.m. and we all trek home via mass transit to prepare for the day to start again tomorrow.

The greatest challenges

The greatest challenge I have found associated with this industry is having to explain why a piece of music is on rental and not available for purchase through the standard channels. The complexities of the copyright world are still very murky to many people and, given the rental fees associated with acquiring materials for performance, it is easily understandable why individuals paying these amounts do not understand why they don't get to keep the materials. Too often we have heard individuals threaten to just extract the parts from the sales score or "borrow" the set from an organization already renting the title. From our end of the spectrum, it is quite disheartening to hear such disregard for the rights of the composers who should fully reap the benefits of their compositions.

Another challenging aspect is that these renting parties often think that we as a company are making enormous profits from these transactions, which is simply not the case. Speaking solely from my experience, a rental agency's profit from a rental transaction is minimal at best, especially given the amount of time and number of parties involved in a rental transaction. The whole process can be a bit of a tightrope walk in that you have to be patient and understanding of a client's concern about what they perceive as exorbitant fees and expenses, but firm in explaining the process in such a way that continues to provide mutual communication and understanding of the system. It is a hard line to toe, but it must be done for the preservation of the rights of the composers and integrity of the musical performances.

What part of the job do you enjoy?

I can sum this up in two items: the people I work with and the concerts I get to attend. We are very fortunate to have the staff we do and having such accomplished, funny, entertaining, caring, and intellectual people surely helps to make the day go easier. I will admit there is a giant perk in being a rental librarian in that you do have the opportunity to go to concerts for free which you normally would have never been able to afford. As a result of my work, I've gotten to see and meet some of the world's major artists and hear some of the most beautiful music ever produced by some of the world's most competent performing groups.

What best prepared you for this job?

My musical background and training were good preparation, along with an excellent set of organizational skills. A good sense of humor helps, as well.

What did you wish you'd known before taking this job?

That "must be able to lift 50 lbs" would forever be in my job description, and the requirement is mandatory.

What would you tell a person interested in this field?

That the smartest thing you'll ever know is to know what you don't know. Hopefully this will give you the impetus to research the matter and ask the appropriate parties for guidance. Mistakes in this field are either minor or catastrophic, so it is best to triple check before chancing anything.

What kinds of job opportunities are available in this career field?

> Rental librarian
> Promotion
> Library Maintenance
> Grand Rights Licensing
> Permissions

Where would you look for job openings?

I would contact the companies directly. We generally post via college campuses when need be or on the MOLA list, but I would as a general rule always contact the publisher directly—both the human resources department and the head of the rental library.

Is there room for advancement?

Absolutely. I started at the bottom and worked my way up. If I can do it, anyone can.

What resources are valuable in this job?

> ASCAP (American Society of Composers, Authors and Publishers), www.ascap.com
> BMI (Broadcast Music, Inc.), www.bmi.com
> David Daniels, *Orchestral Music: A Handbook*. 4th ed. Lanham, Md.:
>   Scarecrow Press, 2005. Online version available by subscription at http://
>   www.orchestralmusic.com.
> Publisher catalogues and websites
> Sheet Music Plus, www.sheetmusicplus.com
> Hal Leonard Corporation, www.halleonard.com

Amy Diane Dickinson is the Head of Rental Services for Schott Music Corporation and European American Music Distributors LLC.

College and Conservatory Librarian

by Erika Kirsch

Personal background and work experience

I am a bassoonist originally, with bachelor's degrees in music performance and music education from Southern Methodist University in Dallas, Texas. While there, I had lots of freelance work in local orchestras. I moved to Rochester, New York, and started my master's degree in bassoon performance and literature at the Eastman School of Music. I started looking around for a work-study job and found one at the Ensemble Library. The Ensembles Librarian at the time was Bill Pottebaum and he was very keen on training the students who worked for him. When I graduated, he offered me a full-time job as his assistant, and mentored me through all the particulars of dealing with rental agents and acquiring performance licenses.

I've also worked at the American Symphony Orchestra in New York City, where my duties initially included assisting the Director of Production. The repertoire of that orchestra included many rarely-performed works, so I really honed my music-searching skills during that time. At the Houston Grand Opera, I learned about preparation of opera materials, including vocal scores and chorus parts, and all of the markings that have to be placed in the music to reflect cuts, inserts, and transpositions. I worked for a summer at the Aspen Music Festival where I was the librarian for the American Academy of Conducting at Aspen (AACA). This ensemble had a wide variety of activities each summer, all of which served to train young conductors. The orchestra met nearly every day of the week, sometimes for rehearsals, but also for readings, concerts, opera scenes, and student composition readings.

Finally, I moved to Montreal and began working for the McGill University Library and Collections as a cataloger at the music branch, later moving within the university to the Gertrude Whitley Performance Library at the Schulich School of Music. The performance library is part of the Department of Performance which provides its budget. This library is considered completely separate from the large university library system and has its own searchable online catalog. The performance library supplies music to the performing ensembles at the school in which the students are required to perform, earning credits toward their degrees. There is a wide range of ensembles, including the orchestras, wind symphony, contemporary music ensemble, opera, choirs, jazz ensembles, and instrument choirs, such as trombone choir. The ensembles play a large variety of music spanning time periods from the Renaissance to present-day, including student compositions, and sometimes serve as a training ground for student conductors. The library also contains chamber music needed by ensembles of five or more members.

A typical day in the library

The typical day in the performance library is a hodgepodge of activities. This job involves circulating materials, acquiring materials from both rental and purchase sources, cataloging, processing, preparing materials for performances and auditions, maintaining the collection, keeping track of the budget, acquiring performance licenses (including those for dramatic productions, recordings, broadcasts, and Internet transmissions), coordinating the activities of student assistants, and fielding requests and reference questions from faculty, staff, and students. Each day involves some combination of those tasks. I have a few student assistants who help with shuttling music back and forth between rehearsals, but the budget doesn't allow for them to spend significant time in the library doing any in-depth projects. The library is heavily used by students preparing for auditions—they often need separate parts from this or that symphony or overture to learn excerpts. If the library doesn't have a particular work, I try to point the students in the right direction to buy it or I'll try to rent it on their behalf from an agent. Students are increasingly interested in renting contemporary works to perform on their degree recitals and I make arrangements for the delivery of those works.

The greatest challenges

One of the challenges of this job is information. Performance librarians need to know everything about a concert or rehearsal: repertoire, personnel, dates, times, locations, etc. A good ensembles manager is indispensable; librarians rely on them to help keep them up-to-date with any changes to the concert or rehearsal information. By the same token, the ensembles manager relies on the performance librarian for information coming from the sheet music or publisher about instrumentations, titles, suggested stage setups, durations, and any instructions for performance.

What part of the job do you enjoy?

I like the variety of tasks associated with this work, but I mostly like interacting with the students and faculty. It is gratifying to know that I'm contributing to the performances at the school and the enthusiasm of the students, especially the younger students, is catching. I've particularly enjoyed helping composition students with the formidable task of formatting and binding their parts and scores for the premieres of their works with our ensembles.

What best prepared you for this job?

My experience in different types of ensemble libraries helped prepare me for the all-encompassing nature of the repertoire needed for a university ensemble library. However, I would say that in this profession, next to experience, the best quality you can have is to be tenacious. Years of making bassoon reeds probably predisposed me to this kind of work. Some projects really require determination to see them through.

You have to be willing to keep at it sometimes to make sure you find the edition you want. Finally, you have to be proactive and patient when seeking information.

What did you wish you'd known before taking this job?

Before taking this job, or any of the other ones I've had, I wish I had known a little bit more about the music publishing industry, specifically about all the different types of scores that are available. I think it would have saved me some time and effort. I would tell a person just starting in this field to try to gain experience at their university ensemble library (if the person is a college student), to try to get an internship with a professional ensemble, or to apply for ensemble librarianship work at a summer festival. In addition, getting involved in the Major Orchestra Librarians' Association (MOLA) is a great way to make the acquaintance of other performance librarians, whom I have found have a very altruistic attitude toward helping out their colleagues.

What kinds of job opportunities are available in this career field?

In this specific position, the opportunities are quite limited. Salary-wise, the next level involves library administration and/or teaching, which requires a master's degree in library and information science. Even so, to acquire one of those positions would mean leaving the domain of ensemble librarianship. To find another position, I would look for job openings on the MOLA website or on the websites of hiring institutions.

What resources are valuable in this job?

There are several useful resources I use quite often. The one I turn to the most is the MOLA membership. When I've searched for something and just can't find it, I'll ask one of my colleagues. More often than not, someone has come across that item before! In addition, I sometimes need clarification on a procedure concerning performance licenses and an experienced colleague can usually shed some light on the subject. The second resource I often use is the music-in-print database Educational Music Service (EMS) provides to its frequent customers. In addition to the database, the reliable purchasing services provided by EMS are very valuable.

A word about MOLA: the existence of this organization is essential for those working in the specialized field of ensemble librarianship. There are, as of this date, no university-level courses available in ensemble librarianship. Therefore, the practice has been training through mentorship or on-the-job experience. Membership of an organization in MOLA is invaluable to ensemble librarians as it provides contact with a network of accomplished professionals with whom to share experience and gain knowledge.

Erika Kirsch is the Senior Specialized Cataloguing Editor and Acquisitions Assistant and Performance Librarian at McGill University in Montreal, Quebec, Canada.

How to Run a Choral Library

by Sally Millar

The following advice is based on my eighteen years of experience as a self-taught choral librarian. Being free of formal training in the field has its advantages and its drawbacks. I can only say that these methods have worked well for me in my particular circumstance, a college choral department.

Assess your collection

Unless you have inherited a well-run choral library with a recently updated inventory, it would be a very good idea to spend the time getting to know both what you have and the physical shape of your collection. Choral music can deteriorate quickly, depending on the care given by its temporary owners (the chorus), and some editions just have shorter life spans than others. The obvious things to check are:

1. The number of copies you own

    a) Is your working inventory up to date?
    b) Are there copies in poor condition which should be retired?
    c) Are all of the copies complete? (A missing cover can sometimes mean that the last page of the piece is also missing.)

2. The edition

    a) Do you have more than one edition? If yes, how many copies of each?
    b) Is the text in all of the editions in the same language(s)?
    c) If the piece is *a cappella*, do all of the editions provide a piano reduction?

3. Duplications

    a) Be alert that you may own copies of the same piece published under two different titles. For example, Beethoven's "An die Freude" may be also listed as "Symphony No. 9 (last movement)." Different editions of works in foreign languages may have differently translated titles while still containing the sung text in the original language.
    b) Watch for different spellings of the composer names. This often applies to publishers using a non-Western alphabet (Russian, Asian, etc.).

Assess your inventory

I inherited a card catalog which I converted into a database. Therefore I had the privilege of deciding how much and which information to include about each piece. If your library already has a database, you might consider additional fields which could be helpful with specific repertoire searches. If you do add data fields, you could enter this information gradually, as you come into contact with the specific works. The fields I include are:

Box number. The specific location of the music in the library.

Composer's first name. A quick way to avoid confusing all the members of the Bach family!

Composer's last name. Choose a spelling and stick with it (and convert all other entries to this spelling).

Title. I try to choose the title which reflects the first language when two are offered. Also, put the indefinite article last, e.g., Celestial Country, The.

Alternate title. If there is a translation of the first title, I enter it here; or, if this is part of a collection of pieces, I will enter the collection title as well as the piece's number in the series, e.g., Six Chansons, no. 2.

Category. I use sacred, secular, Christmas, folk song, opera, Hanukkah. Choose others which are helpful to you.

Voice. The voicing for the chorus as well as soloists, e.g., SAATB; SA soli.

Copies. If there are two or more editions, I *try* to break down the number of each accordingly (e.g., 15, 7). Be sure the numbers are in the same order as the listing for each edition.

Publisher. Be consistent because your computer doesn't know that G. Schirmer is the same as GSchirmer (if you ever want to sort your list by publisher, that is).

Instrumentation. Enter accompanying instruments here. I use "orch" or "ch orch" if the number is more than 5 or 6 separate instruments. My abbreviation for *a cappella* is "a/c."

Language. List the language of the text(s) in the order in which they appear, such as: English/German/French.

Piano part. This lets me know whether an *a cappella* piece has a piano reduction, an important feature for your accompanists!

Movement/excerpt title. This field is for multi-movement pieces, published as a whole, with movements that could be performed separately; e.g., Bartók's *Four Slovak Folk Songs*. I enter the individual movement title here so they are also searchable.

I find that the task that I forget most often is that of updating the inventory after a performance, when there is often a slight reduction in the number of copies in the collection. I do keep a separate database for borrowed materials, but unfortunately it is not linked to the primary database. This would be a helpful feature when designing your own catalog.

I keep two printed lists of the catalog and update them by hand, adding the information for newly-acquired pieces, and then reprint the list every few years. I print only those fields of the catalog that I need to see when using it to search the collection, and I do not include some of the less important fields.

My predecessor had established a single-copy file in my office filing cabinet. This has proved to be extremely helpful, especially since the choral library is located on a different floor. This file contains one copy of each piece in the library, organized alphabetically by composer and then by title. These copies do not circulate outside of my office, but they are available for study and perusal and as a reference when gathering information for concert programs.

Ordering new music

It is very helpful to get as much information as possible from the conductor (or the person requesting a new piece) before you place an order. Some people want a particular arrangement or have a strong preference for the language display (i.e., is the language to be sung in a prominent position, on the top line?). Some need an edition with a piano reduction or one which matches the orchestra parts already in the library. It is easiest when they can hand you a copy and say, "Please order fifty more of this," but often you may need to do some additional research. Ordering music directly from the publisher has its advantages, but I find that using a music dealer where you can work directly with a person who can do the research for you is best. The dealer should also be able to advise you about realistic shipping costs and delivery timelines, track down obscure pieces and publishers, and provide you with other information not usually available on the publisher's website. And don't forget to search the Choral Public Domain Library (http://www2.cpdl.org/wiki/index.php/Main_Page) for music that is out of copyright. There are some good, free editions available there!

Processing new music

When new music arrives, I stamp it on the outside (or, if the cover does not easily absorb ink, on the inside) with our library property stamp. If the piece is large with a thick spine, I will often cover the spine with a strip of two-inch wide book tape. This gives the spine some protection from the wear and tear of normal use. I put aside one copy for the single-copy file, writing "file copy" in red on the cover, and enter the information into the catalog.

Distributing music to the chorus

Even with the best will in the world, most chorus members will leave their mark on and in their scores. Here are some preventative steps which have worked well for me:

1. A plastic envelope. Plastic envelopes, with string ties, keep the music together and protected from the weather, food, pets, and accidents. I label each

envelope with the student's name and music number and the plea: "Found? Please return to the NEC Chorus Office, Room 2M." I've had several music envelopes returned to me, thanks to this step!
2. Numbering. I assign each student a music number and make sure that each new piece they receive has the same number on it. This makes owner of "found" copies easily identifiable.
3. Colored dot labels. The music numbers are written a brightly-colored dot label which is affixed to the front of each part (with scotch tape over the top to keep it from falling off). The next time the piece is used, a different numbered label can be put over top of the first, if the parts must be renumbered.
4. Pencil markings only. Chorus members are warned that only pencil may be used to mark their music. Excessive or indelible markings means that the chorus member must purchase the music.

Collecting the music after the concert

Whether you use choral folders or black three-ring binders to hold the music for concerts, I have found that collecting the music immediately after the concert works best. There will always be a few who forget to do it, but the majority of the chorus members are usually happy to be relieved of their folders. In our case, this gives them both hands free with which to help themselves to the post-concert reception food.

After I have taken apart the folders, checked the copies returned against the roster of the chorus, contacted those with missing folders or parts, and come to the point where I feel that no further copies will be returned, I can re-shelve the music and update the database with the revised information (if any).

I find that it is helpful to stack the music in their storage boxes or on the shelves in groups of ten, alternating the orientation of the copies (spine on the left vs. spine on the right) so that you can quickly count the copies.

Sally Millar is the Administrative Assistant for Choruses at the New England Conservatory in Boston, Massachusetts.

Ballet Music Librarian

by Matthew Naughtin

Personal background and work experience

Music Librarian, Colorado Music Festival (2 years); Music Librarian, Peninsula Music Festival (2 years); Principal Music Librarian, Omaha Symphony (10 years); Resident Composer and Arranger, Program Annotator, Section First Violin, Omaha Swymphony (20 years); Librarian, Stage Manager, Section First Violin, Lake Forest Symphony, Lake Forest, IL (7 years); Concertmaster, Waukegan Symphony Orchestra, Waukegan, IL (7 years).

How I got the job

San Francisco Ballet advertised the open position of Music Librarian in the spring of 1997 and I sent in my résumé. The Ballet flew me to San Francisco for an interview and I was offered the job. After carefully calculating the probability of my being able to survive on the offered salary in one of the most expensive rental markets in the country, I accepted the offer and have never regretted the move.

My role and duties

I oversee all music library functions for the San Francisco Ballet, one of the three largest ballet companies in the United States. The Ballet has an annual budget of about $45 million and employs an office staff of more than 100. There are more than seventy dancers in the company and an orchestra of forty-nine musicians is contracted for 140 services from mid-December to May.

The Ballet year begins in December with thirty to forty performances of *The Nutcracker*, then the repertory season begins in mid-January with an opening Gala. There are eight programs, usually comprising two or three full-evening ballets and five or six mixed-repertoire programs, each comprised of three to four short ballets. The repertory season ends in the first week of May. There is usually an outdoor performance in August at Sigmund Stern Grove in San Francisco, and the company goes on tour in September and October. The company tours in the U.S. every three years, usually to New York City and Washington, D.C. The most recent international tours have been to Edinburgh, London, Paris, Barcelona, Reykjavik, Shanghai, Beijing, and Copenhagen. The orchestra does not accompany the dancers on tour—local musicians are contracted at the tour venues.

In addition to my salaried tasks as Music Librarian, I also work as an independent contractor, arranging and transcribing music from full scores, tape and piano scores, and adapting existing music to the needs of choreographers.

These are my normal tasks as listed in my job description:

- Contact music publishers, orchestras, and other ballet companies to purchase, rent, or borrow music for use by the Ballet
- Maintain a budget database covering all real and projected costs for royalties, music rental and purchase, and miscellaneous expenses. Report figures for costs and fees to the Music Director and General Manager when requested.
- Prepare music for performance in collaboration with the Music Director, Artistic Director, and Rehearsal Pianists. This preparation includes:
  - Editing piano scores and orchestral scores and parts to conform with choreography
  - Creating legible performance parts for the orchestra and rehearsal pianists
  - Creating back-up and practice parts for use by orchestra musicians
  - Creating extra sets of parts for use on tours
  - Preparing reference scores for use by ballet production department, sound technicians, TV and film production personnel
- Distribute and collect music at performances; be prepared to assist the conductor and musicians during rehearsals and performances
- Prepare and maintain an updated data file for each season listing repertoire, instrumentations, timings, and music sources for reference by the Personnel Manager and other Ballet Association staff
- Prepare and maintain an updated catalog of the music collection and maintain files of correspondence, memoranda, shipping records, and financial records for each season
- Send advance music to players who request it, ship music back to publishers, ship music to tour venues, ship music to guest conductors and others as needed
- Maintain the music collection, repairing and replacing damaged or lost music where necessary; maintain the library space in a clean, orderly condition
- Perform miscellaneous tasks of research, give information about repertoire to ballet staff and audience members when requested, provide music for special projects and events, loan music to other ballet companies when requested, and provide musical materials for auditions
- Perform other duties as required or assigned by supervisor

Working with a ballet company

Music librarians who work exclusively with ballet companies are, admittedly, a rare breed. Only the four or five very largest ballet companies in the U.S. have a resident orchestra on contract, and those orchestras may only work a few months out of the year. The situation is a bit different in Europe, where several theaters have orchestras that work with both an opera and a dance company. In the U.S., music librarians generally deal with dance or ballet programs at most once or twice a year…usually at *Nutcracker* time.

So what's it like working at the ballet? It's different.

My first awakening on my arrival at the ballet was the realization that it's an organization whose artistic focus and corporate culture is radically different from that of a symphony orchestra. When you work with an orchestra, most of your daily interactions are with musicians, ex-musicians, or people with some musical training. Conversely, at the ballet the majority of the staff are dancers, ex-dancers, or people with a dance background. So the three of us in the Music Department—the Music Director, Orchestra Personnel Manager, and me—are exotic beasts corralled in our little preserve and approached with some trepidation by the rest of the staff. The trepidation comes from the fact that dancers speak a different *language* from musicians.

A dancer, choreographer, or Ballet Master (the person who supervises and corrects the learning of the choreography for a ballet) might ask me for a copy of the score of a Pas de deux from, say, George Balanchine's *Stravinsky Violin Concerto*. I will look at him or her and ask, "Which movement is it?" There are two (quite famous) Pas de deux movements in *Stravinsky Violin Concerto*, but Stravinsky didn't label them "Pas de deux." Balanchine did. Stravinsky's titles for the movements are "Aria I" and "Aria II." Similar language difficulties arise when a dance person discusses a "Boy's Variation" or "Girl's Variation" or an "Adagio." This is dance jargon that has nothing to do with actual musical variations or tempos. So the first thing I had to do was learn what Dance People are talking about when they talk about music.

Ballet language and structure

Since its codification at the court of Louis XIV, the international language of classical ballet has been French. Thus, *Pas de deux…trois…quatre…cinq…six*, etc., mingle with *Divertissements*, *Ballabili*, and *Grand pas d'action*, and everything is resolved (or everyone dies) during the final *Apothéose*.

The overall structure of a full-evening classical ballet is fairly standardized. There are usually two to four acts in which Boy meets Girl, complications ensue and are resolved, and there is a big party (usually a wedding) at the end where everybody gets to dance. The center of the evening is the *Grand pas de deux* (usually in the last act, although sometimes, as in *Swan Lake*, there is more than one *Grand pas*) in which the male and female stars show off their grace, technique, and charisma.

A *Grand pas* is often extracted and performed separately, and is structured as an *Adagio* (two or more solo "variations," and a rousing *Coda*). The *Adagio* (which can be any tempo from andantino to lento) is a display piece for the woman, who demonstrates her balance, strength, beauty of carriage, and "line" with the discreet support of the male dancer. Each dancer then performs one or two solo "variations" to show off dazzling virtuoso technique, and the *Grand pas* ends with a headlong *Coda* that often features the woman performing a series of thirty or more bravura *Fouettés en tournant* (spins with leg whips) to express her joy at capturing her man.

Assembling and editing ballet music

Music preparation is the most challenging task I do. Much of the music used by ballet companies is either unpublished or is performed in arrangements and adaptations that are unique to that particular company's productions. Even the familiar Tchaikovsky ballet scores present problems for librarians when they leave the austere, foreign world of the concert hall and return to the comfortable, messy domain of the stage. Every ballet company routinely adapts the standard classics to fit its own personnel and style. Although companies occasionally seek to reconstruct stagings from previous eras, there is no urtext *Swan Lake*, for example, to which Artistic Directors remain devoutly faithful for fear of censure by historical purists. Radical cuts, reorderings, and insertions of foreign material are to be expected, and the librarian's best allies are the rehearsal pianist and conductor, both of whom should be aware of day-to-day changes made in the dance studio.

I always keep this in mind: choreographers don't have ANY IDEA what goes into preparing music. In the studio, if something isn't working, it's easy for the rehearsal pianist to alter the music to fit the choreographer's concept. It's vital that the conductor or rehearsal pianist keep me updated on changes and provide a copy of the working score with cuts and additions marked in plenty of time for the orchestral materials to be prepared and edited. In the best of all possible worlds, there will be time to send a copy of the marked score to a copyist who can create customized parts for the orchestra with good page turns and no paste-overs, hanging tabs, or Byzantine penciled road maps for the musicians to follow.

Compiling and editing the music for a new production of a full-length ballet is a time-consuming and labor-intensive task that can take weeks, sometimes months of preparation. In order to fit the music to the choreographer's vision, entire sections will be shifted out of sequence, innumerable cuts will be made of music that doesn't fit the dramatic or choreographic flow, and music from other sources (often by other composers) will be inserted.

This means that the orchestral parts that come from the publisher must usually be radically and extensively edited. My experience has been that the best solution often is to either create a completely new set of parts or get permission to keep the published parts on permanent loan. Thus the changes (revised sequence, cuts masked over or excised, new music inserted) can be incorporated in a performance set that will be used exclusively by us for that production. There are also the usual, time-consuming issues all music librarians deal with: inserting rehearsal numbers, copying bowings, correcting errata, and erasing markings, cuts, and musical directions that aren't relevant to the current production.

To give an idea of the time and effort involved, let me describe the process I went through for the new production of *Don Quixote* by Ludwig Minkus presented by the San Francisco Ballet in March 2003. I began the task of acquiring the orchestral parts in June 2002. The choreographers were undecided as to which orchestration (there are several) they wanted to use. They settled on a version done for a production created in 1999 by Alexei Fadeyechev for the Bolshoi Ballet in Moscow.

The choreographers gave me a conductor's score they had acquired in Russia as a reference. After four months of negotiations with the Bolshoi management and the RAO (Russian Author's Society), the music finally arrived in December. The parts I was sent were an old back-up set used for tours and were in terrible condition—badly photocopied and scribbled with many years worth of performance markings and graffiti. I immediately had to request better copies of the string parts. I also discovered that the wind, brass, and percussion parts did not have rehearsal numbers, which would have to be inserted. I hired two extra librarians (who work for the San Francisco Opera) to help with this task, which was complicated by the fact that the choreographers were continually changing the sequence of the musical numbers in the ballet even as we were creating the new parts.

There were five musical numbers to be inserted from other sources, which had been orchestrated by a musical consultant, and for which I had to make computer-generated scores and pages for insertion into the orchestra parts. As we approached the first orchestra rehearsal on March 7, I personally worked thirty-five days without a break, sometimes working twelve and fourteen hour days. This was necessary to ensure that the thirty orchestra parts were ready with all fifty-six individual musical numbers in the proper sequence, the five extra pieces of music inserted, and about twenty-five cuts correctly marked.

Since the percussion parts I was sent were so badly copied and scribbled over as to be completely unusable, I also was obliged to copy the conductor's score pages, cut out the percussion lines, and paste them up to create new percussion parts, which took several days. The process of revision continued even after the rehearsals began, with the choreographer changing cuts and sequences in sections he was dissatisfied with right up to the final dress rehearsal. The conductor also requested a different orchestration for one ninety-five-bar section, for which I had to make a new score and parts on my computer and insert them in the performance parts during the rehearsal week. Needless to say, I was exhausted when *Don Quixote* finally began its run.

A day at the ballet

A typical workday at the San Francisco Ballet begins at about 11:00 a.m. with the dancers' communal *leçon* (lesson) or "class," which lasts about ninety minutes. This is a daily series of exercises taken by dancers throughout their career to continue learning and to maintain strength, flexibility, and technical proficiency. It consists of *exercices à la barre* (exercises using the support of the barre) followed by *exercices au milieu* (free-standing practice): pirouettes (turns) and petit and grand allegro (increasingly vigorous jumps and spins). Today class is held onstage at the Opera House since there will be a full-dress rehearsal with the orchestra at 1:00 p.m. After class, the dancers who are working today go downstairs to costume and makeup before rehearsing with the orchestra.

Of course, my day begins a bit earlier. The orchestra has already had three or four rehearsals on its own at a separate venue down the street before joining the dancers in the Opera House. There are at least two rehearsals with the dancers before the opening night performance, a semi-dress, and a full-dress. My duties during the rehearsal week have mainly been transporting the music to and from the rehearsal hall and being on hand ready to deal with musical changes and issues with the orchestra parts (those pesky "bad" page turns).

In the morning I check that the setup in the orchestra pit is correct, deal with my e-mails and invoices, and make sure there are sufficient practice photocopies for the musicians to take home. Because we have a liberal personal leave allowance in the orchestra's master agreement, there can be several substitute players working at every service. This has led to my habit of making practice photocopies of *all* the orchestra parts, which makes it easy to mail a practice copy to a player who has been hired as a substitute. I encourage the musicians to take photocopies home rather than the real parts so we avoid having the performance part turn up missing when a musician is sick or takes a personal day. Once a performance run starts, removal of the real parts from the Opera House is strictly forbidden, since the backup parts won't have the latest edits.

Now I can enjoy one my job's great pleasures. I sit at the front of the house behind the conductor during the dress rehearsal. Next to me is the rehearsal pianist who will help the conductor with tempos and translate the Ballet Master's hums and "where the girl does the diagonal *chaînés*" into bar numbers and rehearsal letters for starting points. Officially I'm there to handle any issues with the music, but really I just enjoy watching the dancers from the $120 seats. Often this will be the first time I see how the choreographer and artistic design team have interpreted the music I've been working on. Typically a rehearsal with dancers will be a straight run-through with the Ballet Master doing "notes" on sections to be fine-tuned at the end. The conductor is usually asked to repeat portions of the music for the dancers and also seizes opportunities to do a little fine-tuning of his or her own.

When we do full-evening ballets, such as *Romeo and Juliet* or *Sleeping Beauty*, my task during performances is simple conductor maintenance. I put up the score for each act on the conductor's desk, and open the library before the performance and during intermissions so musicians can browse the practice copies and complain about bad page turns and too-small notes. If we're doing a mixed-repertoire program with three or four short ballets, my task is more complex. Depending on the orchestration of each ballet, the pit setup may have to be reconfigured two or more times. This often requires me to be poised and ready to rush into the pit and quickly pull music folders off the stands as soon as each intermission (there are normally two) starts. This allows the pit crew to come swarming in and start shoving pianos, chairs, riser boxes, music stands, and sound shields around without fear of music getting dropped and sliding down through a crack into the sub-pit. If there isn't a substantial pit change needed for the next day's schedule, I can leave after the second intermission and avoid the traffic jam after the performance.

Is the ballet world for you?

If you are interested in working as a staff music librarian for a ballet company, job opportunities are limited. In North America, only a few companies are large enough to afford a resident orchestra, much less a full-time librarian. To my knowledge, only the American Ballet Theatre, Houston Ballet, National Ballet of Canada, and San Francisco Ballet have full-time librarians who work exclusively for the company. That said, if you are working for a symphony orchestra, it is very likely that you will have the opportunity to work with a local ballet company, perhaps several times a year. Dealing with the standard ballet repertoire shouldn't present any problems. Your librarian skill set and knowledge are all the preparation you will need. If you're asked to dig up music that's not in the standard symphonic repertoire, I've provided a list of reference sources at the end of this article that will give you a place to start looking. I wish I had had this list when I started at the Ballet in San Francisco. It would have saved a lot of wasted steps. Also, ballet librarians like me are an excellent source of arcane knowledge if you really get stumped. If you're enlisted to work on a new production, it's important to make clear at the outset how much time you have available and insist on being given adequate lead-time and resources to prepare the music.

After thirteen years working with the San Francisco Ballet, I can say that I have never once regretted my decision to jump feet-first into the world of music for dance. Working with world-class artists of such intense focus and dedication always inspires me, and I find dancers to be some of the happiest and warmest people I have ever been around. I came into the job with next to no knowledge of the repertoire and traditions of the ballet, but now I am as enthusiastic a *balletomane* as the folks who sit in the front row next to the orchestra pit at almost every performance and chat with me when I'm changing the conductor's score. The musicians in the orchestra are a happy bunch, too, with little of the grumbling and resentment I often found among symphony players. All in all, if you love dance and don't mind a little stress and anarchy now and then, I can heartily recommend working At The Ballet.

Ballet reference resources

American Ballet Theatre Repertory Index
http://www.abt.org/education/archive/index.html

Balanchine Catalogue
http://balanchine.org/balanchine/search.jsp

New York City Ballet Repertory Index
http://www.nycballet.com/company/rep.html?TierSlicer1_TSMenuTargetID=1996&TierSlicer1_TSMenuTargetType=5&TierSlicer1_TSMenuID=350

New York Public Library for the Performing Arts
http://www.nypl.org/research/lpa
Tel: 212-870-1630

Jerome Robbins Foundation (website has a catalog of works)
http://jeromerobbins.org

Royal Opera House Collections
http://www.rohcollections.org.uk/Collections.aspx

Web links for ballet and dance

Ballet.co (online ballet magazine)
http://www.ballet.co.uk

Ballet Index
http://www.cmi.univ-mrs.fr/~esouche/dance/ballets.html

BalletMet: Ballet History & Repertoire
http://www.balletmet.org/balletnotes.php

Ballet Russes: history & repertoire
http://www.cmi.univ-mrs.fr/~esouche/dance/dance1.html

Ballet Talk: Ballet history and music forum
http://ballettalk.invisionzone.com/index.php?showforum=11

Choreographers Index
http://www.cmi.univ-mrs.fr/~esouche/dance/choreo.html

Critical Dance (online dance forum and magazine)
http://www.ballet-dance.com

Dancer.com dance links
http://www.dancer.com/dance-links/index.php

Paris Opera Ballet (fan page)
http://www.cmi.univ-mrs.fr/~esouche/dance/POB.html

Voice of Dance (online dance forum)
http://www.voiceofdance.com/v1/index.cfm

Publishers and rights administrators of ballet music

Alphonse Leduc/Heugel (handled by Theodore Presser in the U.S.)
http://www.alphonseleduc.com/EN/
Tel: (011)-33-1-4296-8911; Fax: (011)-33-1-4286-0283

George Balanchine Foundation
http://balanchine.org/balanchine/index.html
information@balanchine.org
Tel: 212-799-3196

The Leonard Bernstein Office
Garth Sunderland, Production Director
garthamb@aol.com
Tel: 212-315-0640 x126; Fax: 212-315-0643

Editions Mario Bois (handled by Theodore Presser in the U.S.)
http://www.mariobois.com
editions@mariobois.com
Tel: (011)-33-1-4282-1046; Fax: (011)-33-1-4282-1019

Edwin F. Kalmus & Co. (has many classic ballets arranged by William McDermott which are not available elsewhere)
http://www.kalmus-music.com
Tel: 800-434-6340; Fax: 561-241-6347

Kevin Galiè (Editions AMH)
19 Fort Avenue, Boston, MA 02119
Tel: 617-427-2342

Lars Payne, Music Librarian, English National Ballet
larspayne@btinternet.com
Tel: (011)-44-20-7735-7948

Jerome Robbins Foundation
http://jeromerobbins.org
Tel: 212-367-8956; Fax: 212-367-8966

Russian Author's Society (RAO)
Tel: (011)-7-095-203-3777; Fax: (011)-7-095-200-126

Matthew Naughtin is the Music Librarian of the San Francisco Ballet.

Jazz at Lincoln Center

by Kay Niewood and Christianna English

One thing I like about jazz, kid, is that I don't know what's going to happen next. Do you?

—*Bix Beiderbecke*

In a gathering of stately grandfathers, Jazz at Lincoln Center is still a teenager amongst the constituents of Lincoln Center. What began as a summer program of the Lincoln Center for the Performing Arts in August of 1987 and became a formal constituent in 1996, Jazz at Lincoln Center (JALC) has grown into its own, with programs in New York City and around the world. In 2004, JALC opened its new home, Frederick P. Rose Hall, also known as "The House of Swing," the first hall built specifically for jazz.

The Jazz at Lincoln Center Music Library has grown exponentially as well. It began as a few hanging files in a production office in the sub-basements of the Lincoln Center campus, then became random piles of envelopes haphazardly stacked around. By the time I came to work for JALC nine years ago, it had morphed to newly-boxed music in the early stages of organization, both physically and digitally and has since grown into a full-fledged performance library. I was the second person in the company's brief history to be solely responsible for the music. I believe the first person had begun as a touring intern and had eventually been put in charge of the music.

Personal background and work experience

My background leading to the library was not as direct as some of my fellow librarians. My circuitous route began with a foundation in music and a desire to teach others. Though a piano and trumpet player, voice was my instrument of choice in college. With a bachelor of music degree in music education, I spent the next years teaching and unsuspectingly building my skill set for the music library. As a teacher, I became well versed in the art of multi-tasking, keeping many projects going at the same time. I also learned to plan and work within limited budgets. At each school, I encountered music library chaos, which I reorganized out of sheer necessity. While studying jazz arranging and composition in graduate school, I brought order to an out-of-control wind ensemble library as part of my assistantship. When I applied for the position at Jazz at Lincoln Center, then called a Music Preparation Associate, I wasn't completely sure what I was getting myself into. But from the ability to organize the music to my knowledge of Finale music notation software, I knew I had the basic skills needed for the job description. Figuring out how those skills all work together to do the job has been an interesting journey and one that is still changing.

The job and its challenges have both changed and stayed largely the same. The position began with responsibilities for not only the print music library, but also the housing and organization of the company's recordings and other media. As JALC has grown, both of those roles have grown with it and we have become "Music Administration," a sub-department of the programming team. One of the biggest challenges has been building and expanding the music library to smoothly move into the future while trying to rebuild the past history of our company to better understand what we have.

In 2008, we reached a major milestone in our department when we hired a second full-time staff member. Christianna English came to the role of music librarian through a more traditional path. She holds a bachelor's and master's degree in clarinet performance, as well as a master's degree in library science. She worked in a university music ensemble library in both her undergrad and graduate years and realized she had found her niche. Even with work experience as an orchestra manager and in a large academic music library, the performance library was where she wanted to be.

The addition of Christi to the library was welcome. I have been fortunate to have a number of great part-time staff members and interns in the library, but it had become increasingly difficult to balance the day-to-day running of the library and the overall demands of my department. Christi's role is to oversee the daily operation of the print music library. She maintains the physical collection of print music, including the catalog database, and prepares song credits for our *Playbill* set lists. As we do most of our music preparation in-house, she also edits digital files of music, prepares performance parts for the jazz orchestra, and prepares music folders for each of our shows and tours. Christi attends rehearsals and concerts, and tracks set lists and other performance information for our database. Her greatest preparation for this job was her leadership experience in her university's music ensemble library. Christi's work in her MLS program also honed her skills and attention to detail, especially in organizing and cataloging new music and the collections we acquire. Christi and I need to be able to work independently to get everything done, so this experience is called upon all of the time. As with any library, attention to detail is incredibly important and probably one of the most highly-regarded skills of our staff members. We continue to employ additional part-time staff in the library to help keep all of the tasks at a manageable level, although there are many times we need more help.

Our roles and duties

Cataloging. In my early years, much time was spent fixing and fine-tuning the basic organization and cataloging of the music so that our system would work both in our physical library and while touring. The organization of our jazz library takes a different route than most orchestral libraries I have visited. After many meetings and sometimes heated discussions, we have tried, pretty successfully, to come up with a cataloging system that will both encompass and differentiate any possible variant of music within our library in a logical and usable manner. Rather than being organized by composer, our library is organized by song title. If a piece is part of a larger, multi-movement work, it is categorized under that title. For example, "Come Sunday" by Duke Ellington is part of the larger work *Black, Brown and Beige*, so it is listed under "B." Each chart is given a permanent alpha-numeric catalogue number. If multiple versions of the same song exist, they are given the same alpha-numeric number with a letter after it to indicate a difference, whether it be the arranger, transcriber, or even if it is a transcription of the same arrangement, but from a different recording. If there is a definitive original version this will be the "A" version. Titles within multi-movement works have the same alpha-numeric number, followed by ".1, .2, .3," etc.

We have also built a pretty extensive database of our music library which we use to track everything from the song credits to the particular master take number of recordings used for transcriptions. Over the years this library has been incorporated into our company database and scheduling system. As we have put these various systems in place, we have been slowly trying to connect all of the pieces in our library to the concerts on which they were performed, both past and current. Because we have multiple versions of the same songs, it is even more imperative to be able to track which version was played for which concert, both for the sake of history and also for future programming. For example, the Fletcher Henderson arrangement of Jelly Roll Morton's "King Porter Stomp" has a very different historical role than the Gil Evans arrangement of the same song. It is important for us to know those differences when piecing together the history of our company. Since we do not have an archivist, these questions often fall to Music Administration. By rebuilding our performance history and incorporating that information into our company database so that it is accessible to everyone, we cut down on the many requests that take us away from dealing with the music.

Acquisitions. Acquiring music in a jazz library is a bit different than other performance libraries. Jazz music itself is less than a hundred years old, so compared to the world of band and orchestra libraries the music that we work with is very new. In our everyday planning, it is not usually a question of which historical edition of a work should be used. Our questions usually are, can we track down the original music or will new transcriptions and arrangements be needed? It is a rarity if we need to rent music and a regularity that we will simply have new charts done. Of the concerts in our season for which the library provides music, probably seventy-five percent of the music is new to our library. This may include purchases of published music, acquisitions from estates or research facilities, transcriptions, new arrangements, or new commissions.

One of our biggest challenges in dealing with all of this new music is accommodating the timelines of others. Though our concerts are programmed a year or so in advance, the specific songs that will be played are often not determined until a month in advance—if we are lucky—and changes or final choices may still be requested and incorporated during the last days before rehearsal. We know this scenario is not the norm in other libraries, but Christi and I work hard at remaining calm and doing what we need in order to make it work. As stressful as this can be, one of our biggest enjoyments, beyond the music itself, is the satisfaction of getting things done when it seems impossible to do so. The hardest part is when we collaborate with other organizations that are not normally put in this position. We truly enjoy doing these special collaborations and appreciate their willingness to work with us in these less than normal circumstances.

Finding jazz music can be an investigative process. Many families or estates of jazz composers and arrangers are finally putting these great pieces of music in archives and research facilities. However, we still rely on asking questions of jazz historians or musicians who might know that "the great-grand-nephew of so-and-so probably has that chart in his garage in Anytown, USA, but no one has gone through it, so you will need to call and ask." You never know what treasures you may or may not find.

What resources are valuable in this job?

Finding jazz music can also be as simple as going through a publisher or distributor. One source that does a good job of tracking down and making historic jazz works available is eJazzLines (http://www.ejazzlines.com). A key example is their recent publication of some materials from the *Charlie Parker with Strings* recordings. They sent someone to the archive that houses the materials to rebuild/edit the music for publication.

Other great resources that publish original music directly from estates or archives are:

- Sierra Music Publications. http://www.sierramusicstore.com
- Kendor Music. https://www.kendormusic.com/store/index.php
- Second Floor Music. http://www.secondfloormusic.com/sfm.cfm

Please note, if you are doing historical programming, it is important to read the fine print to know whether you are getting an arrangement that sounds similar to the original, or if the chart came from the original materials. Beware. Don't be afraid to ask questions.

As part of our education programming, Jazz at Lincoln Center has been publishing historic transcriptions and original compositions. The entire catalog is now available through Alfred Music Publishing: http://alfred.com/JALC.

Two main archives that have multiple artists music collections are:

- Smithsonian Institute, American History Museum Archive Center. http://americanhistory.si.edu/archives/d-5.htm
- The Institute of Jazz Studies, Rutgers University. http://www.libraries.rutgers.edu/rul/libs/jazz/jazz_coll_descript.shtml

They each have a great page of links that lead to other collections

Other resources (that we regularly use):

Popular Music: An Annotated Index of American Popular Song, edited by Nat Shapiro and Bruce Pollock. (New York: Adrian Press, 1964– .) We use this set of books for song credit reference. Our Jazz Curator turned us on to this as one of the more accurate sources for song credits.

Allmusic.com (http://www.allmusic.com). We use this as another source of song credits—we usually check more than one for accuracy—as well as a quick research tool for recording information. If we need to go to the next step, we move on to discographies.

Fake Book Search (http://www.fakebooksearch.com). We use this to save time in locating song titles in various fake books. We have also taken the time to create a searchable PDF of the indices of fake books we have on-site. As Christi says, "Fake books are your friends."

Finale Forums (http://www.finaleforum.com/forums and http://forum.makemusic.com). As we handle our own music prep, we continually run across questions or problems that we need help with. If none of us can help each other answer the question, we head to the forum.[8]

What kinds of job opportunities are available in this career field?

The field for jazz performance librarians is still pretty limited, but as more institutions continue to add jazz ensembles or jazz music to their programming, the opportunities will become greater. The access to the music itself is changing all of the time, so it is important to be willing to look to new sources. Roll with it. As Bix said, you never know what is going to happen next.

Kay Niewood is the Assistant Director of Music Administration and **Christianna English** is the Associate for Music Administration at Jazz at Lincoln Center, New York, New York.

---

[8] Forums for the Sibelius notation application include the Sibelius Music forum (http://www.sibelius.com/community/index.html) and the Yahoo! group for Sibelius users (http://tech.groups.yahoo.com/group/sibelius-list).

Does the High School Music Department Need a Librarian?

by Walter O'Keefe

Most high school music directors are required to wear many hats: concert promoter, teacher, counselor, expert about every single musical instrument, repair technician, travel agent, conductor, and performance librarian. *Notice how far down the list "conductor" appears!* A typical high school music program may support as many as fifteen separate large ensembles including, but not limited to, marching bands, pep bands, concert bands, wind ensembles, choirs, orchestras, string ensembles, jazz ensembles, and various chamber ensembles. These ensembles may perform upwards of forty times a year, playing formal concerts as well as every community service event at which music is requested. Given the musical and non-musical demands placed on the music director, the stress can be overwhelming.

One idea, which could potentially ease some of that stress, is to enlist student interns to handle some of those responsibilities. Of all the responsibilities of a "music director," one of the most time consuming, but at the same time crucial for the day-to-day running of a program, is that of performance librarian. If one were to examine musical organizations at both the college and professional levels, the role of performance librarian is essential. However, at the secondary school level it is considered just another responsibility of the music director. If the many ensembles of a typical high school music department perform three to six times a year and play from four to six compositions per performance, it becomes quite apparent that there is a significant quantity of music to be prepared, distributed, collected, repaired, and refiled back in the library. When provided with the necessary structure and resources, a library staff comprised of dedicated student musicians will ease some of the burdens of music preparation and provide a valuable time saving service for the music director.

Qualifications and personal traits

Following is a list of suggested personal qualifications to consider when recruiting students as the high school performance librarian.

Educational and musical qualifications
- Respectable GPA, 3.0 or above. Students who are motivated and successful in their academic work possess the motivation and dedication to do a job correctly the first time.
- Should be a member in good standing of the foundation ensemble.[9]

---

[9] Foundation ensembles are defined as the largest all-inclusive ensembles from which all other small and more selective ensembles are created.

- Should be in the upper grades within the school. In a four-year high school, students in grades ten through twelve would be eligible to work as librarians. In high schools that only have three grades, ten through twelve, only students enrolled in grades eleven and twelve would be eligible for selection as librarians.

Computer and mechanical skills
- Comfortable with the technology associated with photocopiers, computers, and scanners. This would include the ability to diagnose and fix paper jams that occur often with school copiers.
- Experience with computer software programs including word processing, database, spreadsheet, and music notation applications.

Personal characteristics
- Strong organizational skills
- An appreciation for details, especially when preparing parts for distribution
- Ability to work with faculty and fellow students
- Ability to work independently
- Self-motivated
- Strong time management skills

Job responsibilities

The duties and responsibilities of student librarians pale in comparison to those who work at the professional or collegiate levels for several reasons. One is the fact that most high school ensembles perform music that is readily available through most music vendors. It is uncommon for high school ensembles to deal with rentals, commissions, or rare and historic works. Additionally, the size and scope of a typical performance library at the secondary level is usually significantly smaller than those at the university or professional levels.

Another point is that the budget for acquisitions at the secondary level is considerably less than that at the higher academic or professional levels. Most secondary schools may receive anywhere from a meager $500.00 to a generous $8,000.00 to purchase music, although the reality is that this money may be allocated to support all of the ensembles within the department. An annual budget of $8,000.00 to purchase music for one school orchestra would be wonderful, but it most likely must also be used to purchase music for two orchestras, two jazz ensembles, three concert bands, a marching band, a pep band, six choirs, and a variety of student chamber ensembles.

The following list reflects those responsibilities that are required to manage the music library within a high school music department.

Library duties
- Prepare music for distribution to all ensembles
- Distribute music to section leaders to be passed out to players
- Collect and maintain all music after the concert

- Maintain an accurate library inventory
- Maintain a list of lost, missing, or unusable parts that require replacement
- Repair and/or clean parts before returning them to the stacks

Additional responsibilities (optional)
- Create concert programs for each performance
- Research and write program notes for concert programs
- Create and maintain ensemble personnel rosters, which could be used for:
  - Tracking music distribution and return
  - Printed concert programs
  - Rehearsal attendance
  - Sectional attendance
- Prepare audition and performance evaluation materials

Additional responsibilities that should not be assigned to the library staff
- Ensemble setup
- Stage setup

It is important to understand that the student librarian's responsibilities should stay focused on the management of any and all printed music. They should not be thought of as ensemble or facility managers or as department administrative assistants. They are students and even the best, most trustworthy student is still that—a student—and should not be privy to many of the administrative underpinnings of the music department.

Moreover, in as much as they are full-time students and often have a tremendous academic workload outside of the music department, their "free" time is extremely limited. The more structure imposed upon them in the performance of their duties, the more successful they will be in completing their assigned tasks. The performance schedule at the secondary level is, at times, hectic, but it is fairly regular and there are not usually any last minute surprises, as there often are at the professional level.

The bottom line

When all is said and done, the ideal student librarian is one to whom the music director can say, "I want to do Holst's Suite in E-flat next Monday with the concert band," and be totally confident that at Monday's rehearsal he or she can step up on the podium and begin the "Chaconne" with the confidence that every student has the correct music. To ensure that this scenario occurs, the music director must be very clear and outline in detail all that is involved in preparing each piece of music for distribution. Music directors do not like surprises and neither do librarians.

Walter O'Keefe is the Director of Bands and the Music Department Chair at Masconomet High School in Topsfield, Massachusetts.

Film and Studio Librarian: Music Preparation for Film Soundtrack Recording Sessions

by Eric Swanson

Preparing music for motion picture recording sessions is a bit different from orchestral librarian work, but there are certain practices common to both.

One must come to terms with the idea that the music being recorded for a film soundtrack is, most of the time, being premiered at the recording session itself. This means that in a three hour session a dozen works or more may be played for the first and last time. Often the "cues" are short: a few seconds of transitional music to help a scene change. Major motion pictures do, however, usually have a handful of longer cues (Main Titles, End Credits, action/chase scenes, etc.).

In certain cases, musicians will want to see their music ahead of time. We will post PDF files to a secure website, server, or iDisk for download. This is especially helpful for the percussionists, so they can make notes as to which people are to play which instruments at what time. We refer to this as "choreography." Orchestra percussionists have to do this, too, but perhaps not on the fly as often as in a studio situation.

Studio work requires a certain kind of musician, but it also requires a unique kind of librarian. Recording musicians obviously must be great sight-readers. They also excel in instrument doublings. Whereas in most orchestras the principal players only play their primary instrument, sessions require most players to double. It is not uncommon for all three flautists to also bring their piccolos and alto flutes. Clarinetists might bring saxophones. A bassoonist might even have to play something on the baritone saxophone. Brass players need to own and be able to navigate Wagner tubas, flugelhorns, contrabass trombones, and cimbassi.

Traditionally, scores were submitted as pencil on paper. Some composers and orchestrators still work this way but typically music will actually be submitted twice to a copying office. First, as MIDI data with a reference audio recording. This will be cleaned up by an orchestrator and made into a "sketch" which contains all of the notes, but not all of the instrument assignments and dynamics. It is rare for a composer to orchestrate their own music in the Hollywood film industry due to the fast pace at which they are required to compose. The orchestrated scores are then re-submitted to the copyists for part extraction, proofreading, and printing.

The typical process

Music is "booked up" for a session either in numerical order (by reel and part which runs in order of the scenes of the movie) or in a custom order, often starting with the larger orchestrations or longer cues. Sets of scores will be double-checked and cartage may be ordered to transport the music to the scoring stage. It is sometimes too much music to fit into the trunk of a car!

It is important to remember that this whole process can and does often happen in the course of a few hours. Most of the music will be prepared in time for the session, but there will always be a few "stragglers" that are sent to the copyists early in the morning and will need to be at the recording stage by 10:00 a.m. Some cues will also undergo significant changes during the session itself. The orchestration might change. Solo passages might be assigned to different instruments. The key might change. And there is always the chance that, overnight, the film's director has changed a scene slightly by editing. In this case the music needs to be conformed to the new cut of the picture, making sure that it starts and ends at the new timings.

For last-minute changes, a librarian brings a laptop computer with Finale, Sibelius, Digital Performer, and Logic installed, as well as a high speed printer capable of printing on oversized and thicker paper stock. Multiple copies of the fixed score will need to be assembled, as well. In addition to a printed score for the conductor, scores are also required for the recording engineer, composer, assistants, music editor, and engineers in the booth.

There is a great deal of paperwork that goes into preparing for every session. As mentioned previously, many session musicians bring multiple instruments to the studio. The music copying team, much like a symphonic music librarian, is responsible for creating lists of instrument doublings, percussion requirements, and other key data so that the recording engineers can set up the studio efficiently. Large keyboard and percussion instruments will be rented and a truck hired to deliver everything to the studio.

After the sessions are over, the music is returned to the copyist/librarian's office where it is broken down from the instrument folders into cue (numerical) order. It is packed into boxes and sent to the studio which produced the film. For long-term reference, a copy of the printed score and all digital files (Finale, Sibelius, PDF, etc.) are kept at the office. The digital files are stored on a server which is backed up daily for safety.

The last step in a film music scoring project occurs when a CD or download soundtrack album is released. If the album sells enough copies, the musicians (and others who worked on the project) will get a bonus. To determine this, we have to match which raw cues became the commercially-released tracks. Often it is a simple process if each track is a cue from the session. Other times it can get very difficult when overdubs, pre-records, and multiple versions of the same cue are spliced together.

I hope I have shown to a certain degree how film soundtrack recording sessions require many of the same tasks performed by orchestral librarians, but differences abound!

Eric Swanson is the Assistant Manager of the Music Library for JoAnn Kane Music Service.

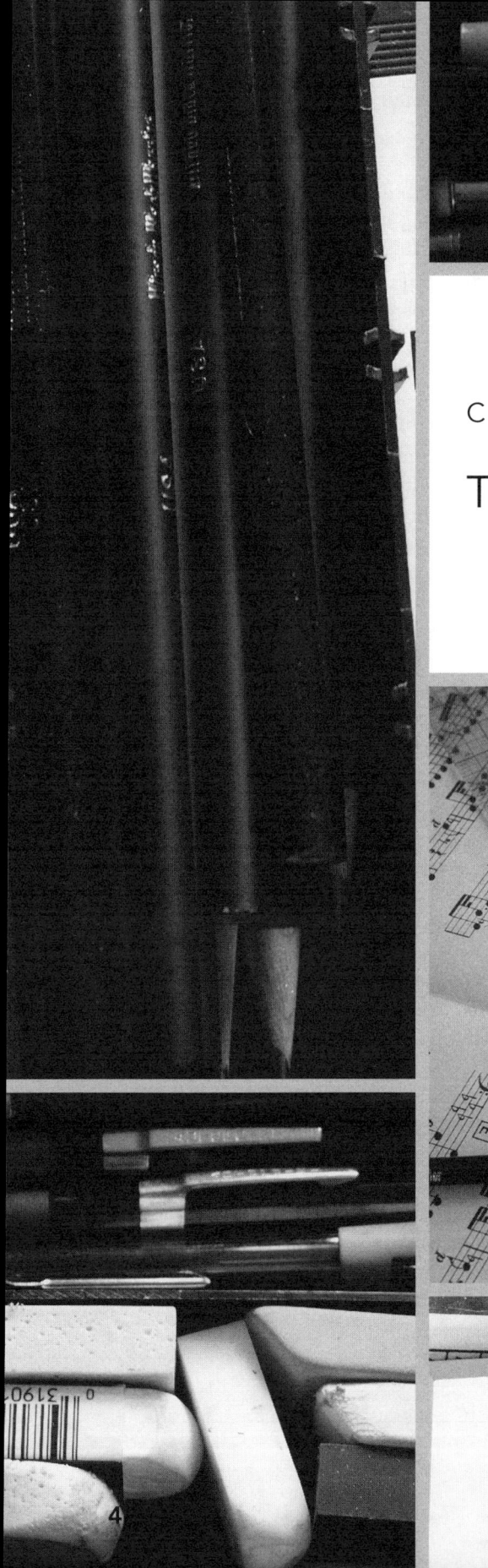

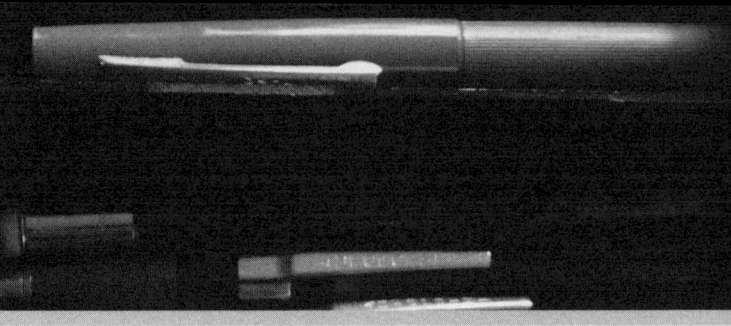

CHAPTER **2**

The Librarian and the …

... ORCHESTRA CONDUCTOR

Librarians are on the Front Line

by James DePreist

Librarians are on the front line of the vital behind-the-scenes preparations that precede music making. Long before the first rehearsal, long before the first sound of the orchestra, a good librarian will already have amassed all relevant information about the works to be performed—editions, revisions, instrumentation, rental costs, bowing options, performance history, the condition of parts, awkward page turns, corrections, cuts, sources, and more.

I have had the pleasure of working with some of the world's very best professional librarians and the trait that sets them apart from their colleagues is their degree of anticipatory thoroughness. Whether preparing material for the Music Director or a guest conductor, the librarian becomes the highly informed guardian at the gate before the first folder is placed on the stands. As a result, rehearsals can proceed with musicians and conductor focused exclusively on music-making.

It is hard to overstate the importance of the collaboration between conductor and librarian and the satisfaction and peace of mind that a conductor can enjoy because of the trust a good librarian engenders.

Considering their value, librarians demand only knowledge, clarity, and decisiveness from the conductor. The amount of time and work required to obtain and prepare orchestral parts can be significant and conductors impede the process when they are less than clear and timely in responding to the librarian's inquiries.

Often programs are established a year or more in advance of performance and it is possible for conductors to forget the specifics of the editions requested. If there is a surprise at the first rehearsal, you can be assured that it's not the librarian's fault. Experience has taught all librarians the importance of keeping meticulous records of communication between conductors and the library to be certain of no surprises.

Of necessity librarians tend to be inquisitive in their research and probe for information beyond that required for the performance at hand. Conversations with them can be most interesting and enlightening for anyone interested in building a musicological profile of a work.

All that I have outlined above would be complicated and demanding were it to have to take place quarterly, but the reality is that these tasks and responsibilities arrive weekly and often on a daily basis.

The very best librarians have established a standard of thoroughness and scholarship that is truly remarkable. I am indebted to each of the fine librarians with whom I have collaborated and for their insufficiently-sung role in making performances possible.

James DePreist is Principal Conductor and Director Emeritus of Conducting and Orchestral Studies at The Juilliard School and Laureate Music Director of the Oregon Symphony.

... WIND BAND CONDUCTOR

The Marine Band Library: The Ultimate Support System for Any Conductor

by Michael J. Colburn

As Director of "The President's Own" United States Marine Band, I am responsible for an organization that performs as many as 700 commitments annually. While these performances range from a 75-piece concert band to a solo piano in the White House private residence, nearly all of these events require some level of support from our highly talented and capable library staff. As with any performance library, their primary responsibility is to provide music to our musicians and conductors, but their contributions far exceed this basic job description. In the paragraphs that follow, you will find an accounting of just a few of their many and varied roles (believe me—there are many more!), as well as my thoughts on the relationships between conductors, musicians, and librarians. Although there are undoubtedly some requirements that are unique to "The President's Own," I hope that readers will find some ideas that are relevant to their ensembles as well.

1. Research assistants for concert programming: Many musicians assume that librarian support for a program doesn't begin until the folders are built for musicians to pick up. For Marine Band conductors, library support often begins long before the musicians show up for the first rehearsal. As soon as I begin planning a program, often more than a year in advance of the concert, it is the library and our librarians that I first consult. Whether it is assistance in finding music that fits within the theme of a program, help in identifying different editions available for a certain work (in the case of band transcriptions, this number can be surprisingly high), or copyright advice for a work we hope to arrange, it is almost always the library that can provide the answer.

2. Research assistants for unusual commitments: As the only musical organization whose primary mission is to provide support to the White House, we are often tasked with supplying the music for a wide range of events, and this support requires a variety of ensembles. Whether it is an orchestra for a State Dinner, a band to play college fight songs for a NCAA event, or a mariachi group to support a Cinco de Mayo celebration, our librarians are always involved. In addition to providing the music, they are often tasked with providing research assistance. When choosing music for a State Dinner, it is not uncommon for our Chief Librarian to contact the appropriate embassy to inquire as to the visiting head of state's musical taste or to ask if a certain selection would be appropriate. As the music advisor to the White House, one of my greatest concerns is that we never play music that would in any way offend or cause discomfort to the President's guests, so this type of research is especially important. When we play college fight songs to honor victorious teams at the annual NCAA event, it is the library that is tasked with tracking each school down, contacting their band department, and doing whatever is necessary to get their hands on the appropriate song. The library provides similar assistance to the various small specialty ensembles that we are often required to provide. In some cases, these ensembles do not exist until there is a specific request, and the library is often the first place our musicians turn when they need to find a style or genre of music with which they have little or no experience. Although an individual librarian is assigned to each commitment, they will often ask their colleagues for assistance, expertise, and advice on how to thoroughly research a new topic. This support often comes from librarians in our sister service bands or from symphony orchestras and universities around the world.

3. Editors/Proofers of musical text: Achieving accuracy and consistency in the appearance of titles, composer names, and other concert program information is a challenge for any ensemble, but because of all of the variables we deal with, it is an especially daunting proposition for the Marine Band. Our librarians ensure that all titles, composer names, dates, and musical terms are checked for accuracy and stylistic consistency. In addition to providing this service for our printed concert programs, they also edit program notes, CD liner notes, and all other Marine Band publications, either in print or on the Internet. The result is a remarkably consistent and accurate treatment of musical information in our publications that is commensurate with the high musical standards of our organization.

4. Liaison for copyright/mechanical licensing: In the late 1990s this responsibility was shifted from our assistant directors to a member of our library staff. Because librarians often deal directly with composers, arrangers, and publishers, it became clear that they were in a better position to identify and communicate with copyright holders regarding permission to arrange and record copyrighted music. This change has greatly streamlined and improved the consistency of this process.

5. Organizational historians: As the nation's oldest professional musical organization, history is very important to us. Our librarians serve an important role as the guardians of much of that history and they do so in a number of ways. They keep meticulous records of Marine Band performances, notating exactly what is performed at many events. In the case of concerts, each selection is timed, and the performance data is maintained with the music for future reference. On some occasions, especially at the White House or during a presidential inauguration ceremony, the sequence of music is often altered on the spot, and I rely upon our librarians to document these changes whenever possible. In addition to adding to the historical record of the organization, this information is often helpful when planning for similar events. It is tremendously reassuring to know that so much valuable information resides in our archives and that I've got a staff of capable librarians to help me find it!

6. Archivists: As one might expect of an organization that has been around for more than two centuries, the Marine Band has accumulated an impressive collection of items that must be carefully preserved and maintained. In addition to the music and books we have in our stacks, we possess old instruments, uniforms, photographs, advertising posters, and a variety of memorabilia that defies categorization. By default, the vast majority of this collection resides in our climate-controlled library, under the careful supervision of our librarians. Just as I need our musicians to have the versatility to satisfy the ever-changing requirements of the job, so too do I expect our librarians to wear many hats. Even though each librarian has a specific area of expertise and responsibility, they all need to have a general knowledge and comfort level in dealing with every aspect of our collection. This concept is very much in line with the philosophy of the Marine Corps, which encourages specialization, but never at the expense of the versatility that has defined the Corps's success.

In the Marine Band we expect and receive a lot of support from our library, but as conductors we need to support them as well. I am convinced that the crucial first step in this support is to afford our librarians (and indeed all of our support staff) the same level of respect and professionalism we show our musicians. Librarians should never think of themselves as second-class citizens simply because their job description differs from that of the performers, nor should musicians treat librarians with anything less than the mutual respect they offer each other. One of the best ways for conductors to achieve an atmosphere of professional courtesy is to do whatever they can to help the librarians to do their jobs. For example, conductors should always do their best to honor deadlines, answer library questions in a timely fashion, and avoid last-minute program changes whenever possible. Of course, there are times when best laid plans and schedules are overtaken by events (especially in the Marine Band), but it is important to avoid a crisis atmosphere whenever possible. It has been my experience that when people work in an atmosphere of professional mutual respect, they are happier, more productive, and more inclined to treat others in the same manner.

Whenever I am asked the question, "What is the best thing about being director of the United States Marine Band," my answer is always the same: The opportunity to work with the finest professionals I have ever met. While their artistry and skill is among the best you will find in any major symphony orchestra, it is their integrity, kindness, and esprit de corps that really define the members of our organization. When hearing this answer, most people assume I am referring to our performers—the instrumentalists who comprise the public face of the Marine Band. But my appreciation applies equally to our incredible support staff, a group that includes the outstanding music librarians of "The President's Own."

Colonel Michael J. Colburn is the Director of "The President's Own" United States Marine Band.

(The information presented in this publication has been prepared solely by the author and neither the United States Marine Band, the U.S. Marine Corps, nor any other component of the Department of Defense of the U.S. Government has endorsed this material.)

... COMPOSER

The Orchestra Librarian— A Composer's View

by Ellen Taaffe Zwilich

I'm a composer who loves writing for orchestra. The orchestra has been in my life since I was in middle school. For a number of years I earned a living as a violinist in New York City, playing, among other gigs, in the American Symphony for seven years under Leopold Stokowski. Despite (or maybe because of?) having had experience as a player and having written over thirty works for orchestra, I never fail to discover something new in each piece I write. For me, the orchestra is an immensely complex organism—never the same from piece to piece and with a special magic when it all coalesces into an amazing whole. (I liken it to a jellyfish, which is not a single creature, but a collection of creatures all working together and seeming to be one.)

As is the case with most "magic," there is much unseen work going on. Some of the most important work is in the hands of the orchestra librarian as well as the composer and the leaders in the orchestra.

My guiding principle is simple: if an orchestra is presented with a set of materials for a piece in the standard repertoire (something many players will have played before or, at least, have heard before) technical issues still have to be addressed, artistic decisions have to be made, and players' understanding of the work has to deepen. For this reason, any potential problems with the materials should be addressed before the first rehearsal. This is particularly important in a premiere performance, in which the performers are, in a sense, creating a new tradition as well as reading the notes. We composers may also be tweaking this and changing that (which adds to the importance of the parts and score being in agreement and accurate). Any discrepancies or anything that elicits questions about notation take away from the rehearsal time needed for artistic matters.

In the current situation in which a composer can select "make parts" in a computer program and instantly have a set of parts, a bit of special vigilance may be needed. A part may look "professional" but the page turns may not be optimum, the cues may be less than helpful, and sometimes an experienced look at a layout will inspire a slightly different configuration that is more helpful to the performer.

The librarian and his or her experienced and watchful eye is my valuable partner in the premiere of a new work. Our partnership, unseen though it may be, makes it possible for magic to occur as a work comes to life in performance.

Ellen Taaffe Zwilich is a prolific composer and recipient of the Pulitzer Prize in Music, whose works have been performed by leading American orchestras and by major ensembles abroad.

... MUSIC DEALER

Music Publishers and Music Dealers: How and Why They are Different and What to Expect From Each

by Carla Boyer

The terms "music publisher" and "music dealer" tend to be used interchangeably, but in fact the two types of companies they describe have very different and usually separate functions. There are few companies that do both functions successfully in a major way. There are simply too many varied aspects and costs associated with publishing music and with being a retail music dealer to permit one company to do it all. Therefore, the music publishing industry has evolved into these two types of companies. Success in acquiring music from either requires specialized treatment on the part of the consumer or librarian.

Music publishers

When dealing with a Music Publisher, normally to negotiate rental fees and terms, you are dealing with the source of the material. What you should expect is information about different versions of a particular title, prompt responses to your inquiries, and being sent music in good repair with all the parts for which the music is scored, along with a full score for the conductor. You cannot expect a Music Publisher to tell you that there may be other editions available. You cannot necessarily expect them to alert you to any problems with their edition, although that would be a big help. You will probably need to consult with colleagues who have had experience with that title in order to avoid unpleasant surprises. As an example, if Kurt Weill's *The Seven Deadly Sins* has been scheduled, the rental librarian may not ask whether you want the high voice or the low voice version and, since the vocal score has both lines, the question may not arise until the first rehearsal. I leave it to you to imagine the details of having the wrong version.

Music Publishers undertake the task of making new music available for performance as either a rental or a sales title. They also supply corrected/updated versions of earlier publications. They are responsible for supplying good materials in either case. By "good," I mean clearly printed materials with all parts included. The rental department of a Music Publisher can also be called upon for recommendations in programming with regard to their own catalog. Music Publishers do not have the luxury of presenting their music to every customer. They must rely on Music Dealers to represent them by knowing the nature of their catalog and also how to obtain music from a specific publisher.

If you want to work well with a rental department, make certain that you have the following information available:

1. The composer and title of the music
2. The date(s) of the performance(s)
3. The date you need the music to arrive
4. The name of the conductor
5. The venue of the performance along with the number of seats and ticket prices
6. Whether there will be a recording or broadcast of some sort

Music dealers

Music Dealers are a horse of a different color. There are many types of Music Dealers. Some specialize in educational materials for the public schools; others specialize in choral publications; others specialize in music for a specific family of instruments (harp, strings, woodwinds, brass); some specialize in orchestral music of various types; and some cover the entire range. As a performance librarian, you need to determine what type of Music Dealer will best serve your needs. One way to find this out is to consult other librarians about what sources they use. I would suggest that you look for a Music Dealer with knowledgeable salespeople who can tell you about the range of editions that can be purchased and who to contact for rental information. That can save you immense amounts of time paging through various publisher catalogs with the hope of discovering the title you want. Your music dealer should be aware of what changes have occurred in the representation of composers and publisher catalogs. There is nothing written in stone about what composer is represented by which publisher, nor is there anything permanent about which publishers are owned by whom. This information can change quite rapidly. In addition, the source for purchasing a particular edition may be different from the source for renting a publisher's materials. For example, purchasable music published by Schott is housed at Hal Leonard Publishing's warehouse in Minnesota, but its rental materials are now handled by the rental department at European American Music Distributors.

The role of the Music Dealer is to sell music, of course, but for certain companies the aim is also to help simplify the daunting task of the performance librarian. Some of the major symphony orchestras have more than one or two librarians to help with getting music ordered, prepared, distributed, corrected, collected, repaired, and filed properly. Although that is a large enough task, it is not the only thing that librarians are asked to do. There is budget preparation, locating the music that has been programmed, negotiating with rental companies (Music Publishers), following up on whether materials have arrived on time and in good condition, and frequently in university, regional, and community orchestras, playing as a member of the orchestra, as well. There is also the challenge of getting information from conductors and soloists about what has been programmed and, if you have a vocal soloist, finding out the key of each work. (For example, Hector Berlioz's *Les nuits d'été* has alternate keys for each song.) You have to do a great deal of preparation so that no time is wasted with tasks that could be delegated to other dependable organizations. One of those organizations could be your Music Dealer.

Music Dealers need to be able to locate materials if they exist or determine that they don't exist. It is an unfortunate fact that just because a work has been recorded, it may not necessarily be available for other performances. In some cases, special musical arrangements may have been made for a particular performance or recording and that arrangement may belong to the performer or the organization (custom arrangements for the Boston Pops, for example) and are not available to anyone else. In some cases, materials have been lost. In other cases, materials may no longer be in print. It is also possible that music may be available from sources other than a Music Publisher. Presently, many composers are taking control of the distribution for their own compositions and so information about how to contact that composer is necessary. Music Dealers should not be asked to create programs—that is the job of the Music Director or Programming Department. However, when a program has been set, your Music Dealer can certainly help locate and supply the materials.

In order to simplify ordering music for sale, here is some information to have available:

1. The composer and title you want to order
2. The edition, if one has been specified by your conductor or if you are adding to materials already in your library
3. Whether a large-size full score is needed (in many editions, this is not automatically included)
4. The TOTAL number of string parts you want (not necessarily the same as the number of players you have)
5. The specific calendar date you want to receive the music you are ordering—not the date of the performance and not "ASAP" or "Regular method." The purpose of this information is to facilitate delivery of the music in a timely and efficient manner without spending unnecessary amounts of money in shipping charges.
6. The address for billing and shipping the music
7. The purchase order number, if your organization is a college, university, or any institution that assigns purchase order numbers to items they buy. This information should be available at the time the order is placed.

If you need information about available editions prior to finalizing an order, you can request it of your Music Dealer. This is generally something that can be done in writing so that you can present it to the music director for decisions on editions. It is also a way to protect the music director's ego in case he or she is not aware of the possible choices available. If you are able to coax specific information from the music director or guest conductor in advance, you will have a better idea of what you want to order or what further information you need to ask of the Music Publisher or Music Dealer.

There is a caveat here, however. While it is appropriate to ask your Music Dealer to do research for you, it is implied that you would then return to that Music Dealer to purchase those titles when they can be bought. It is not really appropriate to ask one Music Dealer to do research and then take that information to another Music Dealer to purchase the music.

There are really no stupid or silly questions, but keep in mind some basic principles:

- NEVER ASSUME that a publication is packaged in a particular way or that it is for rent or sale.
- NEVER ASSUME that music will be readily available; it may be a foreign edition that needs to be imported (this applies to both rental and sale materials), or it may be temporarily or permanently out of print.

Wherever possible, plan ahead to save shipping costs and mental anguish. Never be hesitant to ask for more details or explanations of terminology. Many publishers and dealers may play fast and loose with some musical formats so don't assume that a "set of parts" contains the same thing in all editions or that choral music is consistently formatted.

Keep in mind that your librarian colleagues are a generous group and are willing to be of help. On the other hand, don't expect someone else to do your job for you. Chances are that your colleagues have plenty to keep them busy with their own orchestras. Be prepared to return a favor and don't forget to express appreciation for help, especially help above and beyond the call of duty.

Finally, although it may seem obvious, it is important to keep financial dealings current with both Music Publishers and Music Dealers and to behave in a professional and calm manner. If an error has been made, it can be easily rectified if the facts are presented clearly in a non-confrontational manner and as promptly as possible. No solution can be achieved by making accusations. If an error has occurred, have exact information available so that the problem can be solved.

Working with Music Publishers and Music Dealers can be a productive experience, but you have to be ready to do some preparation on your own before picking up the telephone, sending the fax, or transmitting the e-mail. Time is something almost no librarian has enough of and the more clearly you make your needs known, the more efficiently you will be able to do your work.

Carla Boyer is the Sales Manager for Educational Music Service in Chester, New York.

... MUSIC PUBLISHER

Behind the Scenes at a Publisher's Rental Library

by Rachel Peters

Working with rental music and publishers can be overwhelming. Like snowflakes, no two music publishers are identical, but I hope the examples I provide from Boosey & Hawkes can remove some of the mystery from the rental process and set some effective guidelines.

How big are you really?

Every publisher's rental library facilities and staff are different. The Boosey & Hawkes Rental Library currently houses nearly 40,000 sets of music of over 14,000 titles. Our roster of living composers is very active and prolific, and our catalog is constantly growing. We also act as the North American agent for about fifteen international publishers. We serve around 7,000 North American customers including major symphony orchestras, opera and ballet companies, youth orchestras, schools, conservatories, religious organizations, festivals, and chamber groups. We have five full-time librarians and one part-timer to take care of it all!

How do I know whether or not you carry the piece I need? If you don't, how can I find it?

This can be a daunting process. First and foremost, be sure to have your conductor confirm the orchestration, edition, and key of the piece s/he wants. A perusal score may be a helpful first step. Once you have identified the work, the Internet is your best friend. Most publishers offer their catalogs online. If you are looking for a piece held by a foreign publisher (such as Ricordi) administered by us, you can look at that publisher's website and know that if you place an order with us, we can rent it to you on their behalf. If you cannot find what you're looking for on our website, it may be held by another domestic publisher. Bear in mind that works by the same composer are sometimes split between publishers. For example, many of Benjamin Britten's works are with Boosey & Hawkes, but many others are with Faber Music which is now administered by European American Music in North America. Nowadays most composers have their own websites that list the publishers of each work. We encourage you to pursue any available resources before asking a publisher's librarian to track it down for you. Sometimes a simple Google search will yield the answer.

Okay, I found what I need and it's yours. How do I place an order?

Our rental order form is available online, as are those of most publishers. Many librarians I know pine for the days when they could just call someone, say "Hi, I'm Bob, and I want some Copland for next week." The new way may feel impersonal, but we need a universally formatted, centrally accessible method of receiving your information. It actually does increase our ability to help you faster and prevents us from missing important details (or dropping the order altogether!). And remember: if you have specific questions, there are still human beings here to help.

Should I be the one at my organization who places the order?

Every orchestra's administration is different. We understand that the librarian is rarely the person who ultimately chooses the programming or pays for it. At larger universities with a separate purchasing department, a big faculty, *and* multiple divisions of a music department, this can get especially unwieldy. Before you order, work out who should be the billing contact, the shipping contact, and any contact in between. Conductors sometimes jump into the rental routine before they realize the librarian is already quite well-versed in it. They will really appreciate the help!

How much is this going to cost me?

At Boosey & Hawkes we determine rental fees based upon the duration of the work, the instrumentation, and the orchestra's budget category. You should expect to pay more for a rental set than you would for music you buy through a retailer. **Always ask for a quote first**. Our quote request form is accessible on our website right next to the order form. It's important to have all of the facts *before* you order. Rental contracts are legally binding, and if you sign one, you and everyone in your organization are agreeing to any applicable fees.

Where does the money from my rental fees go?

Our composers' works are under copyright and rental income translates to royalties for these works. We also use these funds to build and nurture relationships with new composers and support our roster's creation of new works for the next generation of audiences to hear. And, of course, just like any other business, every publisher incurs considerable overhead in providing and maintaining materials.

How far in advance should I order the music?

As soon as you have confirmation that it will be on the program! We have orders in our queue for over a year from now. Not everyone has that much advance warning and programming may need to change at the last minute, but "the sooner the better" should be your mantra. Be aware of each publisher's rush policy. There is an additional service charge—*not* the same as expedited shipping—to put your order at the head of the line. Boosey & Hawkes requires ten *business* days before the piece is required to *ship*. Pay close attention to the publisher's rules when calculating the date by which you can avoid a rush fee.

Why do you need so much time? Aren't you just pulling a set of music off a shelf?

Unfortunately, it's almost never that simple. Some librarians imagine that publishers' rental libraries are like Amazon.com and have overstock ready to go at any time, but we simply cannot operate that way. Some pieces go through phases of high demand (and some are *always* in high demand). At the other end of the spectrum, you may be requesting a work that has never been played on this continent. Or the previous customer may have lost several parts to our only set of the piece you want. If we have no (or insufficient) materials on the premises when you order a work we publish, we will have to reprint. If the piece originates from one of our international publishers, we may need to import it, and *they* may even need to print new materials for your order. The bottom line is getting you the right material for your concert requires sufficient lead time.

I got it, but my conductor and/or musicians are complaining about the parts. What now?

Every publisher has a different relationship to its editorial and printing resources. Make sure you find out whether the problem is with the physical condition of the materials or if it is related to layout, page turns, errata, style, etc. It is rare that a rental librarian is personally able to fix materials to your specifications. Re-engraving materials is a labor-intensive process and cannot be done on demand. We do take these requests into consideration and, if the demand is sufficient, we strive to fold it into our existing production schedule down the road. If, however, you are displeased with the physical condition of your set, it is usually possible for us to provide a replacement set upon request. Check your package as soon as you receive it. Sometimes a set of parts will sit in a box until the first rehearsal, and then suddenly everyone panics. Don't let this happen to you!

If I'm renting music from you, do I also need a license from ASCAP/BMI/SOCAN?

Yes, yes, always yes. These are Performing Rights Organizations with whom our composers are registered. When you rent music for a concert performance, we will ask you for a license number, and your performance will then be registered with ASCAP or BMI (or SOCAN in Canada).

We would also like to broadcast/record/stream/synch/our concert OR we plan to add staging or film elements. Is that okay?

Any additional use of rental material must be reported to and approved by the publisher in advance. There are fees associated with these extra uses and you may need to obtain a mechanical or synchronization license. If you are planning to perform the work with staging of any kind, you will need a Grand Rights license and should expect to pay a Grand Rights performance fee in addition to your rental. This applies to all opera and dance performances. Some uses require additional permission from the composer or his/her estate. Do not assume that permission will be granted. As a librarian, you may often find yourself in the awkward position of copyright police for your orchestra. It is always better to be safe than sorry. Again, planning ahead and excellent communication are key. We will be happy to help you navigate these complicated procedures.

Rachel Peters is the Associate Director of Grand Rights for Boosey & Hawkes Inc. in New York.

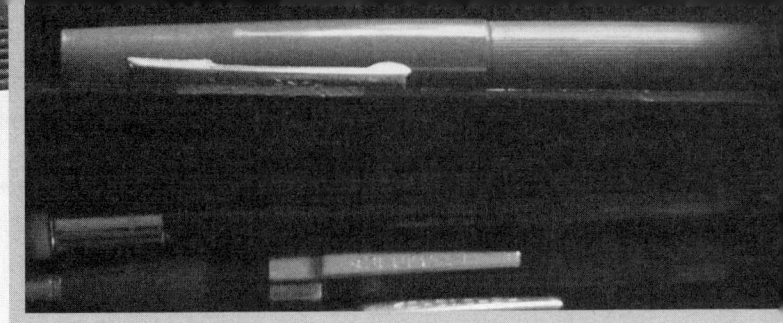

CHAPTER **3**

Aspects of the Profession

So, You Think You Might Want to Be an Orchestra Librarian?

by Lawrence Tarlow

Well, it can be very rewarding. It can also be very frustrating. Let's discuss the most essential skill necessary, the frustrations, and then the rewards, if you're not already thinking of doing something else.

Reading music is the paramount skill necessary for an orchestra librarian. Well, of course! But, there are different levels of ability in reading music. Why is it utterly important for the orchestra librarian to be a good—not good, *great!*—score reader? What does score reading entail? How does one learn to read a score?

The necessity stems from the orchestra library's function in music preparation. Nearly every day, the orchestra librarian makes reference to the score. Why do we refer to the score? Because it's the master copy, the one place where every part in the orchestra is notated. While a player might make reference to something in their part, it's the score to which we librarians generally refer. When a player mentions something in the part that needs to be checked, it's often something to be checked against another part. In the score we can see both parts and make the necessary comparison. When the conductor wants the orchestra librarian to alter something, to correct something, or to check something, it's to the score the conductor will refer. When the librarian is asked about the instrumentation of a particular work, while there are numerous reference materials listing instrumentation, it's the score that by definition has the correct information…if you know how to read it, and where to look.

Once you know how to read a score, it's not so difficult. The same can probably be said of speaking French, producing a television program, or hitting a curve ball. The rub is in getting to that level of ability.

We all know that written music for the most part consists of a five-line staff populated with a variety of symbols. Without the symbol at the beginning of at least the first line—the clef—the notes written can be any pitch. The point of this elementary observation is that there are a variety of clefs used in the orchestral score. Musicians are generally familiar with the treble and bass clefs, used for nearly every instrument in the orchestra, but there are others. We orchestra librarians must read the alto and tenor clefs as well as we read the treble and bass clefs.

To muddy the waters, there are also instruments whose written pitch is not their sounding pitch. Those instruments are referred to as "transposing instruments." When asked by a player or conductor—or another librarian—about a passage for a transposing instrument, there is no opportunity to consult a reference source about the transposition when being asked a direct question in person; the orchestra librarian must know at once what the sounding pitch is. Conversely, the orchestra librarian must also be able to express any given sounding pitch as the written pitch for a transposing instrument.

That's just pitch notation. What else do we have to know about reading a score?

Well, there are the instrument names. Not every score lists the instrument names in English. The orchestra librarian must recognize instrument names in a variety of languages. Familiarity with German, Italian, French, and Spanish instrument names is a must. This isn't just familiarity with standard instrument names, but also with names of auxiliary woodwind and percussion instruments and traditional names not often used. For example, some scores refer to *1. und 2. Geigen.* While it can often be inferred by the placement in the score what the instrument is, sometimes we're looking at a text listing of instruments or an informational e-mail with instrument names out of context and not in score order. The orchestra librarian must know these nonstandard terms for first and second violins [*Geigen* is literally translated as "fiddles"].

There are also performance instructions. This does not refer to interpretative markings, such as *Allegro* or *Sans ralentir* or *Etwas langsam*, but to instructions such as "change to E-flat clarinet," "with mute," or "for continuing." Again, apart from scores whose composers are native English speakers, these instructions are not generally in English. The orchestra librarian must have knowledge of foreign-language performance instructions.

The novice librarian might think that those are instructions for the player and conductor, of no importance to the orchestra librarian. However, the experienced librarian knows that we run across these instructions every time we open a score, and is glad that he or she long ago learned what these instructions mean.

Here's an example: the librarian is asked to obtain a perusal score for a work being considered for performance and the orchestra personnel manager has asked the librarian about the instrumentation. The score arrives as a PDF file and the person making the scan saved time and file size by not scanning the page that lists the instrumentation. The librarian needs to page through the score to make an orchestration listing. Hmm. While paging through the score, the librarian sees the instruction *nehmen Es-Klar.* What does that mean? Probably not important, thinks the novice, or someone else's problem. Well, it *is* important and might have a direct effect on the possibility of performance.

In what language is this? What does *nehmen* mean? Is it an instrument? What about *Es-Klar*? That looks like an instrument, but which one? It's vitally important for the orchestra librarian to alert the orchestra personnel manager that the clarinet player must also play the E-flat clarinet. *Nehmen Es-Klar* is literally translated as "take E-flat clarinet," meaning "change to E-flat clarinet." Knowing the foreign language versions of this sort of performance instruction is a necessary part of score reading.

How does a person interested in becoming an orchestra librarian learn to read a score? There's no better way than by doing. The prospective librarian can develop the necessary ability by getting scores from a library, from a friend, or by downloading scores available online and then finding recordings of the works in question. Listen to the music, follow the score, and it will all be clear. Of course, this isn't a one-week project.

Start with something fairly simple, like a Mozart overture or Haydn symphony. There are just a few lines, but when you hear the music at the same time you see it in notation, you'll start understanding what a score is all about.

Clefs? Violas are notated generally in the alto clef. Follow the viola line in your score-reading studies and say the note names to yourself, whether in *solfeggio* or letter-names. The point is, learn to read the alto clef. Trombones sometimes use the alto clef as well. In certain older Soviet-era scores, the English horn part is notated at concert pitch in the alto clef.

Perhaps the student has started with a Brahms symphony. There will be instruments that use the tenor clef, and the student should be looking at the tenor clef instruments and saying the note names until there is facility in reading that clef.

In nearly any orchestral score, other than the older Soviet-era publications referred to above, there will be instruments that say "in B-flat," or "in F," or in any number of things. The beginning librarian must know what these indications mean and be able to recite the note names of the sounding pitch for these instruments.

Keep an eye open as you move into more complicated scores for those performance indications mentioned above. In even an uncomplicated score by Dvořák, you might see the word Piccolo (or *kleine Flöte*) on the flute line. Your ear should tell you that this indication means a flute player plays piccolo at this point.

So, the prospective orchestra librarian must develop facility in score-reading. It's the foundation of everything done in the orchestra library. Without this skill, very little else matters. If the prospective orchestra librarian doesn't develop fluent score-reading ability, don't bother learning anything else about the profession. It will all be wasted.

Being an orchestra librarian can be frustrating. It's not likely there is any career without frustrations, but the prospective orchestra librarian should bear in mind the following: we orchestra librarians are generally only noticed when something goes wrong. It's a compliment to us that top-level work is the normal expectation, but we're rarely thanked for doing good work. We're not on the stage at the end of the performance when the orchestra is being applauded, but we've contributed directly to that performance. There are no bows for the orchestra librarian. If you need to bask in the limelight, this is the wrong career. There is no limelight for an orchestra librarian.

Also frustrating is the lack of appreciation of orchestra librarians as musicians. We don't play, sing, or conduct in front of an audience, but we are engaged for our musical skills. Our particular skills come from music preparation skills of long ago: music copying, orchestrating, and arranging. These are all skills long since accepted as being of a musical—not administrative or clerical—nature, and our field stems from those skills.

The reward of being an orchestra librarian is put simply: we're a part of creating great music. What other reward do we need?

That said, the rewards relate, naturally, to the frustrations. This relation, however, requires a certain mind-set on the part of the orchestra librarian. *We* have to know what our contribution to the successful performance was, and we have to, in some small way, tell ourselves at the end of the performance that some of the applause is meant for us as well. The audience just isn't aware of it.

In the end it comes down to this: every day that we go to work as an orchestra librarian, we get to hear the greatest musical compositions of the last two hundred and fifty years performed by the greatest artists of the current day.

Lawrence Tarlow is the Principal Librarian of the New York Philharmonic and a Past President of the Major Orchestra Librarians' Association.

Auditioning and Interviewing for the Performance Librarian

by Sara Griffin

Over the past several years I have come up with some pretty good comebacks to the question: "So, what is a library audition?" Rather than try to explain what really happens, I sometimes resort to a joke, relaying accounts of timed bowing trials or of being judged by the committee on speed and accuracy when setting folders on a stage full of stands and extension cords.

The truth is, an audition or interview for a performance library position can come in many different forms. Written tests and verbal interviews covering a wide range of subjects are the most common ways to judge a candidate's knowledge and personality. While it is unlikely that you will know exactly what you will be asked or how you will be tested at your audition, there are areas that can be used as a foundation, countless resources to get the information you need, and techniques for preparation.

Presenting yourself on paper and in person

Your audition process begins with the first correspondence you send to your potential employer and continues with every personal interaction. It is essential that you present a good communication style through your:

- Résumé
- Cover letter
- Verbal interview
- Institutional knowledge

Most organizations require that a résumé, cover letter, and manuscript example be sent in advance of an audition. Because these documents give the first impression of you as a candidate and reflect the quality of your work, they should be professional, concise, and free of errors. If there is a job posting, read it carefully, take it seriously, and note the specified parameters (length of résumé, application deadline, type of manuscript example to be submitted, etc.). Once you have finished preparing your documents, it is a good idea to have a fresh pair of eyes look over your work. Even the most detail-oriented person can miss a typo!

The verbal portion of your audition is critical, especially if an interview is your only interaction with your potential employer. Spend time thinking about possible questions (i.e., personal opinion, hypothetical situation, and technical) as well as your answers. Even if you feel particularly comfortable in an interview situation, practicing your verbal delivery with another person is never a bad idea. You might be surprised that the answer in your head becomes something different coming out of your mouth.

Answers should not be rehearsed, but organized in such a way that you can be comfortable and still be yourself.

Becoming educated about the institution should be an essential part of your preparation. Your research will give you the ability to ask informed questions, show that you are willing to become part of the fabric of the organization, and help you focus your preparation on the written portion of the audition.

Repertoire

Almost everything we do as performance librarians centers around repertoire. Candidates should expect to communicate many details of a given work at an audition including:

- Instrumentation
- Duration
- Editions and publishers
- Revisions
- Unique requirements
- Composer catalogs
- Popular and formal titles of common works
- Common excerpts from large works

As a beginning librarian, it can be difficult to know how to build your detailed knowledge of repertoire. You first need to find a starting resource that will help you become comfortable with standard repertoire in your prospective field. *Orchestral Music: A Handbook* by David Daniels[1] is an example of a basic resource for an orchestral librarian. Publisher and music retailer websites are also useful places to find information. Through this initial research, you will need to become familiar with the standard complement of your prospective ensemble and learn the related instrumentation formula.

Because there is an immense amount of repertoire out there, you should begin your study by focusing on commonly programmed repertoire and works that have certain "red flags." You can determine "red flag" status by researching and using first-hand experiences. Take a stroll down memory lane and make notes of repertoire that has stuck with you. For instance, perhaps you have performed *Fantasia on a Theme by Thomas Tallis* by Ralph Vaughan Williams and you recall the special stage setup for the double string orchestras and solo string quartet.

As you compile information, keeping it all straight can become a challenge. Use notebooks and index cards to develop an organizational system early in your preparation process. This material should be organized in such a way that it can easily be referenced or added to, both during and after the process.

---

1 David Daniels, *Orchestral Music: A Handbook* (4th ed. Lanham, Md.: Scarecrow Press, 2005). Online version available by subscription at http://www.orchestralmusic.com.

Musical instruments and terminology

Perhaps the most critical function of a performance librarian is to communicate musical information between the conductor, playing musicians, and staff. To do this a candidate should be familiar with the following:

- Names of instruments in foreign languages (especially English, French, German, and Italian)
- Written and sounding ranges of instruments
- Transpositions
- Directional terminology (mutes, bowings, stage directions, etc.)
- Publishing terminology

Auditions often require a candidate to read music in different keys, clefs and transpositions, as well as understand terminology in multiple languages. The most effective and practical way of preparing for this is by going straight to the source and sitting down with a variety of musical scores.

Again, keeping track of and organizing the information you are learning is essential for retaining it. Find meaningful and practical ways of reviewing this information with note cards, notebooks, or other methods. Every candidate will go into an audition with different strengths and weaknesses. It is important to spend some time evaluating your own situation to come up with a game plan that will maximize your preparation.

Music preparation

An interviewer or committee is interested in assessing not only your musical knowledge, but also your technical skills as a musician. Working hands-on with material is to be expected at an audition and a candidate should be prepared to complete the following projects:

- Bowings
- Transpositions
- Proofreading
- Marking cuts
- Extended work in a library

Regardless of whether you are performing these tasks on a regular basis, your written work should not be taken for granted while you prepare. Written work is often part of a timed element of the audition so it is a good idea to make sure your work can be neat and accurate when you are working under a time constraint.

Personal tools are generally allowed at an audition to complete projects. Your tool kit should include pencils, pens, ruler, correction fluid or tape, manuscript paper, tape, etc.

Industry knowledge

Becoming familiar with the musical details of a score is important, but it is of little use if you do not know how or where to obtain the material and what to do after receiving the music. At an audition, a candidate can expect to answer questions concerning the following subjects:

- Copyright
- Library procedures
- ASCAP and BMI
- Rental and purchase procedures
- Communication within the prospective institution
- Tour experience
- Computer software and database knowledge

The largest repository of information by far for these topics is the website of the Major Orchestra Librarians' Association or MOLA (www.mola-inc.org). The MOLA website provides links to publisher websites, performing organizations, information concerning copyright and licensing, and the largest amount of information about the profession of performance librarianship.

Another excellent resource for any beginning librarian is *A Manual for the Performance Library* by Russ Girsberger.[2] This manual provides procedural information for large ensemble libraries, as well as a detailed bibliography.

While first-hand experience working in a performance library is the best means of gaining industry knowledge, it is not always possible to find an opportunity to work in a library. Locating a mentor to help guide you and provide insight is of utmost importance in the life of any performance librarian. By reaching out to those more experienced in the field, you will find the best and most important resource available to any performance librarian.

Performance library interviews and auditions come in many forms. No two will be the same. Through thoughtful preparation and organization, you will help yourself find a place in a fascinating field that can teach you something new everyday.

Sara Griffin is the Assistant Principal Librarian of the New York Philharmonic.

---

[2] Russ Girsberger, *A Manual for the Performance Library* (Music Library Association Basic Manual Series, No. 6. Lanham, Md.: Scarecrow Press, 2006).

Teach Our Own

by Paul Gunther

Mentor: A wise and trusted counselor or teacher.

In Greek mythology, Mentor was Odysseus's trusted counselor, in whose guise Athena, goddess of wisdom, became the guardian and teacher of Odysseus's son Telemachus.

The first day I worked in an orchestra library was not actually in the library, and it didn't seem like work. It was copying bowings into string parts spread across the top of the baby grand in the librarian's living room. I was a part-time assistant with an undergraduate degree in music theory and composition—specific knowledge much of which had been obliterated by four intervening, peripatetic years. Decades of performance experience, however, at levels of increasing challenge, not to mention a good word from my former teacher—who happened to be a Minnesota Orchestra musician—had led me to John Tafoya's living room. John was at the time Minnesota Orchestra Librarian; the next year he became St. Louis Symphony Orchestra Librarian, where he continues at the time of this writing.

Never once in my years of performing did I give a thought to who put the music in the folders nor how the folders reached the stands onstage, let alone the source of that music.

Standing at John's piano with the cello and bass parts spread out before me, I thought, "How wonderful! This is a snap. I'm being paid to do work that is ridiculously easy. How easy? I don't even need to go to school to learn how to do it."

Now, many years later, like many in our profession, I still prefer to stand at a table (rarely a piano, however) to mark music. Although the mountain of pages prepared by my colleagues and me at times has seemed a bit more onerous than snappy; and although the seeming simplicity of that first day's work masked a deeper complexity, the overall feeling that it is excellent to be paid for this work has never dissipated.

And while I never did undergo formal schooling in order to learn this trade—this little-celebrated offshoot of the music profession—I did learn to appreciate very much Those Who Had Gone Before. For it has been from them that I began to be able to unpeel the layers, to unravel some of the riddles wrapped in mysteries inside the enigmas that comprise performance librarianship. Because even as my career progressed, so did my exposure continue to arcana I neither could have experienced nor imagined. Thus, I always will harbor feelings of the most intense gratitude toward my colleagues in the field, who held themselves ready to assist, pre-MOLA; and to those who continue to help me to this day.

Every performance librarian, like any librarian anywhere, must become an adept researcher. In our own specialized field, with relatively few reference sources at one's disposal, and no academic resources to speak of, it is people we must depend on, and people to whom we turn in our hours of need. Along with one's knowledge base, one's address book expands over time.

And then something happens, sooner or later. The circle begins to turn, perhaps so subtly you don't even notice at first. You, who have required mentoring—and who will in all likelihood continue to request advice and accept assistance for years—respond to another's inquiry.

It begins innocently enough. Perhaps you begin fielding questions we all will hear at one time or another: "What exactly do you do?" "Do you need any assistance?" "Could I work in your library for school credit?" "Do you ever accept interns?" "Could working in the orchestra library help my music career? My arts administration career? My nonprofit work experience for my résumé?" And that old warhorse: "Where does the music come from, anyway?"

Or you are giving a Library Tour, showing interested patrons, colleagues, friends, or family your workplace, and you are doing your best to explain exactly what it is you do. Or you respond to the arts manager or education director's request to address a group of volunteers, or an entire pre-concert audience. And you realize not only do you not need any notes, but your talk, your explanation, only skims the surface.

Twenty or thirty or sixty minutes pass in a flash. You could speak on this subject for hours. They have to drag you off with a hook.

It was at one of these moments (not the hook, but a speaking experience) that I understood I was teaching a little about our craft. It was then also that I first grasped the notion that I had an obligation and the know-how to return some of the many favors that had been shown me, from which I had so benefited.

Unlike music performance, one cannot take formal lessons in our profession. Unlike traditional librarianship—library and information science—there is no formal academic program available for such a relatively self-contained specialty as performance librarianship. While it has been discussed for years, and although there have been tentative plans, proposals, and the occasional lecture or mini-course, it seems that the strength of the draw is insufficient for an institutional course of study. And if it does happen, I believe it will be a rarity for the same reason.

Useful texts exist both in print and online for anyone desiring to learn the ins and outs of orchestra librarianship; however, they are relatively few, especially considering how complex and wide-ranging this profession is. Pre-MOLA, working performance librarians may have managed to acquire a copy of former Detroit Symphony Orchestra Librarian Albert Steger's typewritten manual.[3] Current noteworthy written materials include a handful of MOLA brochures and Juilliard School librarian Russ Girsberger's more recent Music Library Association *Manual for the Performance Library*.[4]

---

3   Albert Steger, "Manual for the Orchestral Library" (Detroit, Mich.: privately printed, 1983).

4   Russ Girsberger, *A Manual for the Performance Library* (Music Library Association Basic Manual Series, No. 6. Lanham, Md.: Scarecrow Press, 2006).

How, then, do we learn our craft?

With so little in writing and still less in the form of formal instruction, performance librarianship must be taught hand-to-hand, as it were; or rather, mouth-to-ear. And that is how every person in this profession has been taught: through trial and error under the guidance of those who have gone before us, and of those who are walking parallel paths with us today.

Like *mentees*—those who are being mentored—and who work under all sorts of varying arrangements, mentorship itself can come in all shapes and sizes. In my years working with less experienced librarians or proto-librarians, mentorship, the process of imparting knowledge to others has taken many forms.

Generally, a formal mentorship is a temporary arrangement. Whether for a week, a summer, a month, a school term or a full season, the idea is that you, the experienced librarian, agree to take another person under your wing. Although there can be situations where the purpose is undefined or open-ended, usually the period of mentorship will be finite, and it will be set in motion in order to accomplish a specific goal. This goal can be the librarian's, such as a discrete orchestra project that might not otherwise be attainable; or it might be the mentee's, such as capturing credit for an academic course.

These are some possible mentoring situations:

- **Summer intern:** A person will ask or agree to work as a volunteer. Occasionally the intern will be paid, perhaps with a one-time stipend. Often this person is a college or graduate student on summer break looking for work, experience, or both, between terms.
- **School-year intern:** This situation is similar to that of a summer intern, except it takes place during J-term or spring break.
- **Student worker:** A student seeking a supervisor for academic course credit may approach the librarian with an idea, or a professor will initiate contact. The "coursework" or project will be designed in tandem with the librarian. In this case, the librarian will likely be required to report on the student's progress, and evaluate the student's work at the project's conclusion.
- **Volunteer:** A person, perhaps a retiree or an orchestra enthusiast with time to volunteer, who wants to help behind the scenes at the orchestra, or one fascinated specifically by the library, will ask if they can assist in some way.
- **Special project worker:** A person may approach the librarian to request guidance in a related career or as an introduction to orchestra librarianship.
- **Inter-library opportunity:** A librarian from one orchestra may wish to experience the inner workings of another library.
- **Part-time worker:** A spouse, relative or friend of an orchestra musician, orchestra staffer, or other trustworthy source may be available to assist part-time with marking music, shipping, filing, folders, or cataloging.

It is one of the great wonders of this field, and one of my greatest pleasures, to watch a new worker encounter and begin to solve some of the same puzzles we have all faced at one time or another. Whether this is a person seeking a start to a career in music or is someone exploring this field and entering as if from a side door with experience elsewhere, doesn't seem to make any difference. It tickles me to observe someone's deepening exposure to the vagaries of how one particular orchestra string section chooses to manage their bowmarkings; or to take note of how I do my best to handle a Difficult Artistic Situation; or to watch someone's expression after some part that seems to have gone mysteriously missing then turns up, seemingly by chance or miracle, but in actuality ineluctably found by an experienced searcher.

It should surprise no one that various performance library volunteers, student workers, or part-time hourly employees have moved up the ranks in this profession. From summer intern to summer employee, from summer employee to part-time worker, from part-time to full-time: the performance library training system—a system that is neither in place nor formalized in any way—is the source of future professional orchestra, ballet and opera librarians. While there are a few in this profession who have successfully emigrated from academia or administrative areas, there is no other major source of future professionals in this area than our modern version of the apprentice system, on-the-job training.

This is part of my job, to show others how to do my job as well or better than I. I could ask for neither more receptive learners nor better teachers than those I have mentored. It is as pleasing to watch others grow, as it is sad to watch them fly off. It is satisfying to watch them prosper elsewhere, as it is comforting when they return for a visit or when they reach out again by phone or text for advice from afar. For this is true in our profession globally: as we all, without exception, call on others for advice and assistance, so others will call upon us eventually for the same.

> *One of the supreme ironies of mentoring another is how much one learns: about the other, about the process of mentoring, about one's profession, about oneself.*

Paul Gunther is the Principal Librarian of the Minnesota Orchestra and a Past President of the Major Orchestra Librarians' Association.

The Librarian as Mentor—Hand to Hand

by Elena Lence Talley

Performance librarians, by and large, still learn their craft the old-fashioned way. Not unlike the apprentice-master relationship of times past, many librarians in the early stages of their career rely on a more established librarian to guide them in the complex world of the music library. Experience is certainly the best teacher for all jobs—including this one—but surely some experiences (the traumatic ones) are best experienced second hand! The mentor librarian can help the mentee avoid pitfalls and those unfortunate situations. Preventing the dreaded "Librarian to the stage!" announcement is a worthy goal.

The more experienced librarian will pass along their tips and tricks and share their accumulated knowledge. Unlike our days as performers, with years of one-on-one private lessons, master classes, and festivals, we music librarians typically learn the business via full-immersion. One day you are playing the music on the stand in front of you, giving little thought to how it happened to come to pass, and the next you may well be on the other side of the equation. How do you gain the skills you need? Find the information necessary to get the job done? A longer-tenured professional can help the newbie learn the ropes. I have had the pleasure of working with several journeyman librarians and am happy to give some of my thoughts on the mentoring relationship.

Each mentoring relationship is different, simply because we are all so individual. A library team grows and adapts, not unlike a marriage. The older partner develops a sense of when the other partner needs some assistance or guidance, and the junior partner learns when to ask for suggestions and help. Sharing as much of their world as possible allows the more experienced librarian to expose the journeyman librarian to all aspects of the orchestra organism. Even if the mentee librarian is not currently responsible for all of these tasks, they almost certainly will be at some point in their career.

These are the main areas that I emphasize with newer librarians:

- Develop procedures to ensure a smooth sequence of events from the start to finish of a program
- Learn how to prioritize tasks and squeeze the extra hour out of the day
- Utilize or create forms, such as inventory records, performance records, etc., to efficiently access information
- Keep complete records and files. Put notes on editions, errata, inserts, cuts, and anything else relevant with the set of parts, the database (OPAS or the like), and in the concert folder.
- Learn where to look for answers to questions. There are so many sources for information, from terrific websites to references books of all types to experts in the field.

- Participate in professional organizations and discussion groups (like MOLA[5] and OLI[6]). No need to be shy, join your colleagues and you will learn from them, and quite possibly be able to pass along a tidbit that you know.

Each orchestra library has its own systems for getting the music prepared—from acquisition and rental to the bowing process to correcting and proofing. There is no perfect way to do any of this, but providing the mentee librarian with the foundation of a system gives her something to adapt to her own situation. If one follows the same procedures in essentially the same order for each concert program, one is less likely to find oneself missing a crucial step (like ordering the rental music early). Keeping track of the status of multiple projects is a huge component of what we librarians must do. Standardization of procedures can be a boon in keeping all of those plates spinning.

I am a big fan of the belt-and-suspenders system for filing and accessing information. I will make notes on any number of things (cuts, choices of edition, instrumentation needs and quirks, and many others) and keep them with the set of parts, in the OPAS record, and the concert file. Memory is great, but not infallible, considering the amount of music we deal with each season.

And speaking of memory, there is simply no way to keep all of the information, big and small, on all of the music simply in our memory banks. So, when you don't know the answer, knowing where to find the answer IS the answer. Introducing the mentee librarian to a wide variety of the catalogs, reference books, and websites available is invaluable to them.

It is also beneficial to teach by example, sharing the ins and outs of meetings, interaction with staff and musicians, and correspondence with others in the industry. Sometimes the interpersonal relationships with other staff and players are trickier than just copying the bowings. Introducing the junior partner to some of the other orchestra librarians around the country is also a plus. We are an incredibly tight and connected community, not to mention generous with time and expertise. The more librarians you know, the better!

Perhaps the most important gift the mentor librarian can give the mentee is the opportunity to tackle and complete projects with supervision and assistance as needed. Watching someone else organize and complete tasks is not the same as doing it yourself. One feels a real sense of responsibility and ownership when one is the person accountable for the music on the stands. Communicating with staff, conductors, and musicians, ordering music, preparing the parts (bowings, cuts, inserts and all), and unraveling the inevitable knots that come up in the whole process will create an indelible and crucial experience. That being said, the mentor librarian has a responsibility to offer guidance and expertise and to intervene before unfortunate mistakes happen.

Mentor/mentee relationships can endure for years, and contact by e-mail, phone, or other forms yet to come make communication easy and quick. Here is a useful

---

5   Major Orchestra Librarians' Association (www.mola-inc.org).

6   Orchestra Library Information (OLI) Yahoo! Group, an online forum moderated by Clinton F. Nieweg, Principal Librarian (ret.) with The Philadelphia Orchestra. Available online at: http://launch.groups.yahoo.com/group/OrchLibInfo/?yguid=137775693.

bit of advice: gifts of chocolate (frequently given and of the highest quality) will help make any mentor/mentee relationship a success.

Elena Lence Talley is the Principal Music Librarian of the Kansas City Symphony and a Past President of the Major Orchestra Librarians' Association.

Communication: Say What?!

by Marcia Farabee

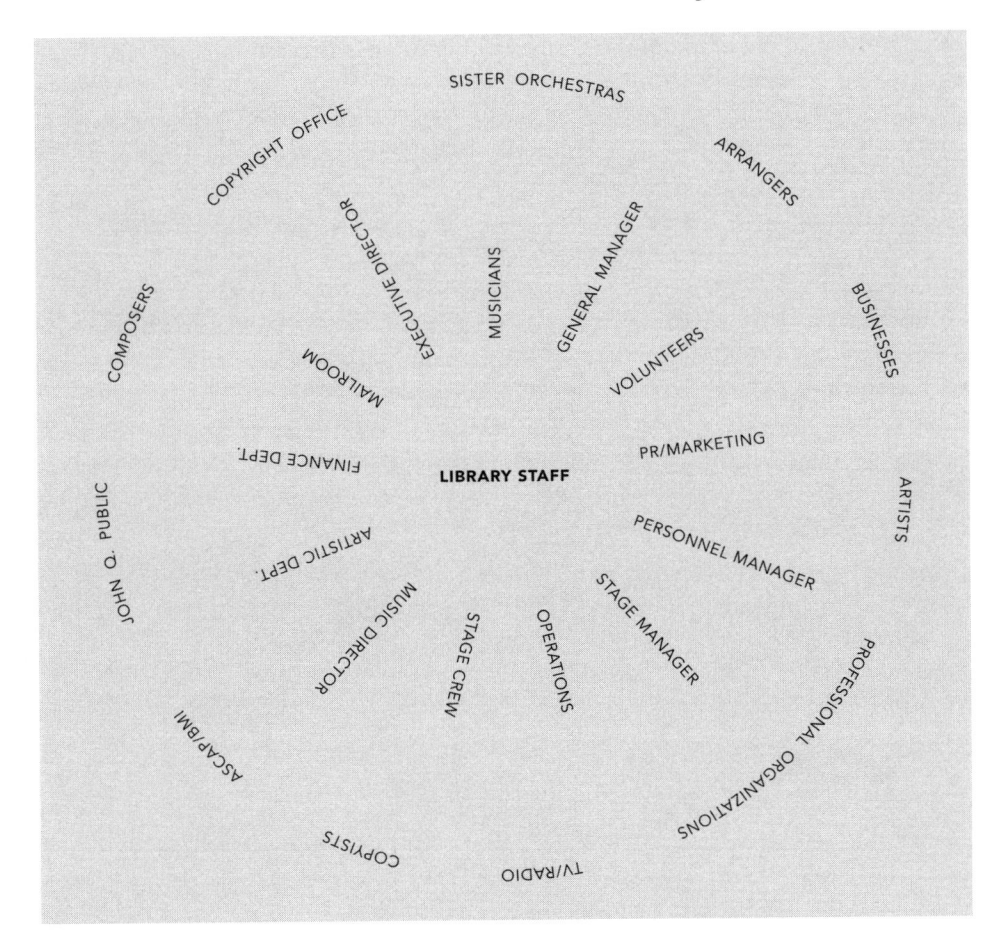

Ah, communication. This is an area that creates a lot of corporate buzz, but unfortunately is not practiced as well as it could be. Whether intradepartmental, interdepartmental, or outside the walls of your organization, written and oral communications serve as the foundation for your performances. Like the story of the servant long ago who could not figure out why her cracked water jar was empty at the end of the journey from the well (the water leaked out along the way), librarians who do not communicate well will not understand why rehearsals and concerts are so problematic.

One of the great ironies of corporate communication is that everyone is expected to know how and what to communicate, but few, if any of us have had any formal managerial training. Accounting, business strategy, conflict management, interviewing, time management, and leadership classes are all available online or as in-person seminars, but what about communication in the non-profit world? The performance library offers many opportunities for its staff to learn and practice communication skills.

It has been my experience that the library serves as the organizational hub. We take the many pieces of information and fit them together, much like a jigsaw puzzle. We are able to pass appropriate information along to others, as well as receive information from those same people. Because the informational flow has several layers, permit me to elaborate on each of them.

Layer one might be called the intradepartmental layer, or the core. This involves the library staff actually speaking to one another! While this may seem obvious, I know from experience that it is possible to be so focused on a particular concert that one assumes the other people in the department already know the details of the project. Some performance libraries function well when each person has a specific duty; others divide duties by concert; still others share all parts of the concert preparation for each program. Regardless of the supervisor's managerial style, instructions, expectations, and feedback are integral components of the intradepartmental dialog. For a supervisor to assume the staff knows its duty assignments cannot be a part of the library culture! Once a program has been determined, the library needs to address who will handle these duties: location/procurement of the titles; processing and preparing the music, including bowings, cuts, starts, stops, edits and the like; and folder compilation, distribution, and collection. It is imperative that each member of the library staff has access to all of the concert program information. Note that I did not say that the entire staff makes all of the decisions concerning the program, only that the entire staff has access to the results of decision-making. An additional communication opportunity takes place at the close of the concert: the library staff has a chance to reflect on the program that has just ended, commenting on areas that might need improvement, as well as on items that were quite successful. It is possible that some feedback would involve other departments, which leads us to our next area.

The second layer of communication is the interdepartmental one. Here the library works closely with the rest of the organization: artistic, operations, personnel, stage manager and stagehands, finance, media/marketing, education, volunteers, and even development. Occasionally the communication flows in one direction, as when the marketing people need to check on the spelling of a title or movement of a work, or when the library submits a requisition or purchase order to the finance officer. More often, it is a multi-department conversation. An example might be the determination of how many wind players are going to be used for a particular piece. This seemingly simple decision is influenced by the number of players required by the score, the number of players available for the concert, and whether or not the conductor is willing to compromise the written instrumentation. Conversely, the instrumentation may require pairs of winds, but the conductor might ask for doubling. These conversations could involve the artistic, personnel, and operations (for stage plots) departments, and possibly even the program note annotator.

Each organization has its own procedures concerning programming questions. While some may prefer that the library directly contact whomever they need to clarify a situation, others may prefer that the artistic or personnel departments act as an intermediary. The critical part of the informational search, though, is making certain that once a decision is reached, it is shared with all of the appropriate people. Also essential to the process is having the entire staff know what the process is!

The outer layer of communication involves going outside the organization. Many times the questions come from outside the building to the library, as in the case of public phone calls, but just as frequently the library can be the instigator of the conversation. Publisher representatives, music dealers, artists, performing rights societies, fellow library colleagues, TV and radio stations, arrangers and copyists, legal counsel, retail establishments, and composers are just some of the professionals with whom librarians interact. Since many of these conversations can be conducted by e-mail or phone, it is important to record the date of the contact as well as the result of the conversation. The immediacy of the Internet and e-mail is both wondrous and problematic: the people involved have nearly instant communication, while those not copied are not even aware that a contact has been made. So, please, keep a record of your contact, but more importantly, let your colleagues know that a dialog has begun.

I would like to spend a moment addressing reference questions that come from the public at large. While these queries may or may not have anything to do with a specific concert program, the interaction can leave an impression on the organization as a whole. Your professional demeanor, honest effort to help, and thoroughness of a reply will make a long-lasting, favorable impression on the caller. This can play out in many ways, including introducing a new subscriber or volunteer to your organization. Contrarily, not responding to a phone message, making it clear that you have "more important" things to do, or being otherwise unprofessional on the phone makes it probable that you will alienate this person. Unhappy patrons write unhappy letters that, in turn, can make supervisors unhappy. Regardless of time constraints and library pressures, every effort must be made to be as helpful as possible. We are, after all, in the customer service industry, even though our medium happens to be music.

To summarize, I offer up these suggestions for improving communication within and outside of your organization:

1. Be sure that your library staff knows who is handling what duties for each concert, and talk frequently about where everyone is in the process. Make sure your staff knows and understands the library processes and procedures, as well as any interdepartmental procedures.
2. Ask questions as early as possible, and ask the appropriate person. Relay the response(s) to anyone who might be affected by it.
3. When contacting parties outside of the organization, be sure to know what your needs are. The who, what, where, when, and why of your conversation should be ready to convey. Sometimes the "how" enters into the discussion!

4. When receiving queries be as polite, thorough, and succinct as possible. If you do not have the information the person needs, make every effort to find someone who does have that information.

Performing arts librarians are known for their attention to detail. Let us add improved communication to our arsenal of skills.

Marcia Farabee is the Principal Librarian of the National Symphony Orchestra in Washington, D.C., and a Past President of the Major Orchestra Librarians' Association.

Strength-Based Organization, Communication Pattern and Work Values

by Kazue McGregor

Performance libraries and library personnel come in all shapes and sizes—and I am not referring to physical attributes! Let me elaborate. Performance librarians for an orchestra, ballet company, opera company, military band, festival, or conservatory share a similar type of work, but no two libraries are exactly the same. We do not share a common database nor do we structure personnel in the same manner. However, no matter their differences, library staff members are expected to work together like well-oiled machines, otherwise there will be trouble on stage or eventually down the road. In our profession there is little room for error. Granted it may not be a life-or-death matter as on an operating table, but it certainly may feel like it for the wind player on stage with a misprint that creates an unintended solo, or the string player with oppositely marked bowings. Worse yet, if the wrong material were to show up at the rehearsal or, in an extreme case, if nothing shows up!

This article focuses exclusively on performance libraries with multiple staff members. What can you do to maximize work efficiency? How do you keep the minutiae of part changes, musicians' requests, music director needs, and endless other details communicated to everyone who needs to know? What are work values and why are they important as part of building a true team effort?

The strengths of the individual

As performance librarians, we were all hired on the premise that we have the qualifications to accomplish the tasks that are required in our jobs. Hopefully, we were hired because we also shared the same goals and definitions of professionalism in the workplace. I dare to add that having a strong dose of curiosity is also a prerequisite. Each librarian must first respect and trust these basic concepts for a library to run efficiently.

It is highly likely that one person may do a certain task better or faster than another person, and the reverse could also be true. That is referred to as the *strength* of an individual. A person may have several strengths. Studies have shown that people generally do well what they enjoy doing. And what they enjoy doing are often their strengths. What is fun for one person may be drudgery for another. For me, accounting is something I could do without. I do not derive enjoyment when working with numbers, but I am certainly capable of creating a budget and balancing the books, which I do regularly. For someone else, budgeting and juggling numbers may be fun and more preferable than marking bowings. I enjoy marking bowings—it's almost meditational—except that I am distracted or interrupted too easily, so I am a good bower only under certain circumstances. What I enjoy doing most is creating systems and facilitating processes. That is probably why I place the rental orders in our library and a co-worker does the purchasing.

To run an efficient, productive, and *inspired* library, I believe it is important to identify and match the strengths of the individual staff to the work at hand and re-distribute assignments when necessary as the work shifts. For example, marking Baroque ornaments in the Bach B Minor Mass takes different "strengths" than marking bowings in Debussy's *Iberia*. For that matter, proofing requires a different set of skills than making audition books. Work will flow more efficiently when strengths are matched to the work, and *not necessarily bound by tradition or seniority*. More importantly, it allows members of the library staff to be recognized for their strengths, to enjoy their work, and to see their contributions in the big picture. I am convinced that this is the start of true team effort in the library.

Let me discuss more in detail how this would apply in a performance library. Generally, our work can be roughly categorized into Music Preparation/Proofing, Administrative, Shipping/Clerical, Communication (internal and external), and more increasingly, Computer Technology. These are very broad categories and you will find overlaps between them. You may think of other areas I have missed or ones that are unique to your library.

Using myself as an example again, I feel fairly confident that I can carry out any of the tasks described above to a certain extent, with the exception of the technology involving computer engraving. However, I am just as confident that one of my co-workers who has an exceptional memory, can remember editions and past performances, and is a perfectionist, will be the best person to oversee our music preparation and proofing. I am equally confident that another co-worker, who dives into large-scale challenges both physical and mental, who is naturally inclined in computer technology, and who also happens to be a perfectionist, is the best person for coordinating complex music projects, expanding our technology usage, and spearheading research. Just as important, our part-time co-worker who has the physical energy of two people and a dogged determination for record keeping that is simply admirable, keeps us up-to-date in filing and shipping, as well as maintaining sanity in our library with her orderliness and upbeat personality. In addition, working in Los Angeles we are fortunate that during critical times there are several local professional librarians we can count on who each have their own strengths that are unique to them.

Leading business thinkers like Marcus Buckingham[7] and Tom Rath[8] have advocated that workplaces playing to the strengths of individual workers are more productive and result in an organization that is more engaged than those trying to fix weaknesses.

---

7 Marcus Buckingham and Curt Coffman, *First, Break All the Rules: What the World's Greatest Managers Do Differently* (New York: Simon and Schuster, 1999).

8 Tom Rath and Barry Conchie, *Strengths Based Leadership: Great Leaders, Teams, and Why People Follow* (New York: Gallup Press, 2008).

Communication

During our summer season, the Los Angeles Philharmonic presents concert programs ranging from classical, jazz, world music, opera, and pops music to a movie night at the Hollywood Bowl, an 18,000-capacity outdoor amphitheater. Our summer season spans from early June through September. There are inevitable overlaps with the Philharmonic winter season that starts in late September and runs through the beginning of June. At the height of the summer season, you can find up to seven librarians working in the library preparing multiple programs. It is at times like these that the pattern of communication becomes critical for us and other similar performance libraries.

Alex Bavelas, a former professor at MIT, and his student Harold Leavitt, concluded that the structure in an organization greatly influences the accuracy of decisions, the speed with which decisions are reached, and the satisfaction of the people involved.[9] They conducted experiments in which they explored different patterns of communication. Even though communication patterns with a strong central figure showed more stability and lower performance errors, they found that the morale of members was relatively low and resulted in decreasing long-term accuracy and speed. By comparison, in organizations where the responsibility for initiating and passing along information is shared more evenly among the members, they found the group morale to be better.

Applied to the library, the idea is to use the entire library staff as a unit to solve problems that no one person could possibly handle.

Informal communication among library personnel becomes even more important for ensuring effective work. The physical layout of the work desks becomes an important feature. While a clustering of desks could pose a challenge to privacy, it contributes toward more informal and frequent communication. A common library e-mail address can eliminate an extra step in fulfilling requests, as long as the information is passed back to everyone once the request is filled.

Sharing coffee breaks is another fun and effective way to strengthen communication and working relationships. In our library, we find daily opportunities to take a brief coffee break together immediately after the rehearsal gets under way. It started years ago as a way for us to compare notes and decompress from the flurry of getting the rehearsal started. We talk about the day's agenda and whatever else comes to mind. Without great effort, this has helped to build a meaningful and effective working relationship in the library.

Work values

In an ideal world, the library will be staffed with highly competent, committed, and like-minded individuals who all get along. But how is that accomplished? Audition

---

9   Alex Bavelas, "Communication Patterns in Task-Oriented Groups," *The Journal of the Acoustical Society of America* 22, no. 6 (November 1950): 725–730.

tests and interviews are limited in their capacity to measure competency and strengths. There are no established methods to measure workers' values that are often intangible and invisible and yet affect us on a daily basis. A trial or tenure process therefore becomes extremely valuable in assessing an individual's work skills, interests, values — and compatibility.

The performance library field is very specialized and openings are rare, but when they occur aspiring librarians may not have the luxury of being selective about applying. In spite of this, I believe it is extremely important to self-reflect on what qualities are most important to find in the workplace. The attitude "it's only a job" will guarantee short-term employment in our business.

So what are work values and why are they important? Throughout the course of our life, all of us have acquired a set of values, beliefs, or ideas that we honor as important. These values can be classified as core values, work environment, work interactions, and work activities. Translating this into the workplace requires clarifying our work values to ourselves. Examples of work value self-assessment tools may be found on the web.[10]

Our work values influence our interactions with co-workers and our overall satisfaction. While we may intend to conduct ourselves professionally and not let our work values interfere should they be different from reality, I believe dissatisfaction with work will eventually arise and compromise the library's team effort. Having similar work values makes compatibility easier to achieve.

Some examples of work values are listed below. Feel free to add your own to this list and then identify the values that you feel are most important for you to find, develop, and exercise in the library.

> **Personal Core Values:** achievement, balance, independence, influence, integrity, honesty, power, respect, spirituality (belief in core values), status, service
>
> **Work Environment:** fast-pace, flexible hours, compensation, challenging, geographic location, predictable, quiet, relaxed, structured, time freedom, security
>
> **Work Interactions:** competition, diversity, friendships, leadership, good management, open communication, recognition, support, collaboration, trust, knowledgeable co-workers
>
> **Work Activities:** analytical, challenging, creative, helping society, leading edge, physical, public contact, research, risk-taking, variety of tasks

I have never asked my co-workers what their work values are and I probably will never need to. I suspect that their top five values will align closely enough to mine to be compatible: knowledgeable co-workers, integrity, open communication, security, and service.

---

10 Santa Cruz County Regional Occupational Program, "Lesson Planning: Understanding Who I Am and How I Work Best. Work Values Inventory," [2006–2007], http://www.rop.santacruz.k12.ca.us/resources/career_planning/step1tool1.pdf.

When performance librarians love their job, are successful in their work, and can find personal meaning tied to their work, then the library thrives. I consider myself lucky to have found this environment.

Kazue McGregor is a librarian with the Los Angeles Philharmonic and a Past President of the Major Orchestra Librarians' Association.

The "One Man" Show

by Patrick McGinn

There are two very important items to remember if you are the only librarian in a performing arts organization: know your responsibilities very clearly and recognize that there may be limitations to how much you can accomplish. **You cannot do everything.** Even in organizations with more than one librarian, they may not be able to do everything necessary to provide the "perfect" set of prepared materials in addition to coordinating all the administrative tasks required. You need to constantly evaluate and prioritize the work that needs to be done. Creating a timeline for the preparation of each work on a program can be helpful and give guidance to prioritizing your tasks.

Communication is key to the success of any size organization, whether with one librarian or multiple librarians. Often assumptions are made by the music director, the management, and the players about what will be done regarding music preparation. It is important to have a clear understanding with the various constituencies about the extent of music preparation that can be accomplished with the resources available to you. Maybe you are only able to get bowings into the string parts. Perhaps you also have time to check rehearsal numbers between parts and the score. Or possibly fix page turns, or check parts for major errata corrections. Being proactive with communications and explanations, and doing so in a positive tone, is a sign of your professionalism and commitment to wanting the best for the organization.

Listed below are guidelines that may be helpful when preparing for any performance.

First, you want to get information as early as possible about what the repertoire will be on a program. Hopefully, management and/or the music director will share this information with you. You may not have been included in the program planning, but don't be afraid to insist on being given information as soon as it is finalized.

Next, schedule a meeting with the music director. Before the meeting you will want to compile information on what materials are already in your library, what is available for purchase, and what will need to be rented. Having an estimate of purchase and rental costs can also be helpful. Decisions are sometimes made based on costs. You will want to review each work with the music director to find out if they have specific editions they want to use. Can it come from your library? Will you need to purchase it? Will it need to be rented? Or does the music director already have his or her own set of materials? Assuming that you know what they want can often lead to wasted effort on your part if you prepare the wrong set.

The cost of renting or purchasing materials can add significantly to any organization's budget, so you will want to share this information with management as early in the planning process as possible. Programming does occasionally change due to the high cost of music acquisitions. Standard reference sources, such as David Daniels's

Orchestral Music: A Handbook[11] and the MOLA publication on reference resources,[12] along with publisher and composer websites can provide valuable information on a work, including the availability of materials.

Your responsibilities may include providing all relevant information about a work, including instrumentation, timings, title, etc., to others in your organization. Instrumentation information may need to be shared with the personnel manager. Many librarians must also provide the proper information for the printed program page, including composer names with birth/death dates, arranger names, complete titles, movement names, and lengths of works. You are often the best source for supplying or confirming this information.

To establish a working schedule for music acquisition, preparation, and distribution, it can be helpful to work backward from the performance date. Listing the following items on a calendar provides a good visual reminder of what and when things need to be accomplished:

- Performance date
- First rehearsal date
- Date music will be available for the players
- Music preparation time, for bowings/errata/edits/cuts/measure numbers
- Music delivery date for rental or purchase materials. You will want to include enough time so you can check over the materials when they arrive to make sure they are the correct materials and are in acceptable condition. If not, you will need to allow time for another set to be sent or to make needed repairs to the materials you did receive.
- Music order date. Some publishers will impose a hefty rush order fee if you require the materials to arrive within a very short period of time, often within two weeks of placing the order. Try to place your order as far in advance as possible. However, there are sometimes last minute program changes or additions that will make it unavoidable.

This list can help you create a basic timeline for each performance. You will also need to be aware of any specific language in the players' contracts that could affect this schedule. For example, is the music required to be available one week, two weeks, or one month before the first rehearsal? If your principal string players mark bowings, you should be familiar with the timeliness of their work habits. You may need to allow more time into the schedule. Also, there may be a few players who ask for their music well before the others, like the principal percussionist who needs to determine what instruments are required and make assignments. You have to decide how possible, or practical, it is to accommodate such requests given the resources you are provided.

---

11   David Daniels, *Orchestral Music: A Handbook* (4th ed. Lanham, Md.: Scarecrow Press, 2005). Online version available by subscription at http://www.orchestralmusic.com.

12   Russ Girsberger, "Reference Resources for the Performance Library: An Annotated Bibliography," N.p.: Major Orchestra Librarians' Association, 2010.

If interns or volunteers are available to you, you may want to take advantage of that opportunity. However, you need to evaluate the person offering aid and what they are bringing to the table before accepting their offer of assistance. If it takes you more time to explain the job that needs to be done and review their work than it would to do it yourself, then the offer may not be worth it. I've had offers of help from people who thought it would be "glamorous" to be around and socialize with conductors, soloists, and musicians, when actually most (or all) of their time would be spent in a room away from the stage, possibly with no windows, putting little marks in the parts. If the person might become a long-term volunteer, then the investment of your time to instruct them may well be worth it. This could also be a way of encouraging someone to enter the field as a possible profession. But always remember, you are the one who is ultimately responsible for the preparation of the music.

Patrick McGinn is the Principal Librarian of the Milwaukee Symphony Orchestra and a Past President of the Major Orchestra Librarians' Association.

Beyond the Library

by Karen Schnackenberg

If there is a stereotypical image of a performance librarian at work, it is probably one of the librarian huddled over scores and parts making detailed markings with a pencil, a Staedtler eraser at the ready. In direct contrast with that picture is the reality of the librarian's professional life which includes the constant challenge of balancing the daily musical work with being an educator and advocate outside the library. The need for such activism is an enduring one, not only within our performing organizations, but also throughout the industry. For the librarian, the experiences enjoyed as a result of these efforts not only lead to tangible improvements throughout the field, but also add a rich and satisfying variety to one's professional life. Some of my most memorable collaborations have come from volunteering as a teacher, mentor, lecturer, consultant, writer, or organizer in our profession.

It may be surprising that many of those with whom we work most closely have little knowledge of what a librarian's job actually encompasses or the musical training and skills that are required to do the work. Players often think we mostly mark bowings, put parts in folders, and make practice copies. Conductors know that we acquire the music they program, but few realize what that entails or how much time it takes to prepare the performance materials to their specifications. Administrators have little awareness of the level of musical detail that our work requires on a daily basis. Board members, as well-meaning and generous as they are, often do not even know that we are musicians.

Such a general lack of understanding can hamper even the most efficient performance library from fulfilling its purpose within the organization. When the administration doesn't understand the library's function and role, it is difficult to get what is needed for budgeting, equipment requirements, hiring of extra help, or ample time for concert preparation, all of which affects the ability to provide the high level of support that is absolutely crucial to players and conductors. We really would like to be able to put measure numbers into every single set, or comprehensively correct the errors in all works that come through the library, but we are often forced by deadlines and understaffing to put parts on the stands that are less than perfect. In short, the work is never done, and we just try to do as much as we can, as well as we can.

When administrators and boards are educated about the librarians' role, it leads to a better understanding of why our work is critical to the success of the overall "product." This paves the way for more support on crucial projects, and more resources committed to the library through increased or, at least, maintained funding. In turn, the organization's stability for the future is enhanced through larger holdings, the latest critical editions, regular data upkeep, and retaining and recruiting talented and experienced librarians. All of this also benefits the performers who can focus on making music, free from the restraints of incomplete part preparation or inferior materials.

It is critically important for librarians to fully understand how they fit into the bigger picture of their orchestras, opera companies, concert bands, or conservatories. In this way, we can be more effective advocates when acting as liaisons throughout our administrations. The truth is, we interact with every department in the organization in ways that still surprise me after all these years. When I got my first professional library job, I could never have guessed how extensive and varied these collaborations would be. I simply didn't know that being an orchestra librarian could mean working with everyone, constantly explaining and showing what the librarians do and how the library works in partnership with the rest of the organization.

But it does. Whether it's presenting budget justifications or proposals to management or finance, providing detailed information to the development staff for grant writing, fund raising, or capital campaigns to acquire music or equipment, working with marketing and public relations by writing for the *Playbill* or orchestra newsletter, advising on copyright requirements for website content, or speaking to the board members, staff and volunteer guilds, it's all about helping to create a more effective organization in support of the art.

We embarked upon a special project a number of years ago, in partnership with the fine arts department of our local public library, to begin a long term process of identifying, collecting, and delivering historical records and memorabilia for the creation of an orchestra archive. We were all complete novices in this venture and had to educate ourselves about what we were doing, how to do it, and why it was important to preserve the history of our orchestra. We taught our staff to think before throwing away or deleting relevant correspondence and project materials, and we set up a once-per-year collection to be taken to the public library. We researched the preservation of data both in hard copy and electronic forms. We learned how to establish a Deed of Gift. We worked with the public library to obtain grants and hire a professional archivist. Now, almost a decade later, the collection is ninety percent archived, we have an established process to research and retrieve material as needed, and we have the satisfaction of knowing that the orchestra's history is being preserved for future generations.

I have also been very fortunate to represent performance librarians in a variety of ways throughout my career, including writing for print and online publications, helping librarians and orchestras in need, consulting on the set-up and organization of a performance library, volunteering through the Major Orchestra Librarians' Association (MOLA) to improve information exchange and resource materials, collaborating with computer engineers to change and upgrade equipment, speaking at affiliated music industry conferences such as the Music Publishers Association and the League of American Orchestras, and assisting orchestra librarians nationally in their working lives through the American Federation of Musicians. It is heartening to see that each effort over time helps in some way to bring improvements in our field and more understanding from our colleagues.

Recently, a special opportunity to share what we do came in the form of an invitation to speak at the annual conference of the Association of Finnish Orchestras in Kuopio, Finland. Fellow librarians, whom I came to know through MOLA, were involved in planning the agenda. The focus was to be on the relationship of the performance librarian with all the other constituencies of the symphony orchestra, and how the libraries might be able to function more effectively for the good of their organizations. The participants were orchestra managers, players, librarians, and civil servants involved with the arts in their home municipalities.

Despite the trepidation I felt that my American experiences would not translate well because of the significant differences in the way symphony orchestras are operated and funded in Finland, I quickly learned that we were all dealing with similar issues and challenges. The message was not that much different on the other side of the world. In our role to provide the musical services conductors and players must have so they can perform at the highest level of artistic expression, it is crucial that we performance librarians have the musical skills, experience, resources, and tools with which to also perform our duties at that same high level. Otherwise, the art suffers.

Performance librarians, by nature, are detail-oriented people. Our tendency, then, can be to immerse ourselves in the music preparation—which is our job, after all—without wanting to participate in the larger goings-on around us. But it's the big picture that gives meaning to our detail work, the overall impact of great live music on the audience. One can either try to avoid the advocacy aspect of the profession or embrace it. We can no longer just sit in the library, hunched over the parts, lost in the minutiae of the endless details of the notes and errors. We need to regularly step out beyond the library (and, perhaps, our comfort zone) and engage with the players and conductors, staff members, managers, board members, and even the public. We must make ourselves available to answer questions, provide information, and bring people into the library and visit their departments to show that we are part of the whole.

Choosing to be an advocate brings an understanding about our jobs and profession that builds relationships and helps to lift up our performers, our administrations, and our industry. In that way, performance librarians have a unique perspective and lasting effect on the art form.

Karen Schnackenberg is the Chief Librarian of the Dallas Symphony Orchestra and a Past President of the Major Orchestra Librarians' Association.

CHAPTER **4**

The Nuts and Bolts

Advance Planning

or How does one proceed without a crystal ball?

by Robert Sutherland

"Advance Planning" is a relative term. It can apply to periods of years or days, depending on the circumstances in which an organization finds itself. How then, does one go about planning in advance, especially when there are so many variables between the now of a plan or decision and the reality of a performance?

The answer will obviously depend on the particular organization and how it operates. But there are some ways to consider the operations involved in producing a performance that may prove helpful.

A method that I typically use when involved in the advance planning of a performance or production is to work backwards from the actual performance. That process will often dictate the timelines for what has to be done by which time in order for the performance to take place. Combined with "if … then … else" analysis, most pieces of the puzzle will become apparent.[1] A very simple example from a library point of view is:

- The performance takes place on xx day.
- The first rehearsal takes place on xx day.
- The very latest I can provide the material to the orchestra members is xx day (depending on contracts, etc.).
- It usually takes xx days to prepare the material for such a concert.
- It takes xx days to get bowings from string principals, concurrent with, it takes xx days to get markings, if any, from the conductor.
- If I can use a set the organization owns, I will be fine to start work on that date.
- If I have to order music, I have to allow another xx days to order and receive the music.
- If I am renting music, I have to allow xx days for the various rental agreements to be sent to me, signed and returned before the music will be sent, which will take xx days.

Following this sort of logic, one's basic timelines become clear. Add to that other library obligations and, if one is fortunate to have the time to allow for contingency, one can set out one's timeline for each program fairly easily. Of course, the more programs that are being performed, and the busier the organization, the more modifying factors enter into the equation.

Those modifying factors are often the very things that make our individual organizations unique. It is the knowledge of those factors that ultimately will make us successful

---

[1] "If…then…else" is a conditional statement in many computer programming languages. The structure is: If (predicate) then (consequent) else (alternative), which is the important sequence in advance planning.

as librarians within our organizations. That said, there are certain types of musical activities for which I will attempt to list some considerations when planning ahead.

Opera/Symphony/Ballet

I will start by discussing opera which, because of its complexity, covers most of the areas involved in planning ahead for symphonic programs and ballet productions. The analytical principles remain the same even though the form of the productions will be different.

Opera companies have to plan years in advance due to the availability of principal singers. If a company is in a position to create new productions, these also require planning years in advance. Often the new productions are directly connected with the principal singers involved (or soloists, conductors, or star dancers in the case of symphonic programs and ballet). So, how does one plan ahead in such a situation?

My experience has been that the same considerations apply, whether for a large house with a large budget or a smaller house with a smaller budget. The difference may lie in how many years out the planning will begin.

Ideally, one will have a relationship with whomever is in a position to make artist and repertoire decisions to ask the following questions:

- What are you planning to do during the next four or five years?
- Are there vocal scores that I should have in my library for consideration?
- Are you planning to use any special editions? (It is very important to establish which edition of the vocal score will be used before sending out all of these scores so that everyone is, literally, on the same page.)
- Will you want scores sent to principal artists for consideration? (This will give you an idea of how many scores you need to have on hand or obtain. Do not expect to get scores back from an artist who has turned down a role in time to send to another artist being considered.)

The same applies to the director and creative team that is conceiving the production. Creating and maintaining good lines of communication with the artistic administrator, music director, and others who make such decisions is of paramount importance.

Things to listen to and watch for are: Does the company seem to favor certain artists (or stage directors, or stage designers) and want to bring them back? What repertoire do those singers sing? In what roles does he or she excel? Will he or she be in the same place as a conductor or director that is being considered? (This will inevitably lead to discussions of future collaborations and, for a librarian, requests to provide material with little notice.)

I find it helpful to maintain an awareness of current and new editions of repertoire. It is worthwhile to make sure that one is receiving the promotional e-mail or regular mail from publishers announcing new works and editions and also keeping track of who is performing a piece that may come your way.

A conductor or a singer may insist on a particular edition. The choice of edition will affect the company and library budgets, as well as the librarian's ability to provide material to all of those involved in a production.[2] If a production is being rented from another company, there may be issues involved if one's own company decides to use a different edition of the score. All of the stage directions, technical cues, cuts, etc., will need to be translated to the page coordinates of the different edition before getting to the stage.

The language in which an opera is to be sung may provide some challenges to the librarian. If an opera is being sung in the original language it is relatively simple, but one must ask whether the production team is conversant in that language. If the production team is relying on an English translation to make important directorial and design decisions, the English translation in a vocal score is usually not accurate when compared word for word with the original. Inevitably it will be a singing translation made to transmit the story line, more or less, but mostly to lie well for the voice. To this end a literal translation of the original language is much more useful, but very difficult to find. A literal translation may need to be commissioned, which adds time to the process.

Another thing to consider when singing in languages that are not familiar to artists or music staff is the need for a transliterated vocal score.[3] It may take time to locate a suitable transliteration, obtain rights to use the transliteration, or commission a transliteration.

Other ways to anticipate and plan for future programs or productions are to keep track of any anniversaries that your organization may wish to honor, such as composer births and/or deaths, important local history events including one's own organization, the honoring of a conductor or artist, etc. Are there ethnic, religious, or cultural theme concerts that one's organization may wish to produce? Taking a moment to imagine oneself as the person making the programming decision and looking ahead at possible "hooks" or themes to attach to different performances can help one be proactive in assembling resources that will assist when it is time to be reactive in the library.

Pops/Gala

Advance planning, as it applies to pops and gala programs, can refer to days rather than years. These programs can be among the most harrowing for a librarian as repertoire can, and often does, change up to the actual performance. It is not uncommon to be sent a repertoire list that has as many "possible" pieces listed as confirmed repertoire. I have found it best not to take the "confirmed" aspect literally.

When faced with such programs, the first thing I do before seeing the repertoire is assume that I will prepare 50–75% more material than will actually be performed and budget library time accordingly. In the case of pops, find out whether the artist has a pre-packaged show that they are performing with a number of organizations. Get in touch with other librarians who have either performed the show or are about to perform the show. Find out when the music is likely to arrive. It may be traveling

---

2   See the article on "Grand Rights" by Robert Sutherland in Chapter Four.

3   What is commonly called "transliteration" in opera circles is technically considered "transcription" in linguistic circles. Most systems of (operatic) transliteration map the letters of the source script to letters pronounced similarly in the goal script. For example, a text in Cyrillic will be written in Roman characters that should result in the word sounding the same despite being written in an different alphabet.

with the artist which means you may not see the folders until the day of the rehearsal. Will the orchestra be performing any works by themselves? Get these prepared as soon as possible so that one can focus on the late-arriving material when it finally arrives. Breathe a sigh of relief if you are performing a show that has material prepared by one of our professional colleagues on behalf of an artist.

In any performance involving one or more singers, remember to ask: which version? which language? and the standard "keys, cuts, start, stop" for each piece being performed. Check the repertoire list for material under copyright or available on a rental basis only. Even if an artist or conductor insists that he/she will provide the material for such pieces, make sure that the proper rights have been obtained so that you or your organization is not held liable for copyright infringement. Consider pre-typing an instrumentation and program order sheet for the folders that contains all the possible selections. This way, when it is time to prepare the sheet for the folders immediately prior to the concert, all one has to do is cut, paste, delete, and print. (I time and date stamp such documents because they can change many times in the course of a day.)

Young Persons Concerts/Educational Programs

These concerts can take many forms and can be set well in advance or change from performance to performance. They often involve audio-visual or dramatic elements to enhance the performance. The best advice I can offer is to try to communicate as much as possible with the people involved in creating the program, prepare as much known repertoire as you can in advance (for any programs that are being performed by the organization) so that you can have contingency time available to make changes during the rehearsals and performances. When assembling material it is good to do so in a manner whereby pieces can be easily added, taken away, and the order changed. Flexibility is the key.

Commissions

It is important to have specific timelines for performance material included in any commission agreement. That does not mean, necessarily, that those timelines will be met by the composer and it often falls to the librarian to perform the heroic measures necessary to get the parts on the stand for the first rehearsal. Circumstances will differ depending on whether the composer is represented by a publisher and editorial department or is self-published, and whether there is a vetting process before the work is confirmed. Working back from the first rehearsal will once again dictate when material is needed. Factors to consider are whether the organization or person commissioning the work has a right to look at the first draft of the work and decide whether the commission will continue to move forward or whether there may be a workshop or reading of the first draft to help refine the piece. Soloists (instrumental or vocal) may require approval of, or input into, the piece. Some composers start with sketches and a short score, others compose directly to a full score. In the case of vocal music, a piano-vocal score will be necessary, usually before the full orchestral score is required. In such cases, a piano reduction will need to be created. Time must be allowed for proofreading and printing of performance material before the usual preparation can take place.

If one's organization is in the process of commissioning any piece, I recommend that the librarian try to be included in the planning process. It is usually those steps between the delivery of a score (often late) and the first rehearsal that get compromised. It is the librarian who is usually the most aware of all of those steps which should be voiced as part of the discussion of timelines for the delivery of performance material.

Guest conductors

Each organization will have its own procedures in obtaining and disseminating information with guest conductors. Given the importance of music preparation in allowing a guest conductor to do his/her best work with an orchestra, I have always believed in the librarian and conductor communicating directly. To this end I have included a sample letter that I send to guest conductors well in advance of his/her appearance with an orchestra. (See example below.)

Sample conductor letter

Conductor: [name]

Performance Dates: [performance dates]

PROGRAM

    [composer]   [piece]

    [composer]   [piece]

    ——— [= intermission here]

    [composer]   [piece]

    [composer]   [piece]

    [composer]   [piece]

MUSIC POLICY
[Obviously one's own contractual or preferred policies should appear here. I am including generic wording.]

Guest conductors are encouraged to send their own marked orchestral parts in order to reduce problems and maximize rehearsal times. Your marked music must be received at least 2 weeks prior to the first rehearsal [month/day] and if any bowings or editings are required, a score with complete bowings and/or editings or a set of bowed string masters must be received at least 6 weeks prior to the first rehearsal [month/day].

The conductor will provide music for the following works:

The conductor will provide a marked score or string masters for the following works:

If we do not receive parts or bowings from you as suggested above, we will use the [One's organization name here] parts. This music will be bowed by the concertmaster and principal strings.

The [One's organization name here] owns the following orchestral material:

    composer   title – publisher

The following is available on a rental basis only:

    composer   title – publisher

Will the conductor need any scores provided? Please indicate which works and by what date the scores are required, and where to send them:

STRING SIZE
The [One's organization name here] basic string compliment is [Add your string size here]. Please list any string reductions or special needs:

Please complete this form and e-mail or fax it to [One's contact information here].

Thank you for your attention to these matters. I am looking forward to working with you.

                                      Yours truly,

                                        [your name
                                        your organization]

Budgets

One is often required to provide a budget without knowing all of the repertoire or activities for a forthcoming season. There are various ways in which to come up with a figure. One is to compare the probable activity with a previous year or compare the type of concert with one previously performed, adjust for inflation, and use that figure until more information is forthcoming.

When budgeting copying costs for a commission, one should ask what the instrumentation and length of a piece will be. Even if a piece is not yet composed, the composer should be able to answer that question with reasonable accuracy. The librarian will then have to imagine what the final material will resemble. Once again, using the process of imagining the performance and working backwards, figure out approximately how many bars of music will be written to occur in the estimated time, given the compositional style of the composer based on previous works. Depending on the complexity of the writing, estimate how many bars will appear per page of score or orchestral part, factor in the going rate per page, or hourly rate if extracting parts from a computer engraved score, and come up with a rough estimate of the costs. If you correctly estimate within a few hundred dollars for a major commission, you are truly psychic and have a great future in orchestra management.

Robert Sutherland is the Chief Librarian of The Metropolitan Opera and a Past President of the Major Orchestra Librarians' Association.

Where are Those Orchestra Parts?

A Primer for Researching the Availability and Details of Orchestral Scores and Parts

by Clinton F. Nieweg and Jennifer A. Johnson

An orchestra librarian should develop a working relationship with a music dealer and purchase the orchestra's music exclusively from that company. Works on rental can only be ordered directly from that publisher or its agent (see entry no. 18 below).

Databases and catalogs used to research orchestral works include:

1. **EMS Database.** Gives the details of 250,000+ titles for orchestra, chorus, and band works. This information is updated daily, which makes it most valuable.

   Educational Music Service (EMS): "Printed Music of All Types, from All Publishers." 33 Elkay Drive, Chester, NY 10918; Tel: 845-469-5790; Fax: 845-469-5817; E-mail: sales@emsmusic.com; Web: http://www.emsmusic.com

   The database is available to regular customers via a computer disk for an annual fee. A video presentation of the database can be found at http://www.emsmusic.com/Mip.html. Also available are the **EMS Catalogs** at http://www.emsmusic.com/catalogs.html. In addition, EMS rents some works that were once for sale and are now permanently out of print.

2. **WorldCat (WorldCat.org).** Searches 1.5 billion items in more than 10,000 libraries worldwide. Useful for finding which academic libraries own music that is or was for sale. These entries will often guide the orchestra librarian to the original publisher. http://www.worldcat.org/advancedsearch

3. **"Daniels 4": David Daniels, *Orchestral Music: A Handbook*, 4th Edition.** The current standard book for finding orchestra repertoire. It is recommended that this book be on the desk of every orchestra librarian. This handy reference has the most correct instrumentation listings for both standard and non-standard orchestral works. It has been expanded to 6,400 entries and almost 900 composers from the 4,200 titles that were in the third edition.

   Lanham, Md.: Scarecrow Press, 2005. ISBN 978-0-8108-5674-5. 640 pages. http://www.scarecrowpress.com

   3a. **Orchestral Music Online.** The most recent iteration of David Daniels's classic repertoire reference work used by conductors, orchestra librarians, musicians, and musicologists throughout the world. This online version, based on the critically acclaimed fourth edition of the printed reference work *Orchestral Music: A Handbook*, provides greater and easier access to even more information on composers and works. More than 2,000 changes since publication of the fourth print edition have been made. As of May 2012, Orchestral Music Online lists 7,456 titles and 1,086 composers. http://www.orchestralmusic.com

David Daniels, formerly Professor of Music at Oakland University, retired in 2010 from the Music Directorship of the Warren Symphony (Michigan), a position he held for thirty-seven years.

4. **Manning "Pops": Lucy Manning, *Orchestral "Pops" Music: A Handbook.*** This 2009 publication is the first reference book to concentrate on popular orchestral music publications.

Lucy Manning provides a comprehensive and informative repertoire list for orchestral pops concerts. This volume alleviates the time-consuming work related to programming a successful pops concert. Manning has collected over 2,000 entries, representing the work of more than 650 composers. Each entry supplies detailed information about the work, including composer name and birth/death dates, duration, instrumentation, vocal needs, publisher, and thematic suggestions. Other information, such as medley contents and dedications are noted when available. Four appendices follow the main text, allowing for easy cross-referencing and accessibility.

Lanham, Md.: Scarecrow Press, 2009. ISBN 978-0-8108-6380-4. 364 pages. http://www.scarecrowpress.com

Lucy Manning is Orchestra Director and Assistant Professor of Music at Old Dominion University, Norfolk, Virginia.

5. **Meyer, Dirk:** *Chamber Orchestra and Ensemble Repertoire: A Catalog of Modern Music.*

Dirk Meyer provides conductors, musicians, and librarians with all the information needed to plan their performances of modern chamber music. Meyer lists almost 4,000 works written during the 20th or 21st centuries, representing more than 1,100 composers. Entries are divided into three categories: Chamber Orchestra, String Orchestra, and Ensemble. Presented alphabetically by composer, each entry fully describes the composition, including its duration, year of composition, availability and publisher, and the complete instrumentation. The comprehensive appendix allows users to search for repertoire based on a variety of criteria, including instrumentation, duration, solo instruments, and solo voices. As a catalog of modern music, the appendix also provides categories for 21st-century repertoire as well as compositions that require the use of electronics.

Lanham, Md.: Scarecrow Press, 2011. ISBN 978-0-8108-7731-3. 444 pages. http://www.scarecrowpress.com

6. **Yaffé, John, and David Daniels:** *Arias, Ensembles & Choruses: An Excerpt Finder for Orchestras.*

   "AEC" is a valuable reference for those who prepare programs that include voice and orchestra, and is most helpful in solving the problems that librarians and conductors face in those dreaded "Gala" programs. It is thoroughly researched, vetted by editorial experts, and indexed in every conceivable category. Yaffé and Daniels have used their expertise as conductors, and their passion for musicology, to bring to light important details on more than 1,750 excerpts from more than 450 works from opera, operetta, oratorio, and musicals. Extensive and fascinating notes are included for many entries, such as "This duet contains a significant solo part for the principal violin" or "In solo concert performance, one generally stops at the B-major chord at fig. [94]" or "In solo concert performance cuts are made in both sections reducing the duration to 6 minutes." Each entry contains information about language, voice type, timings, excerpt location (in both the full scores and vocal scores), instrumentation (in the standard Daniels format), starts and stops, cuts, keys, and sources of orchestral materials for the excerpt.

   Lanham, Md.: Scarecrow Press, 2011. ISBN 978-0-8108-8166-2. xxiii, 523 pages. http://www.scarecrowpress.com

7. **emusicquest.** The home of the **Music-In-Print Series**™ books. A large music database with over 933,000 titles, including 134,000 orchestra titles and 83,000 chamber works, which are accessed by an inexpensive yearly subscription: http://www.emusicquest.com/pricing.htm

   This database is fast, easy to search, and provides access to the publisher, instrumentation, and duration for works as listed in publishers' catalogs.

   emusicquest, P.O. Box 112, Lansdale, PA 19446. Donald Reese, Owner and Database Administrator. Toll Free Tel: 1-866-387-7639; Tel: 215-855-0181; Fax: 215-855-0182; E-mail: info@emusicquest.com; Web: http://www.emusicquest.com

8. **Fleisher Collection.** The largest lending library of orchestral performance material in the world, for which music organizations pay only a handling and shipping fee. The collection is also a great resource for public domain orchestral music that is now permanently out of print and currently on rental. Search the Fleisher Catalog before you rent from the original publisher; if the work was for sale at one time, you may be able to borrow it from Fleisher.

   - To search, go to https://catalog.freelibrary.org/
   - Click "Enter"
   - Under "Enter a word or phrase to search," type in your search requirements (e.g., for *La Valse* by Maurice Ravel, type in, say, "Ravel La Valse")
   - Under "Search by," click "Add Limits"
   - In the left-hand column, under "Limit Material Type," click the drop-down list to select "Fleisher Collection"

- Back at the top of the page, under "Search by," click on "Author" or "Keyword" if you have included the title
- In the result, click the title or MARC Record to the left for more information

Remember to use the "Fleisher Collection" limiter, and you can also combine that with Author or Title searches.

The Edwin A. Fleisher Collection of Orchestral Music in the Free Library of Philadelphia. Free Library of Philadelphia, 1901 Vine St., Philadelphia, PA 19103-1116. Tel: 215-686-5313; Fax: 215-686-5314; Curator: fleisher@freelibrary.org; Stuart Serio, Assistant Curator: serios@freelibrary.org; Web: http://libwww.freelibrary.org/collections/collectionDetail.cfm?id=14

9. **KVK Library (Karlsruhe Virtual Catalog).** A global WorldCat which searches more than 500 million books and serials in library and book trade catalogs worldwide. Titles that are cataloged in over sixty academic libraries can be found here. This database specializes in European libraries.

   Hints: set the timeout to 300 seconds in order to prevent the search engine from stopping prematurely. Then check mark all the catalogs shown. You must check mark at least one catalog. The search includes orchestral scores, CDs, and DVDs. At the end of each search the number of hits and how many sources queried are summarized. http://www.ubka.uni-karlsruhe.de/kvk_en.html

10. **Kalmus.** E. F. Kalmus is a reprint music publisher whose standard catalog of orchestral music can be used identify works that are in the public domain in the United States. With over 8000 titles in print, the Edwin F. Kalmus catalog includes high-quality reprints of standard editions along with completely new orchestrations, performance, urtext and critical editions, and new works published for the first time.

    Edwin F. Kalmus & Co., Inc., Music Publishers, P.O. Box 5011, Boca Raton, FL 33431. Toll Free Tel: 1-800-434-6340; Fax: 561-241-6347; E-mail: info@kalmus-music.com; Web: http://www.kalmus-music.com

11. **Luck's.** Luck's Music Library is a reprint music publisher whose standard catalog of orchestral music can be used identify works that are in the public domain in the United States. Luck's is also a music dealer that rents some works that were once for sale and are now permanently out of print.

    Luck's Music Library, 32300 Edward, P.O. Box 71397, Madison Heights, MI 48071. Toll Free Tel: 1-800-348-8749; Tel: 248–583–1820; Fax: 248-583-1114; E-mail: sales@lucksmusic.com; Web: http://www.lucksmusic.net

12. **Broude.** Broude Bros. is a reprint music publisher that also publishes facsimile editions for scholars and performers. To access their list of catalogs, visit http://www.broude.us/retail.html and click on the buttons. Catalogs of scholarly editions are available at http://broudeeuropa.com.

Broude Brothers Limited, 141 White Oaks Road, P. O. Box 547, Williamstown, MA 01267-0547. Tel: 1-800-525-8559; Fax: 413-458-5242; E-mail: broudebrothers@verizon.net; Web: http://www.broude.us/index.html

13. **MOLA (Major Orchestra Librarians' Association).** The international organization for librarians of larger performing ensembles has a public website and a members only section where librarians can ask questions about repertoire. The collective knowledge of these professionals is invaluable when one needs to find publications that no other reference source has listed. See the Resources links in the left sidebar of the main page. http://www.mola-inc.org

14. **OLI (Orchestra Library Information).** This Yahoo online forum group for librarians of regional, community and university orchestras has, as of February 2012, ca. 5,800 searchable posts of information about orchestral works. Use this link for an invitation to access the OLI listserv: http://launch.groups.yahoo.com/group/OrchLibInfo

15. **ASCAP (The American Society of Composers, Authors and Publishers)** website. The ASCAP ACE Title Search will list the original copyright owner of a work, as will BMI (see entry no. 16). http://www.ascap.com/ace/search.cfm?mode=search

16. **BMI (Broadcast Music, Inc.)** On the website, scroll to the very bottom right corner of the website and check "Repertoire," followed by "Songwriter/Composer" or "Title." http://www.bmi.com/search/?link=footer

17. **LC Online Catalog (Library of Congress Online Catalog).** This catalog lists the name of the publisher in the "Full Record" about a work. To fully investigate the music collections at the Library of Congress (Washington, D.C.), a researcher should make a personal visit. Only then will the enormity and scope of the various collections be appreciated. The music may be published or unpublished; some can be examined only on microfilm. Music with active copyrights may not be photocopied without written permission of the copyright holders. LC does not hold a copy of every work published. http://catalog.loc.gov

17a. **Library of Congress Authorities.** When using this site you can browse and view authority headings for Subject, Name, Title, and Name/Title combinations. http://authorities.loc.gov

18. **Publishers' websites**. Most publishers will list their catalog of publications on their website. See below for those that are the most often used. For current contact information about publishers of orchestral music, see the **MOLA Publishers, Agencies & Dealers** (PAD) list. http://www.mola-inc.org/cgi-bin/fudpaddb/fudpadndx.cgi

Direct links to some often-used Rental Publisher websites:

Alfred Music Publishing Rental Library: http://www.alfred.com/rental

Bärenreiter/Alkor: https://www.baerenreiter.com/en/sheetmusic [On left sidebar limit to rental/ hire material]. U.S. rental agent: EAM.

Boosey & Hawkes: http://www.boosey.com/pages/licensing/catalogue/rental_search.asp

Breitkopf & Härtel KG: http://www.breitkopf.de
U.S. rental agent: G. Schirmer.

Doblinger Musikverlag: http://www.doblinger-musikverlag.at/Verleih/index.php?sp=2&kat=1
No U.S. agent.

Durand/Salabert/Eschig: http://www.durand-salabert-eschig.com/english/search.php
U.S. rental agent: Boosey.

European American Music (EAM)/Schott: http://www.eamdllc.com

ECS Publishing: http://www.ecspublishing.com

Carl Fischer: http://www.carlfischer.com/Fischer/lib_composerindex.html
Rental agent: Theodore Presser.

Alphonse Leduc/Robert King: http://www.alphonseleduc.com/EN/orchestre_recherche_oeuvres.php
U.S. rental agent for Leduc, Hamelle and Heugel.

Oxford University Press: http://ukcatalogue.oup.com/category/music/hire/orchestralensemble.do
U.S. rental agent: C.F. Peters.

C. F. Peters: http://www.edition-peters.com/hire.php [Use links on right sidebar]

Theodore Presser: http://www.presser.com/Catalog/Rental/RentalWebIndex.cfm

Ricordi: http://www.ricordi.com [Click EN in upper right corner]
U.S. rental agent: Boosey & Hawkes.

G. Schirmer: http://www.schirmer.com/default.aspx?tabId=2420. Click on "Advanced Search."

Universal Edition: http://www.universaledition.com
U.S. rental agent: EAM

Note: Daniels's Orchestral Music Online also has updated publisher information under Sources (see entry no. 3a above).

18a. **Publisher Print Catalogs.** Collect printed catalogs at conferences, trade shows, and from music publishers. These hard copies can often be clearer than the websites and contain valuable details about orchestral compositions.

19. **OPAS (Orchestra Planning and Administration System).** A comprehensive software program specifically designed to manage virtually every facet of orchestra administration. OPAS seamlessly integrates the repertoire, artistic, scheduling, personnel, finance, library, and tour operations of any performing ensemble. Repertoire from Daniels's *Orchestral Music* can, in whole or part, be imported directly into your own copy of OPAS (see entry no. 3a above). Distributed by Fine Arts Software. http://www.fineartssoftware.com/index.htm

20. **MPA (Music Publishers Association Directory of Publisher Imprints).** Lists the U.S. agent for each publisher. As this information changes often, some contacts and agents will not be up-to-date. http://mpa.org/directories/publisher_imprints

21. **IMSLP (International Music Score Library Project/Petrucci Music Library).** The free public domain sheet music library. Each work scanned gives the original publisher and information about public domain or non-public domain U.S., or non-public domain European Union status. http://imslp.org/wiki/Main_Page

22. **Buschkötter.** Wilhelm Buschkötter and Hansjürgen Schaefer, *Handbuch der Internationalen Konzertliteratur, Instrumental-und Vokalmusik* [Manual of International Concert Literature, Instrumental and Vocal Music]. Includes movements, duration, instrumentation, and publisher information for 640 composers and 3,600 works. Forward and table of contents in English and German.

    Berlin: de Gruyter, 1996. Reprint 2010. ISBN 978-3-11-080845-2. http://www.degruyter.de; Direct link: http://www.degruyter.com/search?q=Buschk%C3%B6tter&searchBtn=Search

23. **Bonner Katalog**: **Verzeichnis reversgebundener musikalischer Aufführungsmateriale** [Bonner Catalog: Index of Musical Performance Materials Available for Rental]. Ed.by Deutsche Nationalbibliothek. The Bonner Katalog, providing the information necessary for performing groups wanting to rent musical performance materials, continues to be published in print form as well as in CD-ROM format.

    The 15th CD-ROM-Edition (2012) of the Bonner Katalog lists about 80,000 actual available works of over 8,500 composers. Numerous searchable fields allow targeted questions about composers or some 9,500 other persons (librettists, arrangers), titles, title-elements, settings, durations, and publications, and make accessible the comprehensive and refined information potential of the Bonner Katalog. The collected descriptions of the works are linked to the complete actual addresses of the publishers.

    München: de Gruyter Saur, 15th ed. 2012. ISBN 978-3-11-027569-8. http://www.degruyter.de

24. **IAMIC (International Association of Music Information Centres)**. As of 2010, IAMIC supports the work of forty-one member organizations in thirty-eight countries. Use these sites for finding published or unpublished manuscripts from the member countries: http://www.iamic.net [Click on the country to see the direct link for each member.]

25. **Heritage Band Guide**: William H. Rehrig. *The Heritage Encyclopedia of Band Music: Composers and Their Music.* Edited by Paul E. Bierley. Westerville, Ohio: Integrity Press, Volumes 1 and 2, 1991. Volume 3 Supplement, 1996. All of the information from the original three volumes is now expanded and revised with an additional two volumes worth of new information on one CD-ROM for use in any PC (not compatible with Macintosh). Useful for finding band works that could be arranged when an orchestral edition has not been published. Contains composer dates and bios that are not in the orchestra databases.

Oskaloosa, Iowa: Walking Frog Records, 2005. Item no. WFR339. http://www.walkingfrog.com

---

Clinton F. Nieweg is the Principal Librarian (retired) of The Philadelphia Orchestra and a Past President of the Major Orchestra Librarians' Association. **Jennifer A. Johnson** is an Assistant Librarian with the Metropolitan Opera.

Choosing Editions

by Ronald Whitaker

One of the important responsibilities of an orchestra librarian is the procurement of music, and with that the question of editions continually crops up. Almost all of these questions are concerned with music that is in the public domain, as music still under copyright is usually only available in one edition.

When a work is available in several competing editions, does one go with the newest, with its "latest critical edition" label boldly announced; an older critical edition that has been widely used; an even older "standard" edition from one of the venerable publishing houses; or one of the various reprints, which has the advantage of a less expensive price? Unfortunately there is no ironclad answer, as what suffices for one composer will prove to be a disaster with another. This article will attempt to give some guidelines, but in the end there is no substitute for individual research and the close examination of the materials themselves. No matter how good the scholarship an editor has given a particular work, if the implementation by the publisher's engravers, typesetters, and layout personnel is below the standard needed by the musicians on the stage to do their job, the edition is basically useless.

Editions of the standard repertoire

First, we must examine why there are so many various editions of the really standard repertoire. What is so wrong with the older editions of Haydn, Mozart, Beethoven, and Schubert that today's publishers keep bringing out competing editions of the same works? Won't they end up being identical with what we have used for generations?

The answer for many is a resounding "No," as one of the main aspects of any edition is the work of the editor of that edition. Anyone who has examined one of Beethoven's manuscripts will readily understand what the editor is up against. Fairly unreadable to begin with, the massive corrections and erasures compound the problem of deciphering what Beethoven intended. Many different possibilities can be imagined. It is the editor's job to make sense of this chaotic situation, and each one will come up with a different solution. Take for instance Beethoven Symphony No. 9, with many editions available. Among others there are the old Breitkopf and Härtel (reprinted by many reprint houses); the newer Breitkopf and Härtel, edited by Peter Hauschild; a Peters, edited by Igor Markevitch; and a Bärenreiter, edited by Jonathan Del Mar. All of these are different in many details (including the notes themselves), and all are valid.

So how does one choose? For the beginning librarian this is an almost overwhelming question. The most accurate and fortunately useful answer is whatever edition your conductor wishes to use. Even if the chosen edition is not the most currently in fashion, it is still what you should obtain. However, your work is not done. For example, Bärenreiter frequently updates their editions as new sources and scholarship come into play, but often does so without changing the catalog numbers or, in many cases, disseminating that information. For Mozart Symphony No. 36,

Bärenreiter has issued two different scores, with one having radically different phrasing from the other. If one looks at the two covers there is no way of knowing they are at variance with each other, and only by reading the preface of the later score would one realize the possible issue. On the other hand, Bärenreiter maintains lists of revisions and corrections for each printing of Del Mar's edition of the Beethoven symphonies, which are available on their website. As each score and part contains the actual printing information, by using these lists one can ascertain almost immediately how much work is involved in correcting and fixing the materials. Unfortunately this practice is not more widespread.

If at all possible you should examine the conductor's score prior to ordering the music so that problems can be avoided. The confusion over editions of Bruckner symphonies show the value of this. Leopold Nowak edited many of the symphonies, several of which have wildly differing versions. If, for example, your conductor specifies the Nowak version of the Bruckner Symphony No. 3, this gives you some information, but not nearly enough. Nowak edited three versions of this symphony, along with an intermediate version of the slow movement. By seeing the actual score that your conductor is using, you will know for certain which Nowak version will be used, be it III/1, III/2, or III/3. Similar problems exist for all of the Bruckner symphonies, some more extreme than others. The Bruckner problem has been a minefield for decades and will remain one—do not be afraid to ask questions. Mahler symphonies present similar difficulties, with newly revised critical editions constantly appearing, replacing the previous editions.

Many times your conductor may be using a score that has no corresponding set of parts. Eulenburg miniature scores are a prime example of this. They are an excellent reference but are not really intended for conducting use. That has certainly not stopped conductors from using them, especially as Eulenburg has vigorously entered the critical edition realm. All you can do is obtain a set of parts of another edition along with a copy of the score in question and manually match the parts with the score. The amount of work this will entail will obviously vary, but one must allow enough time to properly do the work. It may only involve matching rehearsal figures, but could also mean wholesale changes that will take considerable time.

The most difficult situation is when the conductor states no preference, leaving the decision in your hands. In a few cases, such as Brahms and Schumann, this will not be a problem, as any differences between editions will be minuscule at best. For most other composers this will prove unacceptable—the differences between various editions will be too great for you to take responsibility. Inform your conductor of the available editions and ask for a decision.

Reprint editions

Often you will be dealing with editions from the various reprint houses. These firms provide an extremely valuable service, as they keep innumerable titles in print that would have otherwise disappeared. I must again refute the myth that these firms introduce mistakes into the music they reprint. Besides not having the time, they really have no reason to do so. Just remember that these reprints can only be as good as the original, which for some titles is fine but for others extremely variable. For example, late 19th-century French editions can be problematic, often having faint staff lines and stems. The reprints of these poor originals will often be much worse, so be prepared to spend time filling in those missing items. In the middle of a performance, the musicians onstage should not have to guess what note or rhythm they should be playing.

Besides reprinting other publishers' editions, reprint houses also will produce their own. While some of these in-house materials can be quite good, one must also be prepared for shoddy scholarship, bad manuscript, computer engraving of dubious quality, and a presentation that is not user-friendly. While good editions of some Rossini overtures are desperately needed, some recent ones from the reprint houses do no one any good with note heads so small that they cannot be easily read, page turns not well thought-out, and a basic layout that is only gauged at saving paper over everything else.

Critical editions

Be careful with critical editions, not because they are not good, but rather their intention. Many critical editions seem to be aimed for the musicologist, not for the performing musician. Implementation can be a real problem, with scores not having matching parts (too many to mention), materials having multiple versions combined in one volume (Berlioz *Benvenuto Cellini*), and illogical layout (Wagner *Das Rheingold* in two smallish volumes—it easily could have been in one). Several critical editions offer what the composer originally wrote instead of his final intentions (Bizet *Carmen*, edited by Fritz Oeser). These problems do seem to affect the opera world more than the orchestral one, but they are symptomatic of the attitude of many critical editors. While extremely interesting for study and research, in the end many of these publications are more than frustrating for the performer, who must jump through hoops to perform these works using these editions.

Another problem with recent critical editions is questionable proofreading. Almost all new editions are computer-engraved, meaning that parts are probably generated from the computerized score. Any mistakes in the score will be reflected in the parts, making quality proofreading at the initial stage mandatory. Major mistakes can completely undo the editor's efforts, and again complicate the rehearsal/performance process. As with all music, adequate planning and preparation time on your part is essential.

If you are confronted with one of these editions and problems look about to arise, a pleasant but frank discussion with your conductor may be necessary. Finding a solution sooner rather than later will save you many headaches.

It is of utmost importance that you establish a relationship with a reputable music dealer, one that deals with orchestra music on a regular and ongoing basis. This dealer will be your greatest asset in determining what is available and the best way of obtaining it.

Do not be afraid to contact other librarians with questions. They can be one of your major sources for answers concerning editions. However, please be respectful of their time—they are just as busy as you.

As I stated earlier, nothing will replace the work and study you do yourself. As you progress, no one will know your conductor and musicians as well as you, and you will be able to anticipate and avoid problems that certain editions create.

Ronald Whitaker is the Head Librarian (retired) of The Cleveland Orchestra and a Past President of the Major Orchestra Librarians' Association.

Proofreading

by Bill Holab

It was an innocent ad on the Juilliard bulletin board that caught my eye: "Wanted. Experienced draftsperson with musical knowledge." I had taken an architectural drawing course when I was ten, so I figured that made me qualified. I put on my one white dress shirt and went for an interview with Paul Sadowski, an expert autographer who did some of the most beautiful work I had ever seen, far better than any of my samples. Paul had me do some drawing while I was there and I *very* carefully drew staff lines. Pens are notorious for spraying ink around (I was sure I would ruin my one dress shirt). To my surprise, Paul called a few days later to say I got the job. I asked him why and he said, "You were the only one who could draw a straight line."

Eventually there would be a team of a dozen people working with us autographing scores, each apprenticing and doing different tasks. One person might do "casting off" or layout, another drawing staff lines, yet another doing note heads. With this type of workflow, there had to be an overseer who carefully looked at the final product to make sure that everything was accurate and correct. We found that one of the composers we worked for was exceptionally meticulous about checking his scores and parts, finding errors that were minute and detailed. When we queried him about this, he said that people were looking for ways to discount his music so he felt it vitally important that his materials be as perfect as possible. We specialized in complex scores and often did works by Carter, Babbitt, Wuorinen, and Druckman. But the composer who gave us this unique proofreading method was John Cage.

Proofreading a musical score is a discipline that requires practice to master. When a musician attempts it, they often make the mistake of trying to "read" the music. That invariably does not work as there are too many detailed elements to check and the eye often fills in things that aren't there. The essence of this system is that you don't read the music as a score. You isolate specific elements and focus on just those elements, making multiple passes through a page. By breaking it down this way, you stop looking at the page as music and focus on details. I'll describe the process as we used it: checking an autographed score against a composer's manuscript.

Begin by making single-sided proof copies of the music you are checking. Using a red pencil, write the following letters at the top of the page: **P R D A M Pd T Ex**. These are the elements you are going to check. The letters stand for:

- **P**—Pitch (clefs, clef changes, accidentals)
- **R**—Rhythm (rests, multiple-bar rests, ties)
- **D**—Dynamics (including hairpins, *cresc.*, and *dim.* indications)
- **A**—Articulations (including expressive text markings)
- **M**—Measure numbers (and rehearsal letters)
- **Pd**—Pedal markings (keyboard music)
- **T**—Text (lyrics, titles, tempi, instrument labels)
- **Ex**—Extremities

This means you proofread the page eight times. The first time, you only check pitches and ensure that the clefs are correct. You look at accidentals and also check for cautionary/courtesy accidentals. When done, cross off "P" at the top of the page so you know you've checked that element. The second step is to just check the rhythm, making sure it matches the manuscript and also making sure each bar adds up to the stated time signature. Cross off "R" when done, and so on, for the other stages. Dynamics would be the next pass, and we also look at text associated with dynamics (e.g., *p, espr.*). In the articulation stage, we look at articulations and slurs (as they are a part of articulation) plus playing indications like "sul pont." If you have a piece with mutes, you check those too, and also check continuity throughout. Next is measure numbers which we count to ensure they are accurate. Pedal markings are for piano parts. In harp parts, they are used for tunings.

Text would cover the typical elements in a score for spelling/capitalization, plus lyrics and correct hyphenation of lyrics. Use a dictionary to hyphenate lyrics. Don't trust your own experience on how to break a word unless you are a professional typesetter. Words are never broken by the way they are sung; they are hyphenated exactly the way a professional typesetter would break them at the end of a line so they are legible.

There is no exception to this rule, despite countless composers who have told me words should be broken differently ("Wa-lking" is a common example that novice composers think is correct). You don't need to tell singers how to handle consonants, but they do need to know what they are singing. Imagine a word break over two pages and the bottom of the first page just has "Wa-." How do you pronounce that? If they see "Walk-" instead, they'll instantly know what vowel sound to use.

Foreign languages pose some interesting challenges. Spanish tends to be hyphenated differently based on the region of the author. Hebrew must be done in English transliteration, which is also true of Chinese (usually written in Pinyin Romaggi, a type of English transliteration). It's best to get information on the language used if you have a project that involves a lot of text in a foreign language.

The last category in our list, extremities, covers the things that many people miss. Items at the end/beginning of a system/page tend to be glossed over, yet they are often the most crucial areas to check. In autographed works we checked:

- Ties
- Cautionary accidentals
- Clefs
- Key signatures
- Reminder time signatures at spots where the meter changes
- Trills/pedal lines/slurs
- Instrument labels, particularly for instruments that double, and percussion

And of course, you would skip a step if it doesn't apply (e.g., you don't need to check **Pd** for scores that don't employ them). For some works we might add a step. For example, a guitar piece with extensive fingerings would require a separate pass just to proofread fingerings.

Proofreader's markings

It is customary to mark corrections in a contrasting color (red pencil is preferred) so that it's easy for the person making the changes to spot all of the corrections. When a work has few corrections, we put an X in the right-hand margin near the spot to help identify where the corrections are, plus an X in the upper right hand corner of the page, since a score with few corrections might not have something to adjust on every page. When there are many corrections, don't bother to write in X's for everything.

The markings we use come from typesetter's markings for correcting text. I've included a chart to illustrate the most common ones:

Symbol	Explanation	Example
ℓ	delete	
⌐⌐	move left	
⌐⌐	move right	
W.O.	write out	
F.S.	flip stems	
X NOT Y	wrong note	E, NOT F
U.C.	upper case	richard U.C.
/ l.c.	lower case	richard l.c.
S.C.	small caps	Richard s.c.
∿ B.F.	bold	Richard B.F.
∧	insert letter or object	Ricard
⌃#	insert space	Runnow!
⊙	add staccato dot	

⌣	close up space	wel⌣come
∩	transpose letters/objects	tr∩ouble
‖ F.L.	flush left text	‖ What is the best way to mark a ‖ paragraph to be flush left? F.L.
‖ F.R.	flush right text	What is the best way to mark a ‖ F.R. paragraph to be flush right? ‖
⌐ ⌐	center text	⌐ What is the best way to mark a ⌐ ⌐ paragraph to be centered? ⌐
‖ ‖	justify text	‖ What is the best way to mark a ‖ ‖ paragraph to be centered? ‖
STET	leave as is	[music notation] STET

Proofreading computer-typeset music

Over the years, as computer typography software has changed the methods used to typeset music, we adapted our proofreading methods, as well. It's important to understand what you are working with. If possible, find out which software program was used to prepare the work and ask whether or not it was done by a professional.

For many years, Score was the predominant program for music copying/engraving, favored by many publishers. It was a wonderful program with many advantages, but it was primarily a graphic program with few large-scale niceties to automate things like bar numbers, page numbers, instrument names, etc. So, we would rigorously check everything, much like we were working with an autographed score. The possibility of errors was high and you had to be vigilant.

Programs like Sibelius and Finale are better in terms of global elements, like page/bar numbers, instrument names, etc., so certain things are less likely to be incorrect. It is possible for errors to occur, though, so we do have to keep an eye out for problems. And the part extraction process is much cleaner in Sibelius and Finale versus Score, so we have a lot less that we need to check. If the person preparing the materials used the linked/dynamic part feature, for example, one would not proofread the content of the part, but would instead look for collisions, page turns, layout, etc., without proofreading the content for pitch and such, since that would all match the score faithfully.

Using playback for proofreading

This is one of the most unreliable ways to proofread a piece of music. You might catch a wrong note or rhythm, which is helpful, but there are so many other elements one should check, that this can only be used as a supplement to printing out proofs and carefully looking at them. Don't forget that the playback features are not perfect; sometimes we have to use workarounds to make something look right, even though it means it won't play back correctly.

Proofreading onscreen

For a first proof of a score, proofreading on screen is impractical. There is too much to look at and the ever-shifting position of a piece when displayed almost guarantees things will be missed. This might be practical for a final proof when you are just checking a few things and no longer need to look at every item on the page. In that case, using the program's navigation features to jump to a specific bar can be very helpful.

One exception is what I call "continuity" proofreading. If I want to check brass mutes for a long work, say an act of an opera, I will use the panorama mode of Sibelius or the scroll view in Finale. This is an endless view that does not delineate pages. I restrict the view to just a few instruments, say just the horns. Then I scroll through and look at continuity. When they change to "con sord." I make sure there is a "senza sord." to cancel it out. I also add courtesy indications ("al sord." and "via sord.") to tell the player when to put mutes in or out. The same method can be used for arco/pizz. indications in strings, wind doublings, and so on.

This is the one case where proofreading onscreen is better than proofreading on paper. Because of the restricted view, it's possible to "see" the music in a way that would be much more difficult when looking at a printed score. Of course, it's only applicable when you have computer files in a suitable program.

Proofreading parts

One must use some judgment when deciding how to proofread parts. As mentioned above, the method used to create the parts, as well as the software employed, will dictate some of the choices the proofreader makes. Hand-copied parts can be checked with the P-R-D-A-M-Pd-T-Ex method. More important though, are certain key elements for good parts:

1. Are there suitable page turns on right-hand (odd-numbered) pages? Remember to be aware of the tempo; a two-bar rest might look like an acceptable page turn, but not if it's in 2/4 time and the tempo is quarter note = 160. Page turns are *not* optional. They must be worked out so that the music can be performed without interruption. The one exception would be in string parts (we frequently see 500-bar cello parts that never stop playing). In that case, one player on each stand drops out to turn the page while the stand partner keeps playing. But this can't be done when the section is playing divisi, only when the section is playing together as a tutti.
2. Are there good cues? If a part rests for an extended period, say thirty measures or more, are there landmark cues along the way so the player doesn't get lost? Cues are essential and not optional.

3. Are the cues transposed correctly (e.g., a flute cue in a horn part would be transposed up a perfect fifth)? My preference is to write cues at sounding pitch for octave-transposing instruments like contrabass.

When proofreading computer-extracted parts, I strongly recommend checking one part first for all global elements, what we call a "bar count" proofreading. Extracting parts is a technical process and one that only goes smoothly when the score is properly input and coded correctly. Checking one part first checks the setup of the score to ensure things are correct.

Sometimes things drift. Sometimes they are attached to the wrong spot and appear in the wrong bar in the part. And sometimes (in Finale, primarily) people don't code them so they will extract properly or they get hidden inside a multi-measure rest. Look at tempo indications, fermati over barlines/whole rests, time signatures, key signatures, titles, copyright notices — essentially the common elements that appear in every part.

If you do encounter problems in that first part, then the engraver can fix the problem before extracting the other parts. It's much more efficient to fix a typo in a copyright notice once before the parts are extracted, then to correct it thirty times in a set of parts.

One proofreader is good, but two are better

My final advice regarding strategies for proofreading is a simple one. No matter how experienced the proofreader, they always will miss something. The best publishers use two or more proofreaders to check a score if they want to ensure that the work is thorough and that all errors are caught. Since a publisher typically goes through several rounds of proofreading, there is usually an opportunity to use different editors in this role.

Smart publishers apply different levels of rigor to the proofreading of a work based on how it will be used. A new edition of Beethoven piano sonatas must be as clean and accurate as is humanly possible, with a great deal of attention focused on consistent style and good engraving practice. A set of parts to a new work that is being premiered may be proofread under tight deadlines, with musical accuracy and clean, legible materials the priority, not orthographic details.

Proofreading is a process. We all make mistakes, but with experience and care the process can minimize these errors so that they will not impede the performer's ability to read the music and bring it to life. Thanks to John Cage, we don't have to leave this to chance.

Bill Holab is the owner of Bill Holab Music (www.billholabmusic.com).

Orchestral "Pops" Music: Take Nothing For Granted

by Ella M. Fredrickson

"If you're not precise—know what you're doing, where you are going and observing the rules—you're going to fall off the trolley. The same thing happens in the music business. You better be prepared."

—Skitch Henderson[4]

From start to finish, successful pops productions often begin with (and end up in the hands of) the orchestra librarian. Being professional means making it look easy, especially when it is not. In fact, the orchestra librarian's role in producing a pops show is much more than putting the books out onstage.

Working with the late Skitch Henderson, the legendary pops conductor and pianist, was one of my first experiences in the field of symphonic "pops" performances. A show with Skitch was always a lesson in expecting the unexpected. In his own unique way, Skitch tested my ability to anticipate any changes, be flexible, and to always *be prepared* backstage. Sometimes rehearsals were a bit of a challenge, but the end result was truly rewarding.

There are several key elements that can help you and your production team have (nearly) anxiety-free rehearsals and performances: communication, organization, planning, information gathering, and implementation. Your organization may not have the same size music library (or budget) as that of the Boston Pops or Cincinnati Pops orchestras, but that doesn't have to limit what you can accomplish. Learn to be resourceful and take nothing for granted.

Marvin Hamlisch (composer, pianist, pops conductor) believes that the role of the music librarian is essential to a smooth production. During a personal interview between acts of a pops show, Marvin said to me, "Assuming is the mother of all screw-ups." He is totally right. The information may be at your fingertips, but you can't go wrong by asking questions if you aren't sure about something. Study the charts thoroughly when they arrive and look over each part. Did the parts you received match the instrumentation you expected? Are there enough string parts for each stand? Do the percussionists have enough parts to cover all the instruments they might need? Do you really have to find someone to play Theremin? Again, *take nothing for granted*.

An orchestra librarian's knowledge, skills, and resourcefulness can be as invaluable to the organization's production team as the performers onstage. The ever-changing technological resources of the twenty-first century have made music research and production easier, faster, and much more complicated. Knowing where to look and

---

[4] National Public Radio audio interview by Liane Hansen, *Weekend Edition Sunday,* January 30, 2005.

what to look for is a good place to start in the planning process for a pops show. The place to begin might not be on the shelf, but can be closer than you think. *Find resources outside of your music library.*

The definition of symphonic pops has evolved a great deal throughout the twentieth century. For example, five major symphonic organizations have pooled their resources by forming a specialized consortium, called the **Symphonic Pops Consortium**[5] which is managed and spearheaded by the Indianapolis Symphony Orchestra. The trend of orchestra artistic administrators to book a presentation that is a packaged show, for pops programming is a successful combination of both the marketing department and the music library.

Sparkling and successful symphonic pops performances leave everyone happy—the box office, in particular. For the orchestra librarian, the achievement is more than just getting the page to the stage; it means you must always have the right music in the right place at the right time.

Planning and information gathering

Let's trace the steps for music preparation from the beginning. Your artistic administrator or conductor has provided you with a pops program and/or a contract rider for a booked show with a guest artist. You need for everyone to have all the information they need so that the right instrumentalists are onstage and the right music is in place. Now is the time to ask questions, even the ones that may seem insignificant. The orchestra librarian should review and reconfirm the information at hand. Even though the contract rider may state one thing, knowing what to ask in advance may ultimately be your best guide.

The cardinal rules of pops program preparation:

- Know your conductor!
- Communicate with the guest artist, if needed. (e.g., "What key do you sing this song in?" or "Are you providing your own music?")
- Review the composers/titles of all listed works.
- Review and confirm the program and contract rider provided.
- Report accurate information to the personnel manager, stage manager and/or operations manager. This may not only include instrumentation, but also timings and correct titles of works.
- Determine the source of the music. You may need to obtain music through a rental agency, music publisher, or private arranger/guest artist.

Getting organized

Use a checklist to help you fill in the necessary information that will be important as you proceed with your music preparation. Use or customize a template like the one

---

[5] http://www.symphonicpopsconsortium.com.

provided here as a guide for your organization. The more organized you are, the less chance that you or someone else might overlook something critical. You want to avoid any surprises that may "pop" up, so to speak.

[insert Orchestra Name/phone/E-mail here]

SHOW TITLE:
ARTIST: **CONDUCTOR:**
PERFORMANCE DATE(s):   First rehearsal:

CONTACT INFORMATION

Guest Artist	E-mail	Mobile	Office	Fax

Artist Manager	E-mail	Mobile	Office	Fax

Road Manager	E-mail	Mobile	Office	Fax

Librarian	E-mail	Mobile	Office	Fax

INSTRUMENTATION:

Is artist shipping / providing their own materials for the show?	Y / N / Some
Is the orchestra required to do a first-half program?	Y / N
Is stage plot accurate and confirmed ?	Y / N
Have all sound & lighting requirements been received?	Y / N
Is the set list / running order available in advance?	Y / N
Detailed Instrumentation for charts available in advance?	Y / N

SHIPPING INFORMATION

Music is expected to be properly prepared, with correct number of string books (7-6-5-5-4) and must arrive a minimum of 3 weeks in advance of the first scheduled rehearsal.

COURIER (UPS or FEDEx) TO:	Anticipated Delivery Date:
Please indicate where and when artist's music should be returned and provide shipping account information for return of materials, as applicable:	

SPECIAL NOTES:

[insert Librarian contact information here]

Music research tools

Music for a show might be in your permanent music collection or someone else's library. Many titles are available for purchase. Networking with colleagues is invaluable. Don't be afraid to ask for another librarian's help to find a title. Likewise, don't despair if your colleague cannot lend you music from their collection due to legal issues.

Familiarize yourself with helpful pops research tools:

- Search publisher catalogues by theme (i.e., Patriotic, Holiday, etc)
- Visit the guest artists' website(s) and look at their performance calendar to see what other orchestras they have recently performed with
- Read music publisher newsletters to keep current with composers and arrangers
- Get to know your local arrangers and music copyists
- Film music is widely used for pops concerts (watch those end credits)
- Use the MOLA Pops Resource List at http://www.mola-inc.org/Pops/MOLAPopsResources.pdf

Music preparation

The program is confirmed and you have done your research on all the titles. There could be as many as twenty different pieces on the program! So, to help you stay on task, use your checklist to confirm each piece as it arrives or is pulled off the shelf.

You may receive music that has no score, other than a piano reduction or a lead sheet. What happens when you open the box of music that has arrived (sometimes two weeks late) and you find that you have to start from scratch? What should you do? *Don't panic.* Here are a few important things to look for:

- Is the set of parts complete?
- Are the parts themselves missing any pages?
- Are there enough string parts for the number of string players?
- Is there an Assistant Horn book? If not, start copying and taping parts.
- Make note of any auxiliary instruments needed, even though they might not have been originally listed in the instrumentation (e.g., E-flat clarinet or saxophone).
- Do the percussionists have enough parts to cover all the stations in their section?
- If there are cuts in the music, do they all match?

The orchestra librarian has to be able to think ahead and improvise when necessary. You might learn from other people's mistakes or errors, but when you find yourself in a seemingly exasperating moment of uncertainty (for example, the principal oboe thinks he left the folder in the dressing room of the theater you were at the night before), remember to keep your cool. There is nearly always a photocopier or music paper and a pencil around somewhere. *Always be prepared.*

The rehearsal

Marvin Hamlisch prides himself in the presentation of music for his concerts (and he has the librarians and copyists he hired for it to thank). Hamlisch believes that out of respect to the orchestra, the music on the stand should be in pristine condition. The same idea should hold true for every show you put together, but the odds are against it.

Take nothing for granted as you ready the books for a show and move toward rehearsals. If changes happen, as they sometimes do, think about what you can do to improve the situation for the next orchestra that will use the same materials.

- Keep an ear to the progress of the rehearsal
- Communicate any changes made in the show order and make sure everyone knows what the final order is, including your stage manager and guest artist(s)
- Your colleagues onstage will almost always alert you if they really need a page turn or a tacet sheet (a place holder for a title that they do not play)
- Keep track of the timings for each piece. You may find this information critical if there is a concern that the show may go into overtime.

The performance

The stage is set for the show, but your job isn't done until the last music folder is back in the road case or in the library. If the conductor gives you their stack of scores to put out onstage, double check to see if they are in the right order. As you did during rehearsal, keep "tuned" in to the progress of the performance. Make a note of any charts that may have been cut or solo numbers that are added to the show. Seize the moment to sit back, listen, and enjoy the brief results of your hours of labor, as your colleagues focus on making magic with all those little black dots.

Afterglow

Don't stop yet! Music has to go back on the shelf or be returned to the publisher or artist or perhaps sent along to another orchestra. Maintain an accurate performance history of your pops show for reporting to ASCAP and BMI. Include the names of composers and arrangers, instrumentation, and timing. Re-shelve sets of music and return borrowed or rented materials promptly.

Then, as Skitch Henderson so often said during rehearsal, "Upper left" (go back to the beginning and start it again).

Ella M. Fredrickson is the Principal Librarian of The Florida Orchestra and the President of the Major Orchestra Librarians' Association.

Music Information Centres

by Jari Eskola

A Music Information Centre is a gateway to a country's musical life, including creators, performers, and the music industry.

Music Information Centres (MICs) are national institutions that document and promote music of our time in their country of operations. Each of the Music Information Centres advocate for music over a variety of musical genres including contemporary classical, world music, jazz, and popular music. Centres often manage extensive resources (libraries of sheet music, recordings and sound archives, biographical and other research materials) and deliver promotional and artistic projects (festivals, concerts, competitions, conferences) to the professional public.

Music Information Centres have traditionally been set up by composer societies or performing rights organizations. Initially, the Centres concentrated on "serious" music, but the scope and mandates have broadened in the past decades to cover all genres. In some cases, the music industry supports the MIC for their country.

The IAMIC (International Association of Music Information Centres), founded in 1986, is a worldwide network of such organizations. It has forty member organizations in thirty-seven countries as of 2010. Check the IAMIC website for more information and a list of members at http://www.iamic.net.

In addition to the daily customer service, MICs participate in professional fairs, seminars and conferences, launch and manage projects (music export, showcase projects, etc.) and participate in the national music industry structure.

MICs and performance librarians

The customer service department of a MIC is a great source of information for any performance librarian. The MIC databases cover all contemporary music in the specified country, both published and unpublished, and offer plenty of information about titles in other genres, too. Sometimes these databases are available online and contain the most important information for any work: title in the original correct form, instrumentation, duration, availability, and publisher's name, or if not published, the acquisition source. The MIC sheet music libraries distribute those works that are not published by a commercial publisher. The MICs rent symphonic works and often sell scores, chamber music sets, and wind band materials. Because they are not publishers, the prices are much lower than those of the commercial publishers. Some MICs have launched Web shops, such as Finland's Fimic Sheet Music Web shop at http://www.fimic.fi.

The MIC customer service personnel are extremely knowledgeable about the musical life in their country. Their networks span a wide range of industry professionals. They can put you in touch with a composer, publisher, arranger, performer, festival leader, recording executive, or other professional person. They have constant cooperation with other archives containing musical works, and can even track down and, in some cases, obtain rare and unpublished works in manuscript copies from those archives. The MIC personnel are also frequently consulted for information about repertoire, performers, and ensembles.

The MICs publish books, brochures, and catalogues about the composers, music, and musical life in their country. These publications are available free of charge upon request. CD or DVD recordings may also be available, as well as perusal scores.

Some MICs have full scores or score snippets available online on their website. These promotional copies can be printed for free. More and more sound files are being uploaded to the websites, making the music-exploring experience more complete and straightforward. The complicated copyright clearance process has kept the number of sound files rather low in number so far, but there are hopes that in the near future more sound and even video clips of performances could be published on the websites. See the American Music Center site at www.amc.net for an example.

Other services

The following services are not so much for the librarian, but might be helpful in case the program annotator consults you about certain topics. In their offices, MICs have great facilities for conducting research work. Most often they have an extensive music library containing just about every published and unpublished contemporary score written in their country. A library containing books and magazines about the country's music is available to visitors. Listening studios are also common. In these, one can listen to the thousands of audio tapes and CDs available or watch performances on video and DVD. Some MICs have a press clippings archive, sorted by composer or a specific topic. Reviews and program comments are archived, as well as articles from domestic and international publications.

Some MICs have a notation studio which composers, copyists, and publishers can use free of charge. They tend to have both market-leading software and also older and more obscure notation software. Due to their nature as documentation centres, most MICs have great in-house printing and digitization facilities. These are mostly for producing scores and sets of parts, but one can inquire about service prices for outsiders. The MIC facilities often have large-format printers and scanners that are not available commercially everywhere.

Finally, the MICs also know about grants for music, performances, and recordings. If your organization is planning to showcase the music of, say, a more obscure Northern European composer, your organization might be eligible for grants from the various foundations in the composer's country. The MIC personnel will tell you about those possibilities.

The MICs have traditionally kept a low profile, but don't let this fool you—their best product is expertise and their best service is providing accurate information.

Jari Eskola is Manager of Services and Development at the Finnish Music Information Centre.

Small Rights, and Print, Mechanical, and Synchronization Licensing

by Jane Cross

"Only one thing is impossible for God: To find any sense in any copyright law on the planet. Whenever a copyright law is to be made or altered, then the idiots assemble."

—Mark Twain, May 23, 1903

Copyright: Why should I care?

If your organization is caught breaking the copyright laws, they could be held liable for infringement and taken to court. This can get expensive fast, and no one wants the ensuing bad press. Copyright administrators occasionally like to make an example of somebody and you don't want your organization in that situation. You might be thinking, "But I'm just the librarian. Shouldn't this stuff be left up to my administrator or conductor?" Since librarians handle the music before anyone else sees it and deal directly with publishers, especially concerning rentals, librarians are on the front lines when it comes to recognizing situations involving copyright issues. Many unwittingly find themselves to either be the most knowledgeable about it or the one expected to be responsible for ensuring their organization is always compliant.

Copyright: What is it?

Copyright protects published and unpublished literary, scientific, and artistic works, whatever the form of expression, provided such works are fixed in a tangible or material form. This means if you can hear, see, and/or touch it, it may be protected. Copyright laws grant the creator the exclusive right to:

- Reproduce (photocopies, recordings, scans, etc.)
- Create derivatives (arrangements, transcriptions, orchestrations, etc.)
- Distribute
- Perform and display publicly
- Perform sound recordings by digital audio transmission

If anyone other than the copyright holder wishes to do any of the above, permission in the form of a license must be obtained from the copyright holder (or their representative). Licensing can take anywhere from a few days to several months or even years, so planning ahead is always key. You may want to have a backup plan ready in case of lack of response or outright denial.

To determine if a work is still protected by copyright, the following is a good rule of thumb: if a work was copyrighted in 1922 or before, it is in the public domain

(PD) and anything can be done with it by anyone. Research is required to determine the status of works copyrighted from 1923 to 1963 since they may have entered the public domain if they were not renewed. Anything copyrighted in 1964 or after is still under protection. If it cannot be documented that the material is in the public domain, a license must be obtained for its use. The U.S. recognizes the copyright protection of works created in most other countries. For further detail, please see the chart "Copyright Term and the Public Domain in the United States" at http://www.copyright.cornell.edu/resources/publicdomain.cfm.

Please note that the work must be *copyrighted* in 1922 or before, not just *composed* or created, to be in the public domain. For instance, many of Charles Ives songs written between 1900 and 1922 are not in the public domain because they were copyrighted much later and subsequently renewed. Be wary of other compositions from this era.

Examples: Copyright versus PD

- Overture in C for Winds, Opus 24 by Felix Mendelssohn, first published in 1839, *in the public domain*
- Christopher Hogwood's edition of Overture in C for Winds, Opus 24 by Felix Mendelssohn, ©*2005 Bärenreiter Music Corporation* [protected by copyright and not in the public domain]
- "Up on the Housetop," 1860s, *in the public domain*
- "Rudolph the Red-Nosed Reindeer," ©*1949 John D. Marks* [protected by copyright and not in the public domain]

The website for the United States Copyright Office (http://www.copyright.gov) is the most official resource available, though at times, also one of the more confusing. Circular No. 1, "Copyright Basics," in the Publications section is suggested as a good place to start learning more about the U.S. copyright law.

Fair use

Fair use is using a portion of a copyrighted work "as is" for purposes such as parody, news reporting, research, and education about such copyrighted work without the permission of the author. Use of copyrighted works, or portions thereof, for any other purpose is not deemed fair use. Even if you paraphrased the author's original words, or if you feel that you don't need the author's permission because it falls in this vague concept of fair use, you must credit your source to avoid plagiarism. There are four factors one must consider when thinking about fair use:

- Character and purpose of the Use
- Nature of the copyrighted work
- Amount/substantiality
- Effect on market

For more in-depth information, see The US Code, Section 17, Section 107 (http://www.copyright.gov/title17/92chap1.html#107) as well as the Stanford University

Libraries' more explanatory Web page on the topic (http://fairuse.stanford.edu/Copyright_and_Fair_Use_Overview/chapter9/index.html).

Licensing

Licensing is obtaining legal permission to do something. You'll need a license if your organization wants to, among other things: make photocopies, recordings (to include analog, digital, and audio/visual), scans, and so forth; create arrangements, transcriptions, orchestrations, and so forth; distribute sheet music, arrangements, recordings, and so forth; perform publicly; and perform sound recordings by digital audio transmission.

Licensing: How to find and contact a copyright holder

1. Determine that you have the correct information for:

   a) *Title, composer, arranger, etc.* — check:
      - The music itself
      - Trusted reference print and Internet sources

   b) *Copyright status* — check:
      - The music itself
      - Chart: "Copyright Term and the Public Domain in the United States" (see link above)
      - Library of Congress: Anything copyrighted after 1977 is searchable on their website at http://www.copyright.gov/records/cohm.html

   c) *Copyright holder and their contact information.* Usually the publisher is the copyright holder, or they administer the rights, or know who does.
      - Start with the copyright notice on the music
      - Then visit the Music Publishers Association's (MPA) online directory of music publishers and publisher's imprints (subsidiary companies or catalogs taken over from other publishers): http://mpa.org/directories/
      - If there is no copyright notice on the music, or the MPA doesn't list the publisher, try searching the American Society of Composers, Authors and Publishers' (ASCAP) ACE database: http://www.ascap.com/ace/search.cfm?mode=search, and...
      - Broadcast Music, Inc.'s (BMI) repertoire search engine: http://www.bmi.com/search/?link=navbar

2. Contact the copyright holder or administrator.

   a) If they have a website, see if they have a licensing/copyright page that has either online submission forms or instructions on how to submit license

requests. Most major publishers provide "How to License" information along with instructions for submitting requests.
b) In lieu of any information online, call to find out how best to proceed, or mail or fax your license request.
c) If the copyright holder or their representative does not respond within a reasonable amount of time (around three months), try following up maybe in a different method than before. Do not try contacting them too soon after your initial request—multiple submissions of your same request can cause confusion. They are often working several weeks or months behind and there is no law about how fast they have to respond, or even compelling them to respond at all. Lack of response should be considered a denial in order to eliminate your risk of litigation.

3. Track all licensing requests so you can follow up in the appropriate time frame, answer questions from others in your organization about the progress and details of a particular license, remember your points of contact and their preferred methods of communication, and calculate/record fees.

Reproduction: Photocopying

Performing from illegal photocopies of scores and parts puts you and your organization at risk. You never know who is in your audience or walking around your ensemble during a performance. ASCAP has agents, and composers have families and far-reaching estates, that may question the legality of any photocopies they see. It is always safest to purchase as much music as you need. This also helps keep in business the publishers, composers, and arrangers we so heavily rely on and sets a good example for the performers. For works that have gone out of print but are still under copyright, find someone with a set they will let you copy and obtain a license to photocopy it. (With the advent of digital presses and print-on-demand, some publishers may respond to this type of license request by offering instead to print the music and sell it to you.) Remember: Out of print does NOT mean out of copyright. For more information, the Music Publishers Association has "Copying Under Copyright: A Practical Guide" that is available at http://mpa.org/copyright_resource_center/copying. You do not need a license to make an emergency copy for an imminent performance as long as the legal replacement part has been ordered, nor do you need a license to make a photocopy in order to fix a page turn.

Reproduction: Scanning

Copyright holders, which include publishers, composers, owner representatives, and others, may contend that the mere presence of an unlicensed scan of their property constitutes a violation of their exclusive right to reproduce. Technically, by scanning the music, you have reproduced it on the computer's hard drive. Underlying this may be a greater concern that once scanned, music is so much more easily mass distributed. Unlicensed distribution violates another exclusive right of the copyright holder, a right that could involve a much larger diversion of their potential revenue stream and thus, a larger legal risk for you.

Derivative works: Arrangements, transcriptions, orchestrations, etc.

In order to create a legal arrangement, transcription, orchestration, etc. of a copyrighted work, a license must be obtained. People have been sued for creating and performing illegal arrangements, i.e., arrangements created without a license. Please be aware that permission could be denied, so it is definitely worth obtaining the license first before creating the derivative work. Also, most copyright holders will usually contract for ownership of the copyright of the derivative work you create.

1. Make sure an arrangement that suits your needs does not already exist. Many requests are denied because the arrangement is already available either commercially or could be obtained (with the copyright holder's permission) from another ensemble. For example, Wilson Ochoa has already orchestrated Aaron Copland's band composition *Emblems* for the Nashville Symphony, so there may be no need to waste time creating yet another orchestration.

2. Contact the copyright holder/publisher via their preference of online form, fax, mail, or e-mail with the following information:

   a) Your name, your organization's name, and contact information
   b) Type of license requested
   c) Titles(s)
   d) Composer(s)
   e) Copyright holder(s)
   f) Copyright date(s)
   g) Type of ensemble for which work is being arranged

3. They reply with:

   a) Permission denied or granted for the arrangement
   b) Contract terms
   c) Amount of fee

4. If you do not approve of the terms and/or fees, you may attempt to negotiate. If you approve of the terms and fees, sign and return any agreement forms with payment.

5. Keep your correspondence on file, preferably both in print and electronically.

6. Notate in your catalog that the clearance is on file and make sure the copyright information is correct. You may also wish to keep a copy of the agreement with the resulting set.

If you are licensing tunes to be used in a medley, license specifically for that use and list in the request all tunes to be used in the medley. Tunes licensed for use in a medley cannot be used elsewhere for other reasons.

There is a question of liability when an organization performs an arrangement they did not license and create themselves, or purchase from a reputable publisher. Each organization has to weigh their tolerance on the issue and carefully read the contracts of guest artists who supply their own arrangements. In some cases, if you knowingly perform an illegal work, you could be partially liable for infringement. Even if your organization isn't liable and hasn't acted knowingly, your advertising and performance could point a public finger at the infringing arranger. If this person is a friend of yours, you could be landing them in hot water.

Public performance of non-dramatic works

The copyright holder has the exclusive right to perform their work publicly. To perform publicly also includes radio, television, and Internet broadcasting. Therefore, if you want to perform a work, that performance must be licensed. To make such a potentially onerous licensing task less burdensome, there are three performing rights organizations (PROs) that represent the bulk of the world's copyright holders in the U.S.: ASCAP, BMI, and SESAC. In addition to individual single event licenses for those who perform infrequently, the PROs offer blanket licensing agreements and require you to report your performances. Please know that publishers and PROs share information, so if you rent a piece of music (without cancellation) and you don't report the performance, you may be asked about it. **Remember, renting music is only paying a fee to obtain the parts, not the right to perform them unless it is stated specifically in the rental contract.** Performance licensing details often land in the librarian's lap simply because we are the ones with the tools to do the reporting.

There are many exemptions to the public performance right and they are covered in detail in Section 110 of Title 17: http://www.copyright.gov/title17/92chap1.html#110. For very brief examples, military bands are exempt, as are most church services and performances in certain educational settings. It is worth investigating closely to see if your performances are exempt.

An organization may find itself performing in a venue that has a blanket license already in place. The fees may then be included in the venue rental cost or may need to be negotiated with the venue instead of the PROs. In this same vein, sometimes the onus of licensing a broadcast may not be on the organization, but instead on the broadcaster. Always encourage your organization to make sure these issues are spelled out clearly in venue and broadcast contracts and agreements so your organization is not liable for infringement. If the broadcaster covers you under their blanket licenses, you may be asked to provide them the title/composer/copyright information for their reporting purposes.

For information on public performance of dramatic works, see the monograph by Tarlow and Sutherland listed in the Further Resources below, and the article "Grand Rights" by Robert Sutherland in this book.

Making a CD: Mechanical licensing

The ability to make and distribute recordings is almost always compulsory, meaning that you cannot be denied the ability to make a recording when you obtain the license and pay the fee. You may only be denied the right to release a recording if you are the first ensemble to do so—the copyright holder has the right to control the first release. Once a work has been released, then anyone may do so provided they obtain the license. Mechanical licenses may be obtained directly from the copyright holder or their mechanical licensing agent, which is usually The Harry Fox Agency (HFA). HFA was established in 1927 by the National Music Publishers' Association (www.nmpa.org) to act as an information source, clearinghouse, and monitoring service for licensing musical copyrights. Royalties are due quarterly. The current royalty rates are 9.10 cents per copy for songs five minutes or less or 1.75 cents per minute or fraction thereof, per copy for songs over five minutes. HFA's website is one of the best resources for more information: http://www.harryfox.com.

1. When applying for a license, have the following information at hand:

    a) Your ensemble/organization name
    b) Your name and contact information
    c) Titles(s)
    d) Composer(s)/arranger(s)
    e) Copyright holder(s)
    f) Copyright date(s)
    g) Exact timing of track
    h) Album title
    i) Number of CDs ("units") to be manufactured

2. Check HFA's Songfile at http://www.harryfox.com/index.jsp. If your song is not listed, contact the copyright holder. They may prefer to administer the license themselves, or they will register the work with HFA and have you obtain the license there.

3. If licensing through HFA, please note that for 2500 units or less you may pay the licensing fees in advance via credit card and the process takes about twenty-four hours. For more than 2500 units, you will need to establish a licensee account, and report and pay quarterly.

4. Keep all licenses on file.

Combining audio with video: Synchronization or "synch" licensing

Music that is synchronized in timed relation with audio-visual images requires a synchronization license. This includes but is not limited to: movies, television, commercials, video displays, and Internet video (i.e., YouTube). The easiest type of synchronization license to obtain, and the type of synch most commonly requested by performing ensembles, may be where footage of the performance is being synchronized with the sound of that performance. Yes, even this sort of obvious synchronization has to be licensed.

There is no overall collection agency such as the PROs or HFA to administer synch licenses, so one must approach the copyright holder or their representative directly, much like for licensing derivative works or making photocopies. There are more details involved with this type of license.

1. Provide at least the following information in your request:

    a) Type of license requested: synchronization
    b) Titles(s)
    c) Composer(s)/arranger(s)
    d) Copyright holder(s)
    e) Copyright date(s)
    f) Timing
    g) Portion used (if not whole, then use measure numbers)
    h) Usage description (concert footage, background for interview, scene description, etc.)
    i) Scope and description of project
    j) Type of distribution: display, broadcast, DVD, etc.
    k) Location, scale, and schedule of distribution
    l) If DVD, the number of units

2. They reply with:

    a) Possibly further questions
    b) Permission denied or granted
    c) Terms/limitations
    d) Amount of fee

3. Communicate denial or terms of license to your "production team" quickly since the project may be on a tight budget and schedule.
4. File all licensing correspondence electronically and on paper.

There are usually many people involved in making a film or video, and getting the answers you need to do the licensing in enough time can be challenging, especially given some copyright holders' licensing backlog. Many times you may find that your "production team" has already set their heart on using a particular bit of music for a scene and will assume they can use it. You will be the one to tell them that the license request was denied and they must find another tune. Denials are most common in synch because a copyright holder may not approve of their music being used to represent a certain product or be associated with particular types of scenes or even organizations.

Further resources

Kohn, Al, and Bob Kohn. *The Art of Music Licensing*. 4th ed. New York: Aspen Publishers, 2009. http://www.kohnmusic.com/.

Moser, David J. *Moser on Music Copyright*. Boston: Thomson Course Technology and Artist Pro Publishing, 2006.

Music Library Association (MLA). "Copyright for Music Librarians." Music Library Association. http://copyright.musiclibraryassoc.org/.

Tarlow, Lawrence, and Robert Sutherland. "The Music We Perform: An Overview of Royalties, Rentals and Rights." Rev. ed. N.p.: Major Orchestra Librarians' Association, 2004. http://www.mola-inc.org/pdf/MusicWePerform.pdf.

Master Sergeant Jane Cross is the Chief Librarian of "The President's Own" United States Marine Band.

(The information presented in this publication has been prepared solely by the author and neither the United States Marine Band, the U.S. Marine Corps, nor any other component of the Department of Defense of the U.S. Government has endorsed this material.)

Grand Rights

by Robert Sutherland

"Grand rights" is the term used to describe works that are under copyright and contain literary or visual elements that go beyond the performance of musical sounds alone.[6] These can include non-musical plays with incidental music added after the play was written, plays where music is an integral part of the play as written, revues comprising stage presentations of separate musical numbers, and dramatico-musical works. Dramatico-musical works are works in which the music is used to carry the action of the story forward. Opera, operetta, musicals, and ballet fall under this heading.

The owner of the copyright for these works has the exclusive right of performance and so their permission is required before a public performance can be legally given.[7] Unlike small rights, where performing rights societies grant licenses, grand rights requires negotiating directly with the copyright owner or the assigned agent. They usually involve fees based on a percentage of the gross box office revenues and can include both royalty fees for use of the intellectual property and rental fees for use of the physical material which represents the intellectual property. The size of the venue, anticipated audience, mean ticket price, number of performances, and stature of the company performing the work can influence the ultimate fee for the royalties payable. In addition, some publishers will add a rental fee per performance for use of the necessary performance materials.[8] All aspects of the grand rights license agreement an orchestra makes with a copyright owner or their agents are negotiable.

Concert performances of ballets or operas in which there are no dancers, or in which the singers appear in regular concert dress and address the audience instead of each other, and in which there is an absence of scenery should not require a grand rights license. Adding projections of images that are not directly related to the telling of a story, but are supplemental to the performance of the music alone, may result in additional rental fees, but not necessarily render the work subject to grand rights. There have been disputes with music publishers regarding these types of performances. This is an area which has rarely been defined through litigation and the discussion as to whether grand rights should apply is subject to negotiation.

It is important to remember that adding any element to a performance of a copyrighted work, beyond musicians giving a performance of only musical sounds, might

---

6   Grand rights only applies to works currently under copyright in the country in which the performance(s) take place. Once a work is considered to be in the public domain in that country, grand rights no longer apply. To this end, a basic knowledge of the applicable copyright laws of one's country is invaluable.

7   Performing rights societies (ASCAP, BMI, SESAC, SOCAN, etc.) have the right to license only non-dramatic performances of the music in their repertoire. The copyright owner or their agent, often a music publisher, retains the right to license all other uses of the music.

8   Rental fees can apply whether a work is under copyright or in the public domain.

make it subject to grand rights and consequently substantial payments of royalties and rental fees.[9]

It is also important to remember that when a grand rights license has been obtained, the income and performance information should not be included in the performing rights society reports that are submitted for non-dramatic performances.

Robert Sutherland is the Chief Librarian of the Metropolitan Opera and a Past President of the Major Orchestra Librarians' Association.

This article is adapted from the monograph, "The Music We Perform: An Overview of Royalties, Rentals and Rights," by Lawrence Tarlow and Robert Sutherland (n.p.: Major Orchestra Librarians' Association, 2004). Available online at http://www.mola-inc.org/pdf/MusicWePerform.pdf.

---

[9] These can include adding a dancer to a copyrighted orchestral work, adding props to the stage so that a direct association with a dramatic work is made, and dressing singers in costumes and have them gesturing to one another during a concert performance of a vocal work.

Important Features to Look for in a Performance Library Copier

by Courtney Secoy Cohen

Despite all the tremendous advances in technology, the copier remains one of the main lifelines for the performance librarian. Librarians spend hours at the copier—fixing page turn problems, creating new performance sets of works, copying practice parts for string players—and the list goes on. The large quantity of output and the high print quality we demand of our machine, coupled with the amount of time we actually expend making copies, dictates certain features that are necessary in any performance library copy machine.

With the vast multitude of copiers out there, how is one to determine which machine is best suited to handle the many tasks of the library? First, there are certain basic features a copier must have in any library setting.

- Scanning screen size of 11 × 17 inches or greater
- Ability to reduce and enlarge copies (Modern machines can usually reduce and enlarge from 25% to 400% in 1% increments.)
- Duplex and collate standard size paper, including 8½ × 11 and 11 × 17 inches
- Good toner fusing to the paper, even on heavier card stock paper (One way to determine this is to rub your finger across the ink immediately after printing. The second way to determine the fusing quality is to look closely at the print job: Does the print quality look clean and solid or is it spotty, like the old dot-matrix printers?)
- Ability to copy on heavier weight paper, such as 60lb or 70lb paper

Most current office copiers meet all of these qualifications. However, the performance library requires many other features besides these basic ones. For instance, music we copy usually measures 9 × 12 or 10 × 13 inches, which does not fall in the standard paper sizes in Europe or America. So, given the option, what additional features are not only beneficial, but also necessary for the performance librarian?

- Capability to duplex and collate any odd size paper (It must be possible to input any odd size and automatically duplex from a tray.)
- Include a paper tray or bypass tray that can accommodate larger paper, such as 12 × 18 inches
- Use a scan speed of at least eighty pages per minute (Scan speed seems more important than print speed for performance library copiers. When we scan hundreds of pages of a score, we want the process to move as quickly as possible!)
- Maintain a print speed of at least ninety pages per minute

- Ability to print on heavy card stock paper from a paper tray or bypass tray, for use when making covers for scores
- Power to scan a document to a computer
- Potential to fax from the copier
- Programming capabilities, so that librarians can save time by storing every aspect of a standard copy job (such as reducing 85%, while double-siding and collating 10 × 13 inch paper from tray 2) and recall that program by pushing one button

Another important feature of modern copiers correlates to an attribute we all look for in our computers—large memory capacity. Inevitably, a librarian will copy a 300 page score only to find out two days later, he/she needs to make another copy of the same score. What memory specifics should one look for in a copier?

- At least 320GB hard disk memory to store copies to print on demand
- Ability to copy first 100 pages of a score in the sheet feeder and save them to memory, so one can continue running the next 100 pages through the sheet feeder before printing

Finally, without a doubt, times will arise when a librarian must produce a set of parts from PDF files. Whether a composer or pops artist sends their music this way, a librarian should be able to create these in the most time effective manner. Therefore, a copier should be able to print an 8½ × 11 inch PDF from an e-mail, enlarge it 118% to fit on 10 × 13 inch paper, and duplex the part or score. Gone are the days where a librarian needs to first print the PDF and then individually enlarge and duplex each part.

A copier can be the thorn in our side or it can be the beloved angel of the library. When choosing a new copier, take the time to look over as many machines as possible. Take stacks of paper, music, and scores to test out all the features listed above on each machine and determine the copier most suited for your library needs. A fully functional copier (and large stashes of chocolate) enable a performance librarian to perform their tasks in a more efficient and effective manner.

Courtney Secoy Cohen is the Principal Librarian of the San Diego Symphony and the San Diego Opera.

Using a Database

by Michael K. Runyan

The Case for Technology

Because of the repetitive nature of what we do—preparing music that gets played repeatedly in cycles over time, and because the pieces we play have ramifications for stage setup, orchestra personnel, concert length, music rental budgets, etc., it is useful to save information about the compositions we play and how we play them.

Saving this information for future reference could be done as simply as filing hand-written 4 × 6 cards in a shoebox. If you wanted to be able to look up information other than by composer, you would need additional shoeboxes—for example, one each to file by artist and date of performance.

Doing this with *electronic* file cards and shoeboxes can simplify repetitive entry and greatly speed up searches. Thus, you would only have to enter "Beethoven, Ludwig van" once; thereafter, Beethoven would be simply linked to his compositions, and his compositions to performance dates. Then searches such as "How often have we performed each of the Beethoven piano concertos in the last ten years with our music director conducting?" are relatively easy.

Terminology

This concept of electronic file cards is termed a **database**. The information stored therein is **data**. File cards are called **records**; individual bits of information within records are written in **fields**; the shoeboxes that house related records are called **tables**.

The "one-shoebox" database is called a **flat-file database** and can be visualized as a spreadsheet, where each row is a record and each column within each row is a field. A library catalog can easily be created using a spreadsheet, where the first column contains a composer name on every row; the second column a work title; the third column a string of numbers indicating instrumentation; the fourth column the catalog number, etc.

Rather than having to enter "Beethoven" in the name field for every one of his works, one might wish to create a second table (spreadsheet), with each row containing a different composer and the various columns showing names, birth and death dates, nationalities, sex, etc. The composer's name would then no longer be stored in the library catalog spreadsheet, but retrieved automatically via a link to the composer spreadsheet.

Databases that do such linking between tables are called **relational databases**. Actually, spreadsheets such as Microsoft Excel are not the best at creating relational links. Better are true database applications such as Microsoft Access, FileMaker, or Base from OpenOffice.org.

Library-only Software vs. Organization-wide Tool

For much of what we do in a performance library, an over-the-counter database (such as those mentioned above) can serve adequately after being set up by an enterprising librarian, spouse, or board member. Such setup is not without significant planning and effort. If the data needs to be accessed quickly, in a variety of ways and by many people within the organization, the additional complexity of user interfaces and links between tables would almost certainly require a professional developer. Even with such assistance, this is a long and arduous undertaking indeed—one that should cause every sanity-loving human to consider an existing package, developed, tested, and tweaked over time "in the battlefield."

Two well-supported systems customized for organization-wide use by performing ensembles are:

- **OPAS**—Orchestra Planning and Administration System (www.fineartssoftware.com)
- **OMS**—ArtsVision from Orchestra Management Solutions (www.omssoftware.com)

Whether for library-only or full-company use, if you do choose to adapt, create, or commission your own database, here are a few tips:

- Walk through in detail what you want the software to do. A good developer or self-help book will guide your thinking about how you work, what information you want to store, and how, when, and by whom it will be accessed. Be open to solutions that might be different than you are used to.
- The ease of data entry is important. A lot of navigation to enter a name or number discourages use.
- Reports are probably more important than the data-entry interface. Determine how you want to see your information (calendars, catalogs, playlists, instrumentation, itineraries, phone lists, season summaries, etc.) and make sure you have easy ways to both see the data on the screen in various configurations and generate it into PDF and paper form.
- Budget resources for continued support. No software is ever finished! One cannot foresee all the possible uses, workflow scenarios and reports. Plus no software is bug-free. Nothing stops the use of software faster than it "not quite" doing what you need it to do.

Following are some snapshots of how a large orchestra could use a full-featured networked database during the course of a season:

Season Planning

Artistic Coordinator
- enters dates into the database for the upcoming season: rehearsals, concerts, holidays, vacations, and number-of-service limits

Artistic Administrator
- using planning screens in the database, starts building "what-if" programs for the upcoming season, attaching conductors, soloists, and repertoire to various dates
- queries the database for work instrumentation, work duration, when pieces were previously played, and when guest artists previously appeared

Librarian
- verifies and updates the database with the instrumentation for the upcoming season's repertoire
- searches the database for music editions owned, editions available for sale, what must be rented, and what rent was previously charged
- creates rental contract records in the database
- generates music quote requests per publisher from the database
- enters rental quotes received from publishers
- attaches music purchase costs to each concert
- generates from the database a music cost analysis for Artistic Administrator

Orchestra Personnel Manager
- analyzes the proposed upcoming season repertoire for extra musicians required
- attaches extra musician costs to each concert
- generates from the database a cost analysis report for Artistic Administrator

Artistic Administrator
- generates from the database an official calendar and list of concerts for the upcoming season (dates, locations, conductors, soloists, and repertoire) and e-mails it to the staff and orchestra

Marketing Manager
- extracts upcoming season repertoire as a word processing document for use in the season brochure
- analyzes repertoire theme labels of last ten seasons and compares with patron attendance and weather logs to understand audience trends

Operations Manager
- runs an instrumentation report of the upcoming season to see when to schedule piano tunings and to rent harpsichords, organs, or other instruments

Finance Director
- budgets for annual maintenance contract of database software

Day-to-day Work Flow

Librarian
- enters catalog and inventory information on newly-purchased titles

- generates from the database an updated library catalog
- verifies in the database the title, movement, duration, and instrumentation details for upcoming concerts
- generates a report showing in-house catalog numbers and rental sources for upcoming concerts
- generates music rental order forms to be e-mailed to publishers
- records rental music payments and return shipments
- records actual concert timings in the database
- generates reports of music played for ASCAP and BMI
- enters into the database perusal score requests; records their arrivals and returns

Orchestra Personnel Manager
- generates from the database the weekly rehearsal schedule
- studies instrumentation required and hires extra players as needed
- generates instrumentation listings for upcoming concerts
- records players assigned to each service
- generates substitute and extra player confirmations/itineraries
- enters player attendance at services
- generates payroll from the database

Orchestra Players
- access the database to see their instrumentation requirements for upcoming repertoire

Stage Manager
- generates report of repertoire, instrumentation, and durations for the week's rehearsals and concerts

Artistic Coordinator
- enters artist itinerary and contract information into the database
- generates artist contracts from the database
- generates artist itineraries
- generates hotel and limo reports for vendors
- generates expense reports of artist costs

Operations Manager
- analyzes each concert and enters special tech and setup needs into the database
- records for each concert durations of stage business: tuning, applause, announcements

Marketing Manager
- extracts upcoming concert repertoire as a word processing document for formatting of print ads and posting on the orchestra's website

Publication Director
- generates *Stagebill* pages from the database
- saves program notes and artist bios in the database for future reference

Development Associate
- enters per-concert sponsor acknowledgements for *Stagebill* and stage announcement
- runs a report of the last four seasons' repertoire with dates of composition and composer nationality to submit with a grant application

Artistic Administrator
- queries database to find a last-minute repertoire substitution based on similar instrumentation and duration

Archivist
- enters into the database the repertoire, dates, and artists from historical programs donated by a supporter
- references database to answer performance history queries from the public and news media

Operations Manager
- enters into the database the details of an upcoming tour and generates reports for booking hotel, travel and cartage, managing instrument and equipment inventory, etc.

Facilities Manager
- links database events to facilities-booking software and generates organization/facilities master calendar

IT Network Manager
- backs up the database nightly

The Cost of Technology

Whether building your own database or using an existing system (or even when using file cards and shoeboxes), thought and planning should be invested to develop your own in-house "rules," ensuring that data can be reliably stored and retrieved. For example, deciding alphabetization conventions can limit duplicate records, such as "Bach, P.D.Q." vs. "P.D.Q. Bach" and "Violin Concerto No. 4" vs. "Concerto No. 4 for Violin." Also, a complex search such as "List all works less than ten minutes with an Americana theme that are in our library," requires that themes and catalog numbers have been assigned to each work.

Using a database as portrayed above creates many efficiencies, but also requires institutional commitment, not only to purchase the software and pay ongoing support, but also to foster the mindset that time spent developing data "rules" and entering and verifying data saves time and increases accuracy throughout the organization.

Conclusion

Databases, like many technologies, provide power, flexibility, and time savings, but require much in return if they are to be truly effective. Perhaps the best advice I can offer is: Be of strong heart and your rewards shall be great!

Michael K. Runyan is Principal Librarian of the Indianapolis Symphony Orchestra.

CHAPTER **5**

Additional Responsibilities

Working With a Composer: The Process of Music Editing

by Charlie Harmon

Editorial work is one step in advance of a librarian's set of tasks, but the general aim is the same: to provide a practical performing edition that fully and accurately represents what the composer wants. The ideal is that there should be no obstacle between the composer and the performer. It's the editor's job to standardize the composer's notation (without changing anything) so that it is completely obvious to any trained musician how to play the music.

What the composer wants to see in an editor

Remember always: discretion is essential. An editor has no opinions about the quality of the composer's work. An editor does not seek publicity. No information about the work-in-progress may be shared, not even with one's closest friends or associates, except for practical questions. Orthography, instrument range, or layout issues may be topics for discussion, but only in an abstract way. The composer places a great deal of trust in the editor, and that trust has only one purpose: to transfer the composer's thoughts to performers, via a practical performing edition.

Here's an example of a question: if a composer writes violin harmonics played glissando, are the glissando lines placed between the diamond-shaped harmonics or between the normal-looking notes? After discussion with several editors and perusing examples from Ravel, Messiaen, and Elliott Carter, it was decided to place glissando lines in both locations. This discussion was an abstract examination of a particular notation detail, and no actual music from the project in question was shared. The solution was obvious and clear to the performers, and no question was ever asked about this in rehearsal.

In some cases, a composer may request a sample of an editor's work. A few pages from a previously edited score gives the composer an idea what the new work will look like. It's always best to use an example from a work that has been performed, corrected, and is ready to print. Sometimes the composer needs a piano reduction—for instance, for rehearsing an opera or ballet. It's a good idea to do a test reduction for piano of a half-dozen pages of full score, so the composer can critique the pianistic aspects of the reduction, the quantity and accuracy of cues, and whether the reduction reflects the original orchestral score. In an opera, the piano reduction is how the singers will learn the music and for many weeks they will hear only a piano. It is important that when the singers hear the orchestra for the first time that they not be confused—that is, the piano reduction must sound enough like the orchestra that nobody ever gets lost.

How the editor should prepare before starting a project

Is the composer self-published or signed on with a publisher? Is there a style guide? If not, familiarize yourself with the style guide from a major publisher such as G. Schirmer or Boosey & Hawkes. If there is a publisher, find out whether the composer may be contacted directly or through the publisher's editorial staff. The publisher must also spell out the copyright line, which must go on the first page of all scores, reductions, parts, and the libretto.

Find out the dates of the first performance, first rehearsal, and the location. If the work is an opera, get the names and contact information for the production staff: music director, stage director, rehearsal pianist, vocal coaches, choral director, assistant conductor. Likewise, get contact information for the librettist, lyricist, and anyone working with supertitles. In fact, the composer may make changes in the text without notifying the librettist, sometimes changing text to suit the music, sometimes making changes by mistake. Keep track of all those changes and share them with all the authors, either directly or through the publisher's editorial staff. Contact the performance librarian about distributing changes to all the production staff through the library, if that's feasible.

Find out the due date for the full score and for the orchestra parts. Include in your plan the time it will take to print, bind, and ship those materials. Then figure a timeline backwards from the due date in advance of the first rehearsal, to allow time for the concertmaster to add bowings, and for the librarian to mark the rest of the string parts. Some orchestras require two weeks for the concertmaster to mark bowings, two weeks for the other principal string players, and two weeks for the librarian. In general, eight weeks before the first rehearsal is adequate time for delivery of the orchestra parts.

Keep in mind that other musicians may need an advance look at their music. For instance, a clarinet player might be expected to make tricky changes of instrument or the percussion could include unusual instruments or a special layout for multiple players. Harp and keyboard parts often require additional preparation. If there are sound effects or other extra-musical devices, prepare those materials first. Ask the performance librarian how to contact those musicians and send the finished edit of the pertinent music as early in the process as possible.

If the composer decides to add a harp halfway through the work, be enthusiastic! Yes, it's extra work, but that's what you've been hired to do: attend to the composer's wishes. Remember that anything can change at any time.

Compensation needs to be set in advance, in writing. Payment may be figured by the hour or by the page, but for a larger work an hourly fee is preferable. Invoices should be sent regularly rather than sporadically. Estimate in advance whether there will be extra charges for small adjustments in the music: re-orchestrations, insertions, or anything that is not an outright error. As the work progresses, think about whether it would be useful to attend rehearsals and what that would cost. Bear in mind that a publisher may send its own editor to those rehearsals instead of any outside help.

Issues to keep in mind when editing:

- Consistency in notation
- Tempo indications: are changes of tempo clear and accurate? (Be sure that an eighth equals an eighth across the bar line, or not.)
- Names of percussion instruments, mallets, and their placement on staves
- Spelling of text (for instance, the letter "w" is three spoken syllables: dou-ble-yew)

Of course ask about anything that is illegible. Question anything that would stop a rehearsal! In general, try to anticipate what a orchestra musician or soloist or conductor would ask.

Finishing the project

Next, contact your most trusted colleagues who are editors and copyists. Extracting or copying parts may take longer than planned. It's reassuring to have trusted colleagues at the ready before the schedule veers out of control.

Keep all computer files, duplicates, e-mails, and all versions of the work as it is written or edited. All correspondence should be archived and be readily available. One way to ask questions of a composer is to write the question on a Post-it placed on the page next to the spot in question, then scan the page with the post-it in place, and attach the scan to an e-mail to the composer. Save everything! The composer may eventually donate these papers to a library or archive and the more complete those papers are, the more valuable they will be to scholars and future editors.

Maintain detailed and dated errata lists. An updated errata list will remind you of the status of changes and corrections. Similarly, include the date on every printing of the score. Put the date on the title page where it can't be missed. If the printing is a draft, include that information, too. If it was used in performance, give the date and venue.

Ask the publisher whether bowings could be printed in the string parts (some composers insist on bowings and sometimes on fingerings!). Will there be bar numbers, rehearsal numbers or letters, or both? Keep in mind that a ballet may require both bar and rehearsal numbers, and that a choreographer may need many more rehearsal numbers than is normal in other works.

For eventual publication, keep track of information for the preliminary pages, including information on the premiere performance: cast, production credits, timings, awards. Examine the publications of reputable publishers for layout examples of these preliminary pages.

Finally, coordinate with the performance librarian. It may be possible to e-mail PDF files of the orchestra parts so the librarian could print and bind performance materials in-house. Ask about that issue well in advance of the due date for those materials. Never assume the librarian can drop everything and help out with editorial work! Also keep in mind that an extra set of eyes looking over the score and parts is always helpful. Always be grateful when a mistake is found—by anybody! In learning and rehearsing a new work, a feeling of camaraderie develops as all the individual efforts come together. Rehearsal pianists and singers may make suggestions, sometimes remarkably good ones. After all, they work with the practical aspects of learning and performing the music.

It's a great service to music to assist a composer through the creation of a new work. In fact, the demands on the music preparation staff can be similar to actual composition. Yet, an editor can never completely second-guess a composer, and the true joy is in the details that come as a total surprise. As long as those details are what the composer wants, then the music preparation has been a success.

Charlie Harmon is a freelance editor and was music editor for the Estate of Leonard Bernstein.

Orchestra Tours

by John G. Van Winkle

So, your orchestra is going on tour. It may be a domestic tour or a foreign tour, but the needs are the same. You are the orchestra's librarian which means you are the one responsible for the preparation and distribution of scores and parts just like at home, but with a few differences and precautions.

During the last thirty-seven years and forty-something tours, I have gained a healthy respect for the phrase, "Be prepared." There is another one to consider and that is, "Learn as you go."

Be prepared

I joined the San Francisco Symphony in the 1970–71 season. My first tour with the orchestra was in 1973. Seiji Ozawa was our Music Director and it was a six-week tour of Europe and the (then) Soviet Union. The previous year I had the opportunity to spend a week each with the librarians of the Philadelphia Orchestra, the New York Philharmonic, and the Boston Symphony. Each one gave me sage advice, not only about being an orchestra librarian (I was green as grass at the time), but what to expect to do and take on such an adventurous tour that the San Francisco Symphony had planned.

From Jessie Taynton, then Librarian of The Philadelphia Orchestra:

> **"Make a 'Switch List.'"** This was a list that detailed where and when titles in the folders were to be taken out and other titles added or replaced. I had hoped that I could fit everything into one folder until I saw our itinerary. Twenty-nine titles were going to be performed throughout the tour! My hopes of everything in one folder being dashed, I drew up my own switch list on Jessie's model. It helped to organize my time, as some pieces needed to be taken out at intermission, some right after the concert if transportation was not an issue, and some could wait until the next stop to be added or deleted from the concert folders *du jour*. The Assistant Librarian in 1973 was Bob Dolan. We decided that all seven of the encores would go in a separate folder on each stand so we wouldn't have to worry about switching them around each night. Jessie cautioned, "It is a good idea to give a copy of your switch list to the Stage Manager and Personnel Manager." It *was* a good idea as the library copy was misplaced somewhere in Switzerland.

From Lou Robbins, then Librarian of the New York Philharmonic:

> **"Take extra parts."** Even your most trusted player could slip up and lose or misplace a part. Changing time zones has a way of making this worse. You, however, are the one a player turns to when he/she realizes said part is not in the right place. I've heard it said that giving the player who "forgot" his part a score to read

off of would teach him a lesson, but that's not what we are about. Chances were, back in 1973, that the local librarian would not be at the hall. That was in the days before MOLA and computers. Even today, I don't really feel like running around an unfamiliar town looking for a part or disturbing the local librarians who may have the night off because we are performing in their hall.

My extra sets include a complete set of winds and two copies of the string masters. Be sure to get permission from the copyright owner before copying their material. It is far better to be prepared with back up parts should a real part go walking. Sometimes they have. As for scores, I do copy the Music Director's score in case his own gets misplaced. It's better to hand the conductor a score with his own markings in case of an emergency. I also carry two or three scores for each piece that we will be performing for those "other emergencies" or just in case.

From Victor Alpert, then Librarian of the Boston Symphony:

"Take along some parts that you have recently performed. Also, take along *Afternoon of a Faun* because your orchestra can play that at a drop of the hat if they need to and take the Eroica, for obvious reasons." I routinely take these even today and throw in the Bach Suite (Overture) No. 3 for the same reason as the Eroica. I haven't had to use these pieces...yet. Victor, who was a veteran of several international tours, also suggested acquiring National Anthems of all the countries listed in your itinerary. Management told us before leaving on the six-week tour that we would not need the Soviet Union's anthem. Whether that directive came from the State Department or not, I don't know, but upon arrival in Moscow, all of a sudden we were supposed to rehearse and perform it the following night. Thanks to the "interpreters" we were able to borrow the parts from the Conservatory with strict instructions that everything be returned at intermission. It was, save one part that a player wanted as a souvenir. By process of elimination, the part was rescued and returned with our thanks to the rightful owner. Learn as you go.

From Jimmy Dolan, then Assistant Librarian of the Los Angeles Philharmonic:

"Take wind clips." Wind clips? Why wind clips? Well, the Los Angeles Philharmonic had just returned from a tour where there was a change of venue from a concert hall to an outside amphitheater where wind clips would be required. Fortunately, Jimmy had them. That definitely goes in the "be prepared" category! Do I take wind clips on tour? Yes. Have I ever had to use them? Yes. Once a flute player came offstage (we were inside) and reported that the music was blowing off the stand. Wind clips to the rescue. For whatever reason, this has happened to other players in different concert halls on a couple of other tours. It has even happened in our own hall. Wind clips do no good sitting in a box at home. Throw a bunch of them in a case and take them along. You probably won't need enough for the entire orchestra, but then....

Learn as you go

Our next tour was a three-week trip in 1975 to Japan. (Six-week tours had by then been outlawed by contract.) This goes in the "Learn as you go" category: Know where the concert is going to be and leave enough time to get there. Wanting to get to the hall early, three of us got together and showed the "greeter" at the hotel our tour book with the name of the hall. The greeter gave the cab driver the information, we piled into the cab, and off we went in what we later found out was the wrong direction.

After a cab ride of about a half an hour the driver let us out and pointed in the direction of the perceived hall and took off. We looked around for a few minutes and, not finding anything that resembled a concert hall or even signs advertising our concert, decided to hail another cab. This time the driver spoke some English and explained the similarities between the names of the halls (only one letter off) and took us across Tokyo again, this time to the right place. You might want to double-check the location of the hall before leaving.

Folders

After the 1975 Japan tour, management decided to only take one librarian on tours. Because of that decision, everything now goes into one folder. No more switch lists. Thankfully, there has been no tour since then that has had twenty-nine titles to be performed.

The folders that I use now were made in-house. I used what was called battleship board or pressboard. It may not be called by that name now, but any good cover stock, trimmed to 11 × 14 inches, will do. I chose a light color, as the folders are easier to see sticking up above the stands when you take that last look around to see if you have collected everything that you had out for the performance. When making the folders, I left a half-inch gap between the sides and used cloth tape to bind them together. I used two-inch tape, but three-inch would be better. The adhesive on the cloth tape has crystallized over the years and I have since taped over it with plastic tape. I used yellow tape for the same reason that I used light colored battleship board. The plastic tape has its problems too as it sometimes cracks. I just tape over the cracks and, though the folders are at times stuffed to the gills, they do hold together well.

Travel cases

Sturdy travel cases are a must! Paper weighs a lot. Just ask a member of your stage crew who has to schlep the music trunks.

For the first two tours we used two old footlocker-style steamer trunks. They were low to the ground, but well built. I still use them for those "extra" items like wind clips, recently performed works that "won't be needed," unused orchestra folders which might come in handy should a guest soloist suddenly decide that their music needs additional support, etc. We also had a 3 feet × 3 feet × 1 foot high fiberboard box for all of the extra parts. The bottom of that box fell out after we got back. I now also use two of the large vertical steamer trunks. One side was for hanging clothes and the other side had drawers. Our Stage Manager remade one of them by replacing the drawers on one side with shelves for the folders, and keeping the other side for hanging concert attire. He also made a table that slips in nicely and prevents the folders from sliding out during transit. In the other trunk, he retained the drawers that I use for library supplies and added shelves for the extra parts in place of the hanging racks for clothes. There are also shelves that handle oversize scores quite well.

Library supplies

What do I take along as library supplies? Here's my list, which has been added to over the years as needs arose. They are in no particular order and you are welcome to add or subtract:

- Staff paper, score paper, writing/note paper, yellow (or color of choice) stickies
- Pencils (of course), pens, marking pens, pencil sharpener (your Swiss Army Knife will do if it hasn't been confiscated at the airport)
- Electric eraser (with proper adapter for foreign currents) and erasers, regular erasers, single edge razor blades (safely enclosed)
- Paper clips (large and small), binder clips of various sizes, rulers, rubber bands of different sizes for different needs yet to be determined, stapler with extra staples
- Tape dispenser, extra tape, 3 inch book tape, double-stick tape, removable tape, correction tape, cloth tape, and plastic tape for folder repair, binding supplies of your choice
- A few DHL or FedEx Boxes (folded), Envelopes, and Packs with waybills (know your account numbers), manila envelopes of different sizes
- Canvas shopping bags (you never know what you may have to carry and they just might make things go a little easier for you)
- Extra batons (the kind your Music Director uses), flashlight (with working batteries and bulb), a box of tissues (for your own use), spare computer parts (who knows, I might even carry one some day), spare glasses if you wear them, and bandages for paper cuts (an occupational hazard)
- A travel light is helpful if you have to work in a dark backstage area of the hall
- Don't forget to take your MOLA Membership List. I put one in the suitcase that goes to the hotel and one in the music travel case that goes to the concert hall

What about medications for minor headaches or fever? What about cork screws and bottle openers? Nope, those jobs belong to someone else.

Programs

I always pick up extra programs at each venue to send to the publishers when I get back. It is likely that your orchestra may need additional programs for their archives and to send to ASCAP or BMI. The Stage Manager and I usually make a request for extra programs from the venue's House Manager, Head Usher, or Stage Manager who have been helpful in acquiring them for us.

Being extra prepared

Several years ago, the Chicago Symphony musicians were on their way to our hall in San Francisco for a concert, but their truck with the instruments, wardrobe, and music was MIA. I got a telephone call early that Sunday morning from our Personnel Manager saying I needed to get to the hall ASAP and lay out the Overture to *Oberon* and Beethoven's 5th along with a set of folders. He explained that the Chicago Symphony truck was not likely going to make it in time, but the performance was still going to happen.

Since the Chicago Symphony incident, as an insurance measure, management has me carry a complete program of music in my suitcase in the event that our truck doesn't make it or the travel cases get left on the loading dock somewhere and don't show up at the next venue or whatever. For this "privilege," I have been allowed a second suitcase where all others in the group are allowed only one. There have been from one to four titles, with corresponding scores that have been carried around in this manner. Fortunately, our suitcases are usually delivered directly to our hotel rooms so there is not a lot of extra lifting or trouble. Depending on how much music goes in that suitcase, I may be able to throw in an extra sweater or jacket, perhaps a coffee pot or other items to keep the music from bouncing around too much.

Carrying an extra program like this also eliminates my having to run around, as mentioned earlier, trying to round up parts at the last minute that would have unfamiliar markings for the players. Have I ever had to use the material from the suitcase? Almost. When we were in London, the truck drivers thought that we were to perform in a different hall in a different city. Wanting to get to the hall early for the rehearsal, I took the extra suitcase and caught a cab to Royal Festival Hall. Fortunately, the truck drivers had gotten the word somewhere along the line and had done an about face. They were unloading just as the orchestra was arriving for the scheduled rehearsal. The rehearsal started late, but the music, both sets, was there.

Some final thoughts

A lot of work goes into preparing for a tour. Most of what an orchestra librarian does happens before the first stage of transportation. Take along some work to do while you are on call at rehearsals and performances.

Getting to the hall early has its benefits. The stage crew is probably already there setting up. They have probably already asked the local stage crew, "Where is the best place to eat?" After enjoying the local cuisine, stroll back to the hall and leisurely change into your concert attire, set up, and wait for the orchestra to arrive. Some orchestras stagger bus departures to the concert hall, so if you can't get to the hall early on your own, at least get on the first bus that goes there. The house has usually not opened by the time you arrive and you can set the stage in your street clothes while others are changing. You can then go and change before the confusion begins as the second bus arrives.

Do eat regularly, get as much rest as you can, get some exercise, wash your hands regularly (also carry hand sanitizer), avoid crowds, be aware of your surroundings, use caution when eating "exotic" foods (getting sick while traveling is not pleasant), don't forget your passport if traveling internationally, arrive early for rehearsals and concerts, and be flexible. Look hot and stay cool! Other than that, always be in good humor and have a good time.

John G. Van Winkle is the Principal Librarian (retired) of the San Francisco Symphony.

Preservation in the Performance Library

by D. Michael Ressler

You want me to do what? I only volunteered to help pass out music folders. Then you asked me to "help catalog a little music." Now I'm learning a new software program and purchasing music too. And now you want me to be a what—a conservator? I don't even know what that means and I'm sure I don't have time!

This may sound familiar. Are you helping with your organization's music library and the job seems to be constantly growing since you first signed on? And then someone brought up the idea of preservation of the music in the library. Is this really necessary? Is the problem such a concern that it should be added to my list of responsibilities?

Unfortunately, the answer is yes—a loud and emphatic yes. Our music libraries are constantly under attack and we, the music librarians, are the first line of defense. So who is the enemy? Where is this attack coming from? What can we do to help?

Preservation challenges

The paper on which our music is printed is our first problem. This paper can vary widely in quality from excellent to terrible depending on the combination of rag content, wood pulp, and chemical additives. Some paper has a high amount of rag pulp and is very solid and stable. Other paper, such as newsprint, is made primarily of wood pulp and seems to disintegrate in days. Just leave a newspaper in the sun for a few hours and you will see how quickly paper can degrade.

Our environment is the next concern. The air we breathe that keeps us alive and singing and playing our instruments can bring an early death to the paper. The sun shining through windows in the library might also be causing big problems with the collection.

Insects are definitely unwelcome guests in your library storage area. Termites, cockroaches, and silverfish are the most frequent visitors along with ants and the common housefly. The ants and flies are not a huge concern, but the others certainly are. They view your library as a five-star restaurant and will do their best to eat all they can as fast as they can.

We musicians are the final enemy—conductors, musicians, and especially the librarians. We tend to handle music roughly, maybe only a little better than yesterday's newspaper. We write on it with things we shouldn't, roll it up and store it in places it doesn't belong, and leave it in places where only bad things can happen.

So what can you, the over-worked music librarian with barely enough time to get music ready for each performance, do to make a difference? Here are a few suggestions that can go a long way to help preserve your library for tomorrow's musicians and audiences.

Environment

The first place to start is to get control of the environment in the library. Try to achieve a steady temperature of between 65 to 70 degrees, and humidity of around 50 percent. Higher temperatures and humidity levels cause an acceleration of the acidification of the paper. Chemicals that were added to the paper to give it a smoother surface and to stiffen it can react with the heat and humidity to produce acid that makes the paper brittle. More important than the actual levels is the steadiness of both the temperature and humidity. When temperatures and humidity levels rise and fall repeatedly, the paper alternately swells and shrinks. This minute motion damages the fibers that give paper its strength. Over time this will cause real damage that you and your musicians will notice, so choose levels that you can maintain with minimal fluctuations. Fluctuations within 2 to 3 degrees of temperature and 2 to 3 percent of humidity are a good goal. Get a quality thermometer and humidistat to tell you how you are doing.

Controlling the environment also includes the quality of the air in the library. Can you smell exhaust fumes in the library from the street outside? If you can smell it so can your music and that is not a good thing. Pollutants from exhaust fumes and industrial smoke just add to the problem of acid in the paper. Combustion of fossil fuels such as gas, oil, and coal creates sulfur dioxide. Paper (including acid-free paper) can easily absorb the air-born pollutants. The sulfur dioxide mixes with moisture in the paper and oxygen in the air and produces sulfuric acid. This is added to whatever other acids might already be in the paper and they gang up together, causing a slow burn of the paper. Paper can also absorb nitrogen dioxide and other pollutants that just add to the nasty mix. If you are in an area where this is a problem and you have windows, keep them closed. If your building has a heating, ventilation, and air conditioning system (HVAC), it has filters designed to eliminate dust and pollution. Ask for the best quality filters available and keep after the facilities manager to replace them regularly.

The light in your library is also a potential problem. Just as our skin can be damaged by over-exposure to the sun, sunlight on the music can cause significant damage over time. If you have windows in the library try to find ultraviolet (UV) filtering film to put over the glass. Install UV filters over the fluorescent lights in your library. These are rolls of film that are easy to slip over the fluorescent tubes. They do a good job filtering out UV light and last a long time. If your music is stored on open shelves, keep the lights off in the storage area when not needed. If you are using filing cabinets or other closed containers, all the better—you are eliminating this problem.

Elimination of insects should be a high priority. Cockroaches, silverfish, ants, and other pests would love to move into your library and take up residence. If you are bug-free now, great! Stay that way. Keep the library clean. If you allow food and drink in the library be sure to clean up constantly. Be careful when you accept a music gift from a person or organization. Make sure all they are giving you is music and no critters. Inspect everything thoroughly before allowing it into the library so no surprise visitors will infest the entire collection. It is much easier to stay bug-free than it is to become bug-free. If you have an insect problem, get professional help.

Steps to preservation

Next, take a look at the paper in your collection. You will probably find a wide variety of types of paper in various stages of deterioration. Never perform from music that is in such bad condition that it might not survive a performance. If the music is no longer under copyright then photocopy it onto a good quality, heavyweight paper (70lb is nice) and perform from the copies. Insist on acid-free paper. It is readily available from most paper suppliers and is worth the slight added expense. You can check the pH (the measure of acidity or alkalinity) of your paper right in your library by using an inexpensive pH testing pen. These are available from archival products distributors such as Light Impressions (www.lightimpressionsdirect.com) and Archival Products (www.archival.com).

If you want to go high-tech, try creating digital copies and storing them in a computer or on a portable hard drive. But beware! Preservation of digital storage media is a completely different problem. You will want to be aware of the advantages and disadvantages of pursuing this course. If the music is still under copyright, purchase new parts if available or write to the copyright holder and ask permission to copy. (It is always better to ask first and keep a paper trail of all of your communication.) If any of your older music is printed on highly acidic paper that appears to be burning images onto adjacent pages, try interleaving the parts with acid-free tissue paper to stop further damage. Remove any old rusty staples, paper clips, or any other fasteners that you might find. If pages are torn they can be repaired with a good-quality transparent tape. I have seen tape that is nearly 40 years old and still in good shape, lengthening the lifespan of the music considerably.

One additional idea will help ensure that the music in your library is available for use for years to come. As pieces are performed, select one original of each different part and set them aside as a preservation set. These should not be used for performance. When purchasing new music, purchase enough extra parts so that you can create a preservation set right from the beginning. Future librarians of your organization will love you for it.

Finally, treat the music with care and respect. When music is issued to performers, be sure that it is in a protective folder or envelope. Insist that they keep the music in the folder while it is in their possession. Do not allow them to roll it, curl it, or fold it so they can fit it into their instrument case. Do your best to impress on them the importance of handling the music with care. Back in the library, music should be stored in a protective folder or box and placed on the shelf or in a cabinet. Purchase acid-free storage materials so that you are not adding to the problem of acid in the paper. There are many companies, such as Hollinger Metal Edge (www.hollingermetaledge.com) and Gaylord Library and Archival Supplies (www.gaylord.com), which specialize in archival-quality library supplies. When preparing music for performance or putting it away after a performance, handle it gently and look for problems with the music that need to be fixed. Rips and tears that are not repaired will just get bigger. Corners that have been folded multiple times to facilitate page turns may need to be reinforced. When music is not in use, put it away where it belongs. When it is sitting out in the open for no good reason, it can collect dust and dirt and, perhaps, turn into a coaster for someone's coffee cup.

We are indebted to the professional conservators who have devoted themselves to studying and understanding the problems of preserving materials that naturally want to degrade and we have much to learn from them. The Northeast Document Conservation Center (www.nedcc.org) is a great source of conservation information for the performance librarian. Another excellent source for help is "CoOL," an online resource from the Foundation of the American Institute for Conservation (http://cool.conservation-us.org). The Library of Congress maintains a very helpful website (www.loc.gov/preserv/careothr.html) that offers great advice on preservation issues.

There is much to learn from the professionals, but the basic steps outlined here will go a long way in helping to preserve your library collection. A performing organization's library is one of its greatest treasures and you are in the best position to ensure that that treasure is protected for years to come.

Master Gunnery Sergeant D. Michael Ressler is the Historian for "The President's Own" United States Marine Band.

(The information presented in this publication has been prepared solely by the author and neither the United States Marine Band, the U.S. Marine Corps, nor any other component of the Department of Defense of the U.S. Government has endorsed this material.)

Using Technology and Community Partnerships to Archive Your Orchestral Collection

by Robert Olivia

This is an account of blending tradition with forefront technology to preserve the Seattle Symphony collection and bring its history and archive to the public. It is also a tale of how something can be accomplished with few financial resources by forming community partnerships, both public and private. Finally, it is a story of one orchestra, its history, and its relationship to its community.

In 2000, Benaroya Hall became the new home of the Seattle Symphony. In the process of moving to the new hall, we discovered boxes of information about the symphony which had gone unnoticed for years, such as newspaper clippings, letters, programs, and photographs. I started sorting through boxes and other materials in my spare time. I was stunned at what I found about the Seattle Symphony's more than one hundred year history.

In photos, newspaper clippings, letters, and programs, we found evidence that, beginning in 1903, the Symphony found support in the new wealth of the industrial Northwest. It was at the center of the entertainment provided on the fairgrounds of the 1909 Alaska Yukon Pacific Exposition. Music directors of the orchestra have included some of the finest conductors of the past century, including Karl Kruger, Basil Cameron, Sir Thomas Beecham, and Henry Hadley. In 1921, during a period of hiatus for the Seattle Symphony, members were organized by Madame Davenport Engberg, who, as a woman, held the unprecedented post of music director. Ironically, the orchestra had no women among its ranks. Legendary performers such as Rachmaninoff, Stravinsky, Fiedler, Kreisler, and Gershwin traveled great distances to Seattle to perform with the orchestra. For them, the journey was literally going to the edge of the continent when the train was the most common mode of transportation. During the 1970s, famed music lover and entertainer Danny Kaye was a strong supporter of the orchestra during his time as part owner of the Seattle Mariners.

This collection of material was a treasure trove that needed to be archived, preserved, and brought to the public. However, the duties of an orchestra librarian are very time consuming. How could I embark on a path of discovery and preservation while attending to my primary responsibilities of preparing music for concerts? And, if I were able to do so, was it possible that in the process of acquiring the needed tools and resources, we could also use them to provide better service to our players?

The answer was yes to both of these questions, but I did not have to do this alone. We would form partnerships in the community by enlisting the help of local professionals who had specialized skills to help us preserve our valuable history.

However, the implementation of this idea was more difficult than it seemed. As with all orchestras, funds are finite and there was simply no money to support such a project. How could we move ahead without funds to pay professional librarians, curators, and archivists? An answer to this was to look outward rather than inward, toward our community programs and investigate whether we could offer opportunities for skilled professionals to volunteer or earn course credit assisting us with our project.

I became aware of a wonderful program at the iSchool of the University of Washington called Directed Fieldwork. It gives graduate students credit at the end of their degree for work in the community. It also turned out that the Dean of the iSchool, Harry Bruce, and his wife Lorraine Bruce, senior lecturer and faculty member, were long-time subscribers to the Seattle Symphony. It became clear that a community of those willing to help was all around us.

After I spoke with Lorraine about our project, she soon arrived at the library with a group of students. They looked over the materials we had amassed and formally listed the Seattle Symphony as one of the school's fieldwork opportunities. Within days of posting on the university's website, two graduate students signed up and an undergraduate requested to volunteer.

This was the first of several community partnerships. I cannot stress enough the importance of making it known to the public what you want to accomplish. Do not be deterred a lack of monetary resources. Invariably, there will be those who will come forward with advice, guidance, and professional personnel resources as a result of your vision, enthusiasm, and inspiration.

With the help of the UW iSchool, we computerized the library catalogue, inventoried boxes of archival materials, and presented a month-long exhibit in our new hall's Grand Lobby which was viewed by tens of thousands of patrons. We also created a library website which enabled the public to access the archive, created a password-accessible SharePoint site for the players and administration, made a thirty-minute narrated DVD of the items in the exhibit, and secured a $100,000 grant from the Mellon Foundation.

These accomplishments were not our goals at the outset. Historians often discuss their work as following a thread that leads from one thing to another. This was also my experience. Our archive exhibit was a tremendous success. It was prepared with the support of our administration and attended by the music director, patrons, board members, and community leaders. As a result, we garnered attention and enthusiasm from many arenas throughout our community. This single thread led us to imagine what else we might be able to do. It was the first step that showed us organically what our second step would be. It was not important to have a detailed plan for everything that was to come, but rather to present it to our community and allow those with specific professional skills to guide us.

Archive exhibit

We wanted to present to the public some of the items we had begun to uncover. Knowing we would eventually need funding, we used this as our guide to find and create resources. As part of the Directed Fieldwork program, we were fortunate to have the skills of Dr. Lia Vella, a National Park Ranger, who was doing her iSchool degree long-distance from the John Day Fossil Beds National Park in Central Oregon. Part of her job was to present interpretive exhibits, tours, and lectures. We also reached out to partner with our neighbors at the Seattle Art Museum. They taught us how to cut acid-free board, how to use the flow of an exhibit to tell a story, and even how to prevent off-gassing from within the antique display cases. The knowledge and experience of these partners were essential to the exhibit. It proved the adage that if you know what you want to accomplish, surround yourself with skilled professionals who can help you.

SSO Library Archive Exhibit with vintage display cases from Seattle's Bon Marché, donated by Macy's.

Each night audience members crowded around the antique display cases which were donated to us by Macy's. The Art Deco building that is now Macy's in downtown Seattle was formerly know as the Bon Marché and there were actually patrons who recognized the beautiful bent glass display cases from the elegant store they once frequented. It was a wonderful way to bring together the history of the orchestra with the history of the city of Seattle.

DVD

Public access to our archive seemed an essential element of our larger goal. A DVD that could be sold in our symphony gift shop and shown on a local PBS station could

Using Technology and Community Partnerships to Archive Your Orchestral Collection 157

generate funding and awareness of our project. Using knowledge I gained from working at JoAnn Kane Music Service in Hollywood helped me create a narrated DVD. There are various types of software available for this, some very sophisticated. However, for someone with basic computer skills, Microsoft Moviemaker is an efficient tool. I made a series of ten short movie clips that used images from programs, pages of music and photographs, with narration. One such example from our archive is this photograph of Danny Kaye and Igor Stravinsky.

Pictured here from left to right: Seattle Post Intelligencer reviewer Louis Guzzo, Igor Stravinsky, Danny Kaye, and SSO music director Milton Katims. Danny Kaye was a great supporter of the orchestra and part owner of the newly formed Seattle Mariners. He did not miss the opportunity to spend the afternoon with Stravinsky before his concert with the Seattle Symphony. (Photo courtesy Seattle Post Intelligencer and MOHAI.)

Patrons who viewed the archive exhibit were fascinated with the many personal notations made by musicians on old, deteriorating parts. While concert attendees are inspired by the music they hear coming from the stage, they know little of what the players see on their stands. The exchange was an opportunity for performers and audience members to interact and raise awareness of our history and tradition.

One such example of how a player personalized his parts stood out to me. We discovered that former principal clarinetist, Ronald Phillips, studiously recorded many performances on the bottom of the last page of his parts. This has given us a valuable performance record. The example that follows is from the Brahms Violin Concerto. The dates range from Joseph Szigeti in 1938 to Yehudi Menuhin in 1983.

Brahms Violin Concerto part performances as recorded by SSO clarinetist Ronald Phillips.

After viewing the video, one elderly patron called me to say she had attended many of the performances documented in the exhibit and she had recorded them in her diary. It was an especially moving connection. It seemed clear to me that the very pages of music were a missing link to our audiences and that the parts themselves had stories to tell. This gave patrons a greater appreciation of the printed music and helped raise awareness of our history and the need to preserve it. This kernel of good fortune developed from simply taking a close look at the treasure trove of music as close at hand as the library shelves.

SharePoint

The attention generated from our archive exhibit prompted others in the community to offer services. Among them was an employee from Microsoft who played trombone in the Microsoft Orchestra. Microsoft has programs that encourage their employees to perform volunteer work in the community. The company also matches gifts their employees make to a non-profit organization. He and Microsoft donated a server and SharePoint software. At first we did not know how we could make use of his skills. A solution was to have him observe what we did and what we needed. The insight someone can have who comes to the demands of orchestra librarianship with a clean slate and no previous knowledge can have great benefits. As a result, a plan was devised to use SharePoint not just for the library, but institution-wide to make our jobs easier and provide a higher level of service to the players. This site is password protected and accessible both internally and externally. We use it to post practice parts and concert information online for our orchestra members. This is a major benefit to string players, who can access parts and begin practicing months before the physical music is available to them. A byproduct of this new service is that it reduced the high cost of overnight shipping and is a tremendous timesaving device for the SSO librarians. The donation of the server gave the software a dedicated host and it is now utilized by each department, including the personnel managers, who post rosters, seating, and other notices.

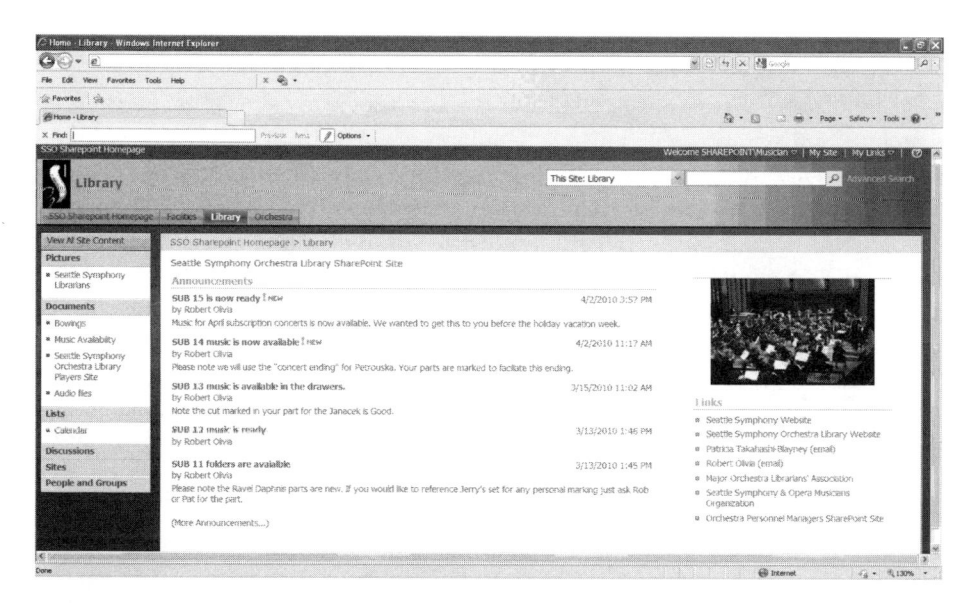

Using Technology and Community Partnerships to Archive Your Orchestral Collection **159**

SSO Library SharePoint site is accessible by members of the orchestra.

Library website

Our next mission was to create a public website. By its nature, an orchestra library is classified as a special collection and is not accessible to the public. However, we wanted there to be some element of public access to the great history and wealth of items we were acquiring in our archive. Our website points out to the public the relevance of the orchestra library, the work the librarians perform, and the Symphony's role in the community, both today and historically.

To accomplish this we again turned to our community partnership with the UW iSchool, which includes a division that focuses on computer programming. We were lucky to have the talents of a librarian/programmer who designed a website for the library that included my short narrated DVD clips, a video tour of the library, and even a demonstration of the age-old craft of hand sewing and making hardbound scores.

Our next challenge will be to find a partner that will agree to host our site since streaming video takes up more bandwidth than our organization's current servers are capable of providing.

SSO public accessible website.

Mellon grant

The accumulation of work over the past five years has clearly shown us the value of our archive and we were encouraged to submit a grant application to the Mellon Foundation. This grant has allowed us to hire professional librarians and archivists to help us create a plan to preserve and manage our collections. Without the support of all levels of the organization, from our music director to the Development and Public Relations departments, such success would not have been possible. We reached out again, this time to partner with the Boeing Museum of Flight which is using Archivists Toolkit (AT) to catalogue their collection. The Detroit Symphony archive is also using this open source software. Our future goal is to use specialized software to link AT and our Orchestra Planning and Administration System (OPAS) software. Ultimately, our entire archive will be able to be searched using a Google inquiry or directly through our website.

I've often noticed that during intermission some audience members gather at the foot of the stage and peer upwards to gain a glimpse of the music. Many are not musicians and yet they feel some intangible relationship or curiosity about the printed page of music they will soon hear. The example of a patron recounting her memories of performances, elicited when viewing the very pages of a clarinet part used in performances she attended, was poignant to me.

Four years ago, the thought of realizing these accomplishments would have seemed more than daunting. At first we simply wanted to protect and preserve the orchestra parts from further deterioration. However the result of one project led us directly to the next project. Attempting this does not mean becoming a super-librarian. You will have to advocate for your library, your collection and archive, your needs, and, especially, your vision. You will be challenged to use your time even more economically and will spend many extra hours beyond your regular duties.

As we continue to comb through our collection, we are reminded that the parts of music is how we began this journey and is the basis of our archive. These parts, with the players' handwritten notations accumulated over many years, have intrinsic stories to tell. The preservation of all these stories is essential to preserving our history and tradition. The respect for tradition has led us forward, with technology, to be able to preserve it. And the fusion of these has enabled us to embark on an exploration of new services to our players. In the end, it is as if the parts of music themselves continue to guide and inspire us.

Robert Olivia is the Associate Principal Librarian with the Seattle Symphony Orchestra.

Input on Your Output: Thoughts from a Professional Music Copyist

by Douglas Richard

A few years ago I was asked to participate on a panel at a MOLA conference. The question was raised as to "how many composers/arrangers/music copyists exist today?" My response: "Everyone who bought the software—just ask!" The availability of music notation software has both increased the amount of printed music being circulated and created a false sense of competency amongst the casual users. Various products have certainly streamlined the process of creating music. That does not mean, however, that the end-user understands the technical and artistic practices a professional copyist has learned over the course of time. Librarians know what I am talking about—you receive material that is abominable ... and then it is up to you to "fix it," "make it work," "research, compile, and distribute the errata sheet"—in essence, doing the work that a professional music copyist would have done.

This text is based on a presentation I was recently asked to give. The mission: discuss the parameters of actual music production with young composers. It is relevant to all of us who have to deal with materials coming from a source other than a publisher, especially since it is becoming common practice. You will probably even be asked to copy parts by hand from a score or run a part extraction from a computer file. It is important to have an understanding of the basics of music preparation in order to provide the best possible materials.

The following paragraphs, as related to the young composers, offer thoughts on important concepts to consider when it comes time to prepare music for performance.

Basic concepts for young composers

Production of "hard copy" is the final stage of musical thought. It is the vital link between a music writer and an audience via performers. Far too often, this final stage is an afterthought that limits the opportunity to have a writer's creativity adequately realized. The purpose of our discussion is to explore aspects of the actual printed page in an effort to give you, the composer, means to provide performance material of the highest quality.

The quickest and smartest route is to hire a professional music copyist. The professional copyist is the best friend of the composer, music librarian, and performer. Unfortunately, you are now at a stage of your career where nobody wants to buy your music because they do not know who you are. That being the case, you probably do not have the money to hire a professional copyist. In the meantime, there are habits you should develop that will enhance the quality of your output.

The biggest benefit of great looking material is that, simply put, it lends credibility to your professional reputation. The fact that you took the time to provide the most professional looking, user-friendly, high-quality parts to the performers will save you valuable rehearsal time. It has been my experience that performers will give you their best if you give them great material to work with. Please understand, I am not talking about your musical ideas at all. There are other people who can and will weigh in on the merits of your compositional ideas. I am speaking directly to the clarity and legibility of your thoughts as you express them to your performers. Software notation programs are very helpful in making your handwriting look neater, but I would urge you not to blindly trust the "factory presets" they offer for page layout! Perhaps this concept is clearer if presented this way: Just because you own a word processing program does not mean that you can write like a best-selling author.

As time passes, your skills will develop and your output will take on a more pleasing aesthetic. Keeping in mind that for every generality presented, aesthetics and musical taste will take precedence over the "rules." The following are some conventions to consider.

Scores

Before the music begins, include this information:

- Instrumentation list/requirements, including percussion and other doubling instruments—saxes, flugelhorns, oboe/English horn, etc.
- Duration
- Is the score in concert pitch or is it transposed? Be clear, especially if you are using a neutral key signature.
- Any additional performance notes, such as unconventional notation, etc.

Score notation conventions

- Use oversized time signatures. The conductors are going to write them in anyway.
- Use readable performance indications. Why not write them in English?
- Performance indications should be located in more places than just the top staff. Depending on the size of the ensemble, you could have the indications in the spaces between instrument families. At least try to have them at the top, middle, and bottom (i.e., above Violin 1).
- Watch spacing between all elements. Try to eliminate collisions and remember that not all system spacing is created equally. Parts with double staves (piano, harp, or solo string/gli altri parts) will have spacing needs specific to what the composer wrote. Many times the spacing of the staves will vary (as opposed to the spacing of the systems on the page). Take care that the staves on the system still look like they are relevant to each other.
- Break barlines between instrumental groupings

- Use individual measure numbers that a conductor can actually read. Times New Roman 8 pt bold, fixed-size seems to work well.
- Should you double up parts or have individual parts on each system?
- Watch the positioning of part-specific information
- Identify percussion instruments on each page
- Lay out material out so that it reads "musically." Be aware of how many measures per page.

Your goal is to deliver parts that leave no room for questions. As you will notice, rehearsal time is non-existent, so maximize that time by having parts that are easily understood. If the performer cannot *understand* what you wrote, then you waste the ensemble's time. So you have a wrong note—it happens—if your parts are clean, the performers will tend to minimize your mistake if it is apparent that you cared enough about your product to give them parts that display *respect for the performer*. Really—it makes a big difference. They are not sitting behind your computer, ready to ask questions nor read your mind. They are sitting three feet away from the music, with poor lighting on the stand and spotlights in their eyes. Plan accordingly.

Conventions for part extraction

Print size. I generally extract parts at about 92% to 94% instead of the default 100% page size. When in doubt, compare the size of your staves to the size of staves on a part by a reputable music publisher.

Font selection. Use "normal" fonts. **Really.** Nobody cares about "cutesy" title fonts. *You do not really believe that I hand-wrote any of this, do you?* **HOW ABOUT NOW?** *Is this convincing?* DOES THIS FONT ADD ANYTHING BUT ANNOYANCE TO YOUR PLATE? Just stick to fonts that are found on all computer platforms.

Font size. I have found that using **fixed-sized** fonts allow for minimal re-working between score and parts.

- Titles—Times New Roman 24 pt, bold, fixed
- Text Tempo Indications—Times New Roman 14 pt, bold, fixed
- Metronome Markings—I use a third-party font—12 pt, fixed—but the fonts packaged in your software program will work just fine
- Headers—either Times New Roman 12 or 14 pt bold, fixed

Page turns. If a part is two pages or less, then you do not have to worry about page turns. You can even go three pages, if you plan on having all three taped fan-fold, so they lay flat on a stand. Page turns should occur on right side/odd-numbered pages. Include a cover page in order to facilitate this publishing convention, if needed.

Try to get as many measures of rest as possible to facilitate the turn. Multi-measure rests at the top of the following even-numbered page are the same as rests at the bottom of the odd-numbered page. It is always nice to add the notation (TIME) in those situations. If it is a lightening-fast turn, (V.S.) is always helpful, too. If page turns mean having only a system or two on a page, then do it. The performer should not have to fight your layout in order to perform your music.

Oversized time signatures are always appreciated.

Performance indications with a "timely" placement. Think of it this way: It is a dark (and stormy) night. You are driving and about to cross the river. Would you rather see the sign saying DANGER: BRIDGE OUT before or after you start across the bridge? The same applies to placement of dynamics and other performance indications (SOLO, MUTE, TUTTI, etc.). Are they readable?

Musical phrases can dictate smart choices about the number of measures per line.

Measure numbers are generally found at the start of every system and demonstrated measure ranges should appear on multi-measure rests. For font selection, keep it simple and clear. I use Times New Roman, 12 pt for parts.

Eliminate collisions. Make sure your performance indications do not collide with your actual music. Take care that text and dynamic indications do not clutter the actual notes.

Do not be afraid of white space on the page.

Hiring a professional copyist

Whether you are a composer or a music librarian, I would urge you to enlist the services of a professional music copyist. I know you have some questions:

How does one find a reputable copyist? I would suggest contacting a music librarian at a major orchestra and asking for recommendations. They should be able to provide names of individuals that they have worked with and can be trusted to deliver an excellent product on time. They can give you guidance on pricing when hiring an individual to provide these services, as well. It will be one of the best investments of time you can make.

Is a professional music copyist expensive? My answer is, ultimately, "No." While the initial quote might seem steep, it becomes very reasonable when considering that an experienced music copyist will work with the composer or music arranger in ways that are supposed to save you and your organization time, money, and resources. A professional copyist will provide parts that are extremely legible and leave no question as to the intent of the writer. A professional copyist will also check for mistakes and ask for clarifications that could waste valuable rehearsal time. It will save you, the composer, time in preparing parts for performance, as the individual parts will be laid out to accommodate page turns in an appropriate manner. It will also provide the musicians the opportunity to do their job with material that is neither confusing nor demeaning to read.

Keep in mind that you are paying for a service that, when rendered by a professional, is well worth it. You can be assured that the price of an experienced music copyist is more affordable in the long term than the cost of wasted resources imposed on your organization by someone who merely "owns the program."

Sergeant Major Douglas Richard is the arranger for the United States Military Academy Band at West Point, New York.

(The information presented in this publication has been prepared solely by the author and neither The United States Military Academy Band, the U.S. Army, nor any other component of the Department of Defense of the U.S. Government has endorsed this material.)

The Art of the *Retouche* (Does Beethoven Know What We're Doing?)

by Marshall Burlingame

Our guest conductor, an eminent elder statesman, smiled, graciously shook my hand, and asked, "Do your parts have the *retouche* in the *Egmont* overture?" "Right...," I thought. "*Retouche!*"

In my first years as an orchestra librarian, I had already been called upon to implement various note changes, additions, re-orchestrations, doublings, etc., all with the intent of strengthening or "completing" a musical passage. None of these alterations had ever been presented as a *retouche*, but when the maestro spoke the word, I recognized the appellation for what I had been doing. The metaphor was perfect: the adding of just a bit of color or definition, obviously intended by the artist, without altering or disturbing in any way the canvas of a masterpiece.

Our conductor was referring to the curiously empty-sounding horn chords between measures 259 and 277 in the *Egmont* overture (Example 1), likely the first passage to be cited if you asked an orchestra librarian to define *retouche*. Of course, our venerable parts had long since acquired the additional notes (Example 2), surely implied by Beethoven, but not available in that key on the instruments of his time.

Example 1: *Egmont* overture (original)

Example 2: *Egmont* overture (with retouche)

Egmont is one of the most impeccable examples of a valid *retouche*: quite necessary and arrived at through respectful consideration of the creator's work. But in the realm of musical revisions, this *retouche* lives in an ivory tower.

Cassell's French Dictionary translates *retouche* as "retouching, touching up; finishing (of garments)." The first two definitions are in keeping with our example of *Egmont*. "Finishing," however, is a dangerous gerund, implying satellite creativity, and encompassing the completions of major works like Mozart's Requiem and his Mass in C minor, Puccini's *Turandot*, Berg's *Lulu*, Mahler's Tenth, et al.

Cassell's presents the transitive verb form as "To retouch; to touch up, to improve." Wait, that issues a subsidiary license to tinker! The intransitive form means, for *Cassell's*: "to apply corrections (to)." This invites the world of scholarship, with its "critical editions," into the "big tent" definition of *retouche*.

The *Random House Dictionary of the English Language*, Second Edition, is even more permissive: *retouche*: verb: "to improve with new touches, highlights or the like; touch up or re-work, as a painting or make-up"; noun: "an added touch to a picture, painting, paint job, etc., by way of improvement or alteration; an act of dyeing new growth of hair to blend with previously dyed hair." (!)

No wonder there is such revisionist zeal among conductors, soloists, and scholars! These nuanced definitions clearly reflect the human compulsion to analyze, interpret, and edit. As a result of this trait, an orchestra librarian's work over the course of a career will always be dotted with renovation projects, some seemingly valid, others ranging from whimsical to clumsy and destructive. Following are a few places, among many in the standard repertoire, where this activity is likely to occur.

Beethoven

The mechanical limitations of Beethoven's instruments have inspired tailoring in more of his works than just *Egmont*. In measures 103 and 107 (there is a corresponding place at measures 373–4) of the first movement of the Ninth Symphony, the timpani is sometimes given the contrabass notes, maintaining its presence in the sonority as the orchestra edges up a half-step. (Presumably, this could also apply to the trumpets in these measures.) (Example 3).

Example 3: Beethoven Symphony no. 9, first movement, Timpani and Contrabass, meas. 103–108

There seems no reason to think Beethoven wouldn't have done this had the instruments of his time permitted it, and there are numerous other opportunities in the movement for a modern timpanist to customize the part. Yet the original timpani line is organic to this titanic movement, every detail of which is chiseled in our memory. This kind of post-creative adjustment always sounds twentieth century and "slick" to me.

There is a familiar retouche in the Scherzo of the Ninth that is often applied in one way or another. It consists of doubling the woodwinds with the horns in measures 93–108 and measures 330–345 (measures 623–638 and 860–875 on the return) (Example 4). As one conductor stated, "This strengthens the melodic material so that the strings can play a full *fortissimo* with the rhythmic figure."

Example 4: Beethoven. Symphony No. 9, 2nd movement, 1st and 2nd Horns, meas. 93–110

The Adagio contains the famous solo phrase for fourth horn (measure 96). Beethoven wrote it for a specific fourth hornist whose technically advanced instrument allowed him to produce those notes. It became established practice for the principal hornist, as customary soloist, to play the phrase, but recent decades have seen a new age of virtuosity and flexibility at all positions and it is now common for the fourth player to perform what Beethoven bequeathed him. If, however, the first and fourth players decide to compete for the solo with a game of darts and the first hornist wins, the librarian will be asked to rearrange the parts in some fashion so that all of Beethoven's horn parts are covered while the principal appropriates the solo.

The *presto* octaves that open the Finale present further opportunities for instrumental revision, particularly in the trumpets, which drop in and out in a sort of stutter because the contemporary instruments couldn't produce all the notes in the phrase (Example 5). This line is sometimes filled in completely (Example 6), with the attendant risk that the trumpet color may become predominant in the sonority. The horns in this place can also be treated to segments of "completion."

Example 5: Beethoven. Symphony No. 9, Finale. Trumpet (original).

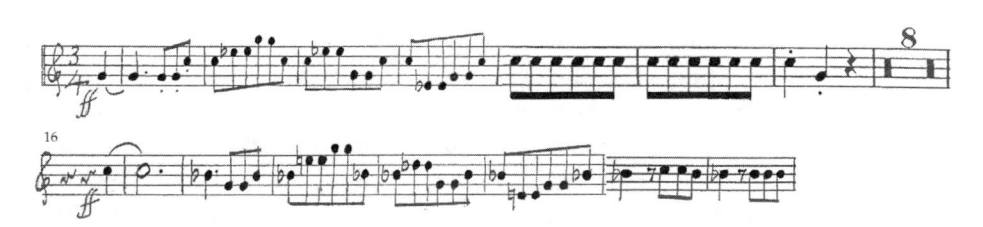

Example 6: Beethoven. Symphony No. 9, Finale. Trumpet (with retouche).

The Finale harbors another possible retouche, called for by Beethoven himself. In the variation of the primary theme in which the first bassoon plays its wonderful counterpoint above the lower strings (measure 116), Beethoven wrote in one manuscript *2do Fag. col B(asso)*, creating a soli bassoon duet. This, too, is beautiful and many people can't decide which sounds "right," the solo bassoon they're used to hearing, or the duet created by Beethoven's eureka moment. One could not be faulted for asserting that Beethoven created two valid choices. In the standard, older Breitkopf edition, the bass part is printed as a cue in the second bassoon part (Example 7). The Bärenreiter edition of Jonathan Del Mar[1] prints the second bassoon line as gospel. In either case, the work is already done for the librarian.

---

1   Ludwig van Beethoven, Symphony No. 9 in D minor, op. 125. Ed. by Jonathan Del Mar (Kassel, New York: Bärenreiter, 1996).

*) Bleistiftbemerkung Beethovens in der Originalhandschrift: 2de Fag. col B(asso); im Erstdruck allerdings nicht berücksichtigt

Example 7: Beethoven. Symphony No. 9, Finale. Bassoons with optional duet cued.

For all the "inevitability" of Beethoven's music, as Leonard Bernstein characterized it in one of his *Omnibus* television programs, people continue to peck away at it, usually in the name of modern instrumental improvements. One guest conductor gave me a list of eighteen revisions for the orchestral parts of the Third Piano Concerto, involving note and rhythm changes and causing the re-voicing of some chords. It all had a kind of logic to it, in the sense of sitting around with some people at a café, looking at the score and discussing what "upgrades" could be made utilizing today's instruments. But it wasn't what Beethoven wrote, and it added nothing to the essence of the piece. I prepared score pages with the changes in red pencil for the next conductor of the concerto, who politely returned them with a request to restore the original in all but two cases.

Schumann

Schumann's music has famously suffered many affronts to its integrity as generations of interpreters have struggled to bring clarity to his thickly orchestrated textures. George Szell's recorded edition of the symphonies was considered definitive in its time. I have never seen the scores, which repose in the Szell collection at Severance Hall. But it was clear when I heard a live performance of the *Rhenish* by Szell and the Cleveland Orchestra that a lot of pruning had been done to feature specific lines, particularly some of the horn passages.

In recent decades, it has become fairly standard practice simply to accept Schumann's orchestration as the composer's unique voice. The feeling is that those rich sonorities are inseparable from the magical atmosphere of Schumann's symphonies which, at their best, represent the essence of a symphony orchestra. Whenever Schumann's music is programmed, however, the librarian has to be aware of the possibility for retouches.

Here are examples of tasteful editing by a guest conductor in recent performances of the *Rhenish* symphony. (Examples 8, 9, and 10)

The Art of the *Retouche* (Does Beethoven Know What We're Doing?)

Example 8: Schumann. Symphony No. 3, 1st movement, 1st Violin, meas. 54–74

Example 9: Schumann. Symphony No. 3, 1st movement, 1st Violin, meas. 143–164

Example 10: Schumann. Symphony No. 3, 1st movement, 1st Violin, meas. 413–438

Perhaps the wildest treatment of Schumann's music occurred at the hands of Shostakovich, who re-orchestrated the Cello Concerto.[2] Schumann's accompaniment acquires the flavor of a Shostakovich orchestra, so that one composer's music is filtered through another composer's voice. Rather than an "improvement" or a "completion," this re-orchestration unfortunately seems more an outright hijacking.

Dvořák

Despite the wonderful and unmistakable sound of Dvořák's orchestration, there are places in his music where retouches seem genuinely necessary. The fabulous *New World* Symphony, culmination of his symphonic achievement, stands very nicely on its own. Only the most compulsive interpreters feel the need to adjust passages in the name of sonority and balance.

A bit more activity seems to have occurred with the Eighth Symphony. An old set of materials in the Boston Symphony library contains some conductorial alterations, including timpani tacets for harmonic clarity and an actual melodic change for oboes in the third movement. The latter falls squarely into the category of "improvements" and presumably was effected without a phone call to Dvořák. Most of the editing, however, involves reinforcing certain passages and there are doubling parts for the woodwinds and trumpets to produce weightier tuttis. The most prominent retouche occurs ten measures from the end of the symphony, where the full sonority suddenly drops out for four bars, leaving the driving rhythm to be played by low woodwinds

---

2   Robert Schumann, Cello Concerto in A minor, op. 129. Orch. by Dmitri Shostakovich, op. 125 (Moscow: Muzyka, 1966; Moscow: DSCH Publishers, in preparation).

and mid-register strings. They are strengthened in the BSO parts by the addition of all four horns, two of whom have just doubled the trombone motive in the preceding four bars (Example 11). The effect of this is undeniably brilliant and clearly thrilled the audience on a BSO tape that I heard, but it's not exactly Dvořák. In any case, the Eighth Symphony is an audience favorite, complete in itself, and is very often performed as the composer left it.

Example 11: Dvořák. Symphony No. 8, 4th movement, 1st and 2nd Horns, meas. 376–383

It is the beautiful Seventh Symphony that is surprisingly in need of help in places and the librarian must always communicate with the conductor about the possible retouches to be applied. Again, the problem seems to arise from the instruments and style of the composer's time. Historically, Czech orchestras have combined light, lyrical brass playing with a shimmering woodwind sound, making for a beautiful, homogeneous sonority that is still characteristic, as anyone who has heard the Czech Philharmonic live can attest. The subtle balances tend to change, however, when Dvořák's music is performed by some modern orchestras with their powerful wind and brass sounds.

This is especially telling in the Seventh Symphony's final bars, where the concluding theme in the woodwinds and second violins is all but obliterated by *fortissimo* whole-note brass chords. The usual remedy is to double the theme with the horns (Example 12) for a majestic peroration (sometimes trumpets are also added, as in Szell's Cleveland Orchestra recording).[3]

---

[3] Antonín Dvořák, Symphony No. 8 in G major, op. 88. Cleveland Orchestra. George Szell, Recorded October/November 1958. Epic LC 3532; reissued CBS Records Masterworks MYK 38470, compact disc.

Example 12: Dvořák. Symphony No. 7, 4th movement, 1st and 2nd Horns, meas. 425–434

One guest conductor asked for the original notation, however, explaining that Wagner's music, in which so much is expressed through harmonic metamorphosis, was the model that composers of Dvořák's time sought to emulate. The Adagio of the Seventh Symphony, in fact, does seem to unfold under a Wagnerian spell. For this conductor, then, the Symphony is a journey from the D-minor world of its opening to a final, glowing D-major in the resplendent brass chords. All this seemed a valid viewpoint to me as I removed the brass retouches at his request. That was the state of the parts for the next guest conductor, to whom I related the Wagner story. "*That's nice,*" he said. "Please restore the horn inserts."

Another common retouche in the finale of this symphony occurs with the rhythmic figure in measures 140–147, notated for first and second horns. The third and fourth horns are often asked to double this figure, giving it more presence against the forceful octave melody played between first and second violins (Example 13). This is a similar balance situation, in reverse, to the horn doublings in the Beethoven Ninth Scherzo (see Example 4). The second time this music occurs (measures 353–360), the violin octaves are a fourth higher and the melody even more sweeping than the first time. Yet here, Dvořák entrusts the rhythmic counterpoint to just oboes and bassoons, so they are frequently doubled by all four horns.

Example 13: Dvořák. Symphony No. 7, 4th movement, 3rd and 4th Horns, meas. 140–147

The horns may be called upon to rescue still another understated figure as they sometimes double, in various combinations, the woodwinds for four measures in the first movement, beginning with the pickups to the second bar of letter C (measures 55–58, plus the pickups).

These are some of the usual revisions to the Seventh Symphony, but there is a passage in the first movement where one Music Director wanted to augment a first-violin melody with half the second violins, leaving the other half to play their accompaniment figure. He asked me to rewrite the second-violin measures for that passage, notating the first and second violin lines together in the body of the part (Example 14).

Example 14: Dvořák. Symphony No. 7, 1st movement, 2nd Violin part.

The Music Director was taking the parts to guest conduct a world famous orchestra. When he returned, I asked him how it had gone and he replied that the passage had worked "beautifully." The retouche itself seemed like a good idea but, to me, the passage looked, and looks, difficult to read and would be much more characteristic of piano notation. I feel sure that our violinists would object to it, and I wouldn't blame them. If I were to do it today, I would put the divided passage on two staves and attach it in the part as a turnable "flap," so that the two lines were clear to both inside and outside players.

Opera

Operatic music can create a type of musical tailoring not covered by our definitions of retouche. Many orchestral programs, both with voices and purely instrumental, consist solely of operatic excerpts. Wagner's music in particular contains episodes of such power that it seems to demand the additional exposure of the concert hall. Stringing together an evening of major Wagnerian segments ("great bleeding chunks from *The Ring*," as it is commonly called) inevitably involves a lot of changes and additions to the music, like concocting an ending for an excerpt or aria, or jumping from one point in an opera to another. There are often passages that need transposing, which can lead to changes in instrumentation and voice-leading. Though such programs are not motivated by the desire to alter or correct a composer's music, they can certainly elicit the full array of retouche activities.

Opera overtures also appear frequently on orchestral concerts. Instead of ending with a flourish, some of them segue directly into the next number in the opera. Providing them with "concert endings" is a long-standing practice, surely a legitimate application of the "finishing" cited in our retouche definitions. This is necessary for Mozart's overtures to *The Abduction from the Seraglio* and *Don Giovanni* (concert endings variously made by Mozart, Johann André, and Feruccio Busoni) and *Idomeneo* (concert endings by Mozart and Carl Reinecke). These concert endings for Mozart's overtures are available from published sources, but some instrumental endings must be created in-house.

Example 15. *Lohengrin*, Prelude to Act III, original ending from the opera.

The Prelude to Act III of *Lohengrin* comes up frequently as an encore and various endings have been devised. Examples 16 and 17 present a longish one, used by Toscanini and available in print, and a rather abbreviated one from the Boston Pops material. Both employ the so-called "Ortrud motif."

Example 16: *Lohengrin*, Prelude to Act III, Toscanini ending

The Art of the *Retouche* (Does Beethoven Know What We're Doing?) **179**

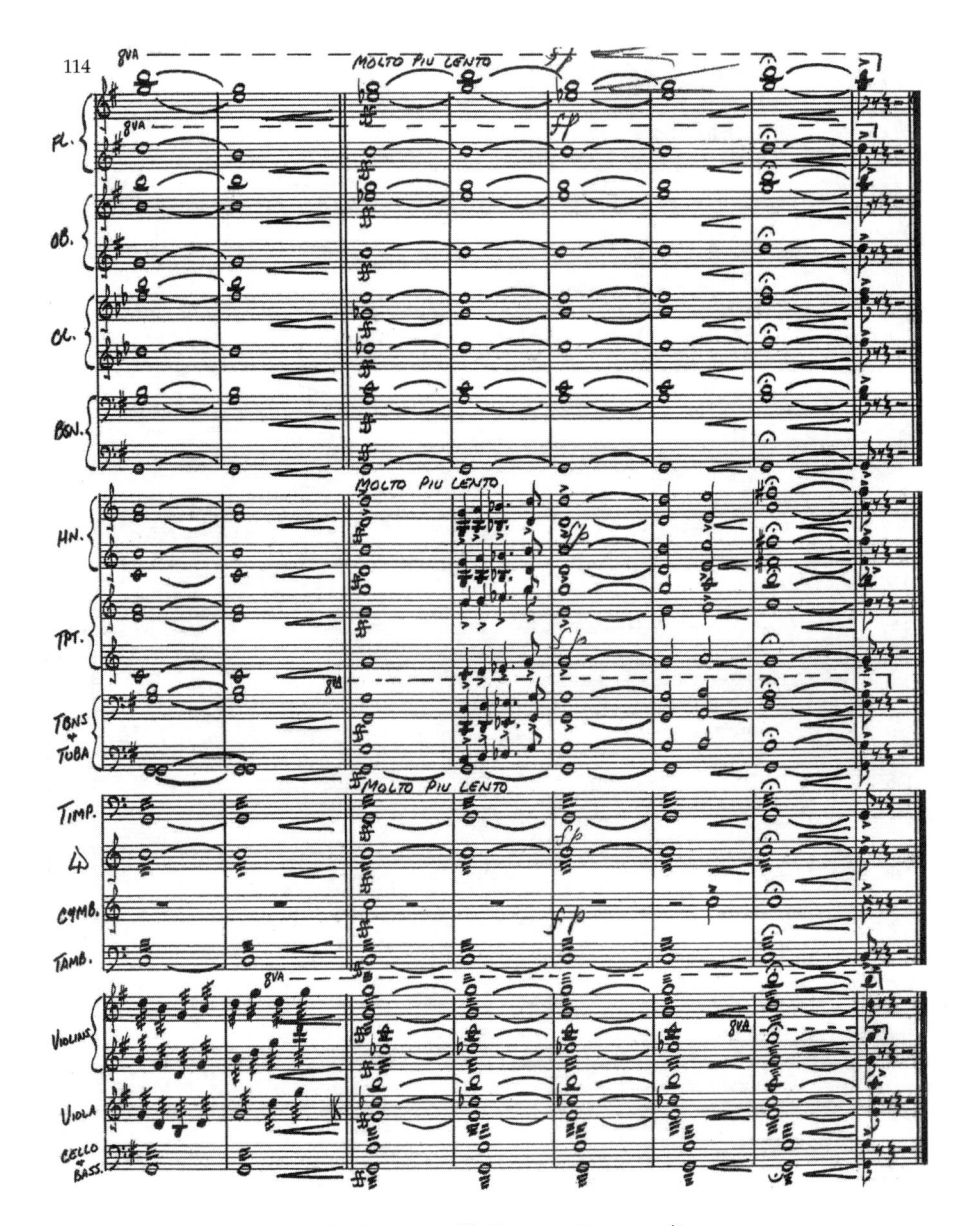

Example 17: *Lohengrin*, Prelude to Act III, Boston Pops ending

The score for this ending bears the inscription "Fiedler–Goossens–St. Louis Symphony ending."

Rossini's overture to *William Tell* already has the ending of endings, but there is a controversy in the Andante that can engender a small "fix." The following excerpt from Luigi Arditi's autobiography, *My Reminiscences*,[4] relates his conversation with Rossini about the famous melodic issue in the English horn solo (Example 18):

> We were chatting together one day about a now well-known passage in the overture of "William Tell" which had always been wrongly played by various orchestras in England. I told him that on my remonstrating during the London rehearsals with my Corno-Inglese player, he replied, "they had always played it thus." On hearing this, Rossini rose from his chair, fetched his *carte-de-visite*, at the back of which he proceeded to inscribe the correct version of the passage in question, while he wrote my name under the photograph. I reproduce, in facsimile, this interesting souvenir. And I also add the bars of music in the incorrect form (B instead of A) in which I had so often heard them played. Need I say that it was not without considerable satisfaction that, on a later occasion, when again conducting "William Tell," I was in a position to triumphantly flash Rossini's photograph and the right bar of music before the stubborn Corno-Inglese, who had formerly presumed to argue the point.

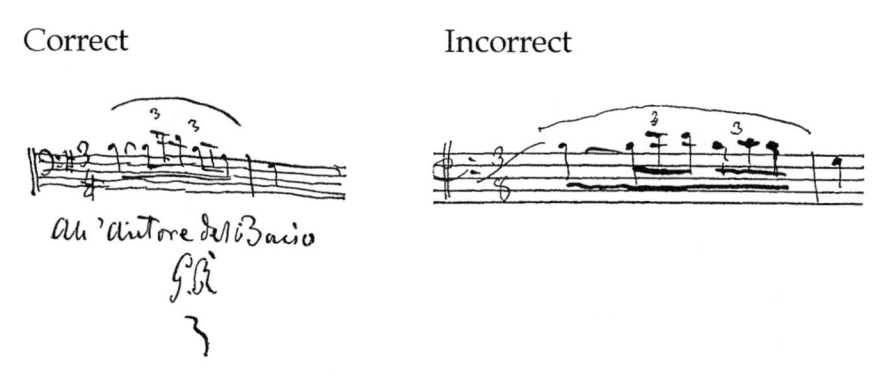

Example 18: Rossini, *William Tell* overture, English horn

Tradition and habit tend to assume the mantle of truth, and though there was a copy of the Arditi anecdote in the Boston Pops materials for *William Tell*, the English horn part stubbornly retained the impostor "B" instead of the "A" vetted by the composer himself. I showed the Arditi to the conductor of a Boston Symphony performance of the overture, who was not receptive to the change. He asked our English hornist to play it both ways and decided that the "B" just felt right. That night, though, he called me in before the concert and said, yes, the "A" was obviously correct once one got used to it and, in any case, we had to do what the composer wanted!

---

4   Luigi Arditi, *My Reminiscences* (New York: Dodd, Mead, 1896), 96–97.

Substituting for the Voice

Voices are sometimes used as a special color in instrumental works. Some examples are the Nielsen Third Symphony ("Sinfonia espansiva"), whose wordless soprano and baritone solo voices are cued into the clarinet and trombone parts; the Vaughan Williams Third Symphony ("The Pastoral"), which can be performed without its solo soprano (or tenor) lines; and Debussy's *Nocturnes*, where the third Nocturne, "Sirènes," calls for eight soprano and eight mezzo voices. Their presence lends so much beauty to the music that it really is not the same piece when they are absent. There *are* purely instrumental performances of "Sirenes," but most conductors program only the first two Nocturnes ("Nuages" and "Fêtes") when voices are not available.

A parallel example is the wordless choral music that creates such an exquisite effect in Ravel's ballet, *Daphnis et Chloé*. There was a letter in the BSO score for the *Daphnis* Second Suite from the publisher, Durand, to Pierre Monteux, granting him permission from Ravel and Diaghilev to perform the ballet at Monte Carlo without voices and describing the instrumental substitutions (Example 19). (The provenance of the letter, now in the orchestra's archives, seems to be: Monteux gave it to Charles Munch, who eventually presented it to the BSO.) Note the reluctance of composer, choreographer, and publisher to allow the retouche, stressing that it was for Monte Carlo *only*. But, of course, it's been performed mostly that way ever since, avoiding the extra hassle of getting singers together. Durand conveniently published the substitute parts, making this another hands-off retouche for the librarian.

Example 19: Letter to Maestro Monteux from Durand music publisher

Composers know all too well the inherent risk in sanctioning "temporary" changes. A score of *Verklärte Nacht* in the BSO library contains a penciled note from librarian Leslie Rogers dated 1934:

Musician in rehearsal: "Will there be a cut, Mr. Schoenberg?"

Guest conductor Arnold Schoenberg: "Cut ... how can I? I wrote the piece. If *I* make a cut, everyone will!"

Brahms

Of course, there are usually many revisions and retouches applied to a new musical work before the musicians and the audience ever hear it. Librarians can get involved in this activity during rehearsals for the premiere, even if there is on-site technical support from the publisher.

The facsimile of the Brahms Violin Concerto provides a fascinating example of "touching up" a work that is already near its final state of perfection. The multi-colored facsimile was produced by the Library of Congress from a manuscript score used by Brahms for conducting the piece.[5] There are annotations throughout in fat blue and red pencil, mostly emphasizing dynamics and structural points to aid Brahms the conductor, and looking very much like the large blue pencil reinforcements in BSO scores used by Serge Koussevitzky. Brahms the composer appears to have made some changes and annotations in a dark grey pencil. And in places, the solo part is revised in a small, precise red ink, likely in the hand of Joseph Joachim, for whom Brahms wrote the work. These are retouches of the most unassailable validity!

In the Preface to the facsimile, Jon Newsom chronicles the Concerto's final evolution, as Joachim takes it to London for a series of performances following the premiere with Brahms in Leipzig. The two friends exchanged suggestions for further revisions in an intimate and feisty correspondence. It's curious to think of this beloved masterpiece crisscrossing Europe as a work in progress.

Yehudi Menuhin's poetic Introduction to the facsimile is full of insight and wonder from an artist who walked, literally, with some of music's masters in his long career. Though addressed to soloists of the Concerto, his final sentence contains words that fairly leap from the page *vis-à-vis* our consideration of retouches: "Let no artist forget how important humility is when facing great works...."

This facsimile (or the original score), of course, would be one of the primary sources for any edition of the piece.

In general, though, Brahms was exceedingly private about the developmental stages of most of his works and he destroyed the earlier versions of virtually all of them. A major exception is the Variations on a Theme by Haydn, which received scholarly treatment as a volume in the Norton Critical Scores series.[6]

---

5   Johannes Brahms, Concerto for Violin, op. 77 (Washington: Library of Congress, 1979).

6   Johannes Brahms, *Variations on a Theme of Haydn for Orchestra, op. 56A and for Two Pianos, op. 56b: the Revised Scores of the Standard Editions, the Sketches, Textual Criticism and Notes, Historical Background, Analytical Essays, Views and Comments*. Ed. by Donald M. McCorkle (New York: Norton, 1976).

Conductor retouches

It was accepted practice until midway through the twentieth century for conductors to exercise a sort of *droit su seigneur* over the repertoire. They approached scores with a free hand, implementing orchestrational and dynamic changes to further their vision of a work. This was seen as serving the composer by enabling the piece to make its best impression in performance.

The tradition of "helping" the composer persisted for a long time. There is an old Breitkopf score of Beethoven's Second Symphony in the Cincinnati Symphony Library. It contains the respectful inscription "Les nuances au crayon sont l'ouvre de Dr. Ernst Kunwald" (an early CSO Music Director), followed by, "And the markings in pencil are the work of an anonymous idiot!"—signed Eugene Goossens (a later CSO Music Director).

Leonard Bernstein had an old set of Beethoven's *Missa solemnis* and I once spent some nineteen out of twenty-four hours restoring the original version by removing various doublings and other re-orchestration. These alterations were made by Dr. Karl Muck, one of the Boston Symphony's early Music Directors. In the Brahms First Symphony archival score in the BSO library, there are penciled horn and other brass retouches by Charles Munch in the introduction and many other places that go far beyond the simple chord completion of *Egmont*. And many of the older sets of standard repertoire pieces in the library contain envelopes of doubling inserts and other retouches by Erich Leinsdorf, one of whose books was entitled *The Composer's Advocate*.[7]

But most of these retouches are like polite suggestions compared to the editing of another prominent conductor. Who would be the likely composer of an orchestral piece that included a woodwind section of 4 flutes, 2 piccolos, 4 oboes, 4 clarinets (4th doubling E-flat clarinet), 4 bassoons, contra bassoon, and that featured devices like "Schalltrichter in der Höhe" and *gestopft* horns? If you guessed Mahler, you're half right. The work is called "Symphony No. 5 in C-minor, Op. 67" by an earlier composer named Beethoven, published by Weinberger in 2011 "mit GUSTAV MAHLERS Retuschen."

Along with the expanded woodwinds, Mahler adds two more horns, utilizing them to reinforce some passages and to aid in re-voicing others, as when he has two of them replace the clarinets so that they, in turn, can double the flutes above the staff in a characteristic Mahlerian wail. And all those extra winds double Beethoven's notes in massive, *fortissimo* sonorities at climactic points, as if segments of the score were written in magic marker. Even the little *fermata cadenza* for oboe in the first movement is marked "a 2" and has wedge accents or dashes over every note except the turn.

Thus, Mahler uses many of his own orchestral techniques in his mission to enhance Beethoven's expression. We should be grateful that someone was able to rescue the original work from its obscurity.

---

7   Erich Leinsdorf, *The Composer's Advocate: A Radical Orthodoxy for Musicians* (New Haven: Yale University Press, 1981).

Mahler didn't hesitate to make such retouches to the music of other composers and he constantly adjusted the orchestration of his own works, sometimes for acoustic or personnel factors related to a specific performance. Many of his works were republished to incorporate the ongoing changes, which have ultimately been assimilated into "critical editions" purporting to be his final word on the pieces. "Maybe," one is tempted to say, "but only because he doesn't conduct anymore!"

The young Bruno Walter and Otto Klemperer spent time as apprentices to Mahler, faithfully executing overnight his retouches in time for the next rehearsal. Significantly, he is reported to have said to them at one point, "Boys, when I'm gone, change anything you want, as long as it sounds good!"

But not every composer is blessed with the enlightenment of a Walter or a Klemperer. One has to think that many composers, finding themselves in the present, would seize the chance to protest the retouches to their music, an opportunity actually afforded Stravinsky:

The prominent theatrical producer, Billy Rose, had engaged Stravinsky to contribute some ballet music (which became ultimately his *Scenes de ballet*) for the 1944 revue *The Seven Lively Arts*. Rose liked what Stravinsky wrote but apparently felt that his orchestration wasn't flashy enough; how to suggest that diplomatically? He agonized over it and finally exchanged telegrams with the great composer, as cited by Eric Walter White in *Stravinsky, The Composer and His Works*:[8]

> *Rose*: YOUR MUSIC GREAT SUCCESS STOP COULD BE SENSATIONAL SUCCESS IF YOU WOULD AUTHORISE ROBERT RUSSELL BENNETT RETOUCH ORCHESTRATION STOP BENNETT ORCHESTRATES EVEN THE WORKS OF COLE PORTER
>
> *Stravinsky*: SATISFIED WITH GREAT SUCCESS.

At least we live in a time when editing music for performance is aided by serious scholarship, resulting in a general desire for informed authenticity. And it is an unshakable tenet for most musicians that the composer's notes are sacred.

One of our Carnegie Hall concerts included the Tchaikovsky Third Symphony, in which the Trio of the Scherzo ends with a sequence of arpeggios dovetailing across the orchestra. The passage sounds somehow incorrect. You can see that Tchaikovsky perhaps was following a linear construct that caused a collateral intervallic oddness. The players were bothered by it but neither they nor the conductor knew what they wanted to do.

After the rehearsal, one of the players said to me, "I saw one of our guest conductors here today. He's a composer and an improviser. If he's still in the building, maybe he would have an idea."

Luckily, I found him, heading purposefully for the exit stairs. "Hey, do you have a minute for a harmonic question in Tchaikovsky?" I asked. He stopped, impatient but intrigued.

---

8 Eric Walter White, *Stravinsky, The Composer and His Works* (2nd ed. Berkeley: University of California Press, 1984), 421.

"A *harmonic* question in *Tchaikovsky*?!" he wondered as he followed me to the music trunk. "But why ask me?"

"Because you're an all-around harmonic genius," I replied.

"Oh," he said. "I forgot."

He glanced at the score page and said "OH!! Well, in the best of all worlds, I would change this and this. But that would be re-writing, and I'd never do it!"

Yet it is true that the conductor's responsibility is to present a piece in its most favorable light. The retouches discussed herein are all manifestations of that endeavor. The common denominator for those who made them is conviction: they earnestly believed they were getting it right. Each retouche is a reminder of the complex, ambiguous nature of music throughout the centuries.

Music is a mirror image of the humans who write and listen to it: its essence is elusive, it exists only in forward motion, and it's always a little different from one occasion to the next. Music is a re-creative art, and despite the black and white documentation that is our touchstone, artistic and interpretive input will always be needed and the application of retouches will continue.

We can only hope for the approach articulated with great respect by a distinguished guest conductor of the BSO, who said (*vis-à-vis* a critical edition of Beethoven 9), "I feel *certain* that some things I do are right. It's an intuition from long study and experience."

In the absence of such hard-won insight, though, it seems best to follow the recommendation of two other astute musical philosophers: *Let It Be.*

Marshall Burlingame is the Principal Librarian of the Boston Symphony Orchestra.

INDEX

A

accession numbers. *See* shelf arrangement
acquisitions 48–51, 64, 81–82, 88–89
  jazz music 34–35
  ordering music 21, 50
  renting music 53–54. *See also* rental music
advance planning 10, 34, 43, 81, 88–94
  management responsibilities 134
  pops orchestra 114–115
advocacy for the library 84–86, 154–160
Alpert, Victor 145
American Society of Composers, Authors and Publishers (ASCAP) 15, 54, 64, 99, 117, 122, 123, 125, 129, 136, 148
arranging materials on shelves. *See* shelf arrangement
ArtsVision. *See* Orchestra Management Solutions (OMS)
audition excerpts 17, 24, 39
auditions (librarians). *See* performance librarian–auditions and interviews

B

ballet
  advance planning 89
ballet librarian 23–31
  grand rights 129
  music preparation 25–27, 142
  terminology 25
band and wind ensemble librarian 2–5, 37–39, 44–46
  acquisitions 95, 102, 118
  performing rights 125
  world parts 4
Bärenreiter 100, 103–104, 121, 169
Beethoven, Ludwig van 19, 103–104, 112, 133, 174
  editions 103
  retouche 166–170, 184, 186

Berlioz, Hector 49, 105
Bernstein, Leonard 130, 143, 170, 184
Bierley, Paul E. *See* Rehrig, William H., *The Heritage Encyclopedia of Band Music*
big band. *See* jazz ensemble
Bill Holab Music (Brooklyn, NY) 112
Bizet, Georges 105
Bonner Katalog: Verzeichnis reversgebundener musikalischer Aufführungsmateriale 101
Boosey & Hawkes 52–55, 100, 141
Boston Pops Orchestra (Boston, MA) 50, 113, 177, 180, 181
Boston Symphony Orchestra (Boston, MA) 144, 145, 172, 181, 184, 186
Brahms, Johannes 59, 157–158
  editions 104
  retouche 183–184
Breitkopf and Härtel 100, 103, 169, 184
Broadcast Music, Inc. (BMI) 15, 54, 64, 99, 117, 122, 125, 129, 136, 148
Broude Brothers Limited 98–99
Bruckner, Anton
  editions 104
budget 11, 17, 24, 38, 49, 76, 84–85, 89, 94, 133, 134. *See also* rental music–fees
  rental fees 53
Buschkötter, Wilhelm, and Hansjürgen Schaefer, *Handbuch der Internationalen Konzertliteratur, Instrumental-und Vokalmusik* 101

C

Cage, John 112
  proofreading system 107–108
care and handling. *See* preservation of music materials
cataloging 17, 67
  database 133, 137
  information to include 19–20
  jazz collections 33
  single-copy reference file 21
Chicago Symphony (Chicago, IL) 148
choral library 19–22
choreographers 25–28, 142

Cleveland Orchestra (Cleveland, OH) 106, 170, 173
climate control. *See* preservation of music materials
collecting music. *See* distributing and collecting music
collection assessment 19
college and conservatory librarian 16–18
commissions 34, 38, 91–92
  budgeting 94
communication 11, 43, 55, 63, 64, 70, 72–80, 81, 85, 89, 91, 113, 123, 152. *See also* conductors–communication with
community ensembles 13, 49, 99
composers 35, 40, 45, 47, 50, 74, 91, 107–108, 114, 116, 119, 123, 140, 183, 185
  rights 13–14, 49, 53, 54
  student composers 16, 161
computer applications 4, 38, 64, 77, 85, 88, 132, 142, 152
  database 133, 155
  ensemble management software 134
  music notation 8, 27, 32, 36, 41, 47, 94, 105, 110, 112, 119, 161–162
  SharePoint 158
  websites 159
concert procedures 7, 24, 28, 117
conductors 21, 26, 37–38, 43, 44–46, 84, 86, 89, 104, 114, 135–136
  and editions 8, 21, 43, 50, 81, 89, 103–104, 105,
  communication with 21, 26, 43, 44, 46, 49, 57, 63, 70, 86, 88, 92–93, 105, 114, 170, 173
  retouche 168, 170, 174, 184–186
  sample contact letter 92–93
  student conductors 16
conservatory librarian. *See* college and conservatory librarian
copyright 8, 14, 44–45, 53, 64, 85, 91, 99, 120–124, 129. *See also* performing rights
  fair use 121–123

public domain 21, 103, 120, 152
reproduction of copyrighted material 123, 145
critical editions 103–105, 167, 185–186

D

Dallas Symphony Orchestra (Dallas, TX) 86
Daniels, David 4, 13, 15, 62, 81–82, 95–97, 100, 101
Daniels, David, and John Yaffé. *Arias, Ensembles & Choruses: An Excerpt Finder for Orchestras* 97
Del Mar, Norman and Jonathan 103–104, 169
distributing and collecting music 11, 21–22, 24, 38, 41, 82
Dolan, Jimmy 145
Durand & Cie. 100, 182
Dvořák, Antonín 59, 172–179

E

editions 43, 44, 48–52, 62, 69, 81, 89, 103–106, 135
  choral music 19–20
  opera 7–8, 89
Educational Music Service (EMS) (Chester, NY) 18, 51, 95
educational programs 35
  advance planning 91
education for the performance librarian 5, 8, 14–15, 17–18, 33, 61–64. *See also* reference materials
Edwin A. Fleisher Collection (Free Library of Philadelphia) 97–98
Edwin F. Kalmus & Co., Inc. 31, 98
employment opportunities 5, 12, 15, 18, 28–29, 36. *See also* mentorship
  internships 6, 10, 67
emusicquest Music-In-Print series 97
environment. *See* preservation of music materials
equipment. *See* photocopier; *See* supplies
equipment and supplies. *See* supplies
errata 5, 26, 54, 69, 81–82, 142, 162

Eulenburg (Edition Eulenburg) scores 104
European American Music Distributors LLC 13–15, 49, 52, 100

F
festival librarian 10–12, 16, 18
film and studio librarian 40–41
Finnish Music Information Centre 118–119
Fleisher Collection. *See* Edwin A. Fleisher Collection (Free Library of Philadelphia)
Florida Orchestra (St. Petersburg, FL) 117

G
Glimmerglass Festival (Cooperstown, NY) 10–12
grand rights. *See* performing rights–grand rights
grants and foundation awards 85, 119, 137, 160

H
Hamlisch, Marvin 113, 117
Harry Fox Agency (HFA) 126
Henderson, Lyle "Skitch" 113, 117
hire music. *See* rental music

I
IAMIC. *See* International Association of Music Information Centres)
Indianapolis Symphony Orchestra (Indianapolis, IN) 114, 138
instrumentation. *See* orchestration
International Association of Music Information Centres (IAMIC) 102, 118. *See also* Music Information Centres
International Music Score Library Project (IMSLP) 9, 101
interview. *See* performance librarian–auditions and interviews

J
Jazz at Lincoln Center (New York, NY) 32–36
jazz ensemble 2–4, 16, 37, 118
jazz ensemble librarian 32–36
Juilliard School (New York, NY) 6. 9, 43, 107
JoAnn Kane Music Service (Culver City, CA) 40–41, 157

K
Kansas City Symphony (Kansas City, MO) 71
Karlsruhe Virtual Catalog (KVK) 98
Kaye, Danny 154, 157

L
Leinsdorf, Erich 184
library
    as information hub 2, 7, 17, 24, 72–75
Library of Congress (Washington, D.C.) 122, 153, 183
    online catalog 99
licensing. *See* performing rights–licensing
Los Angeles Philharmonic (Los Angeles, CA) 78, 80, 145
Luck's Music Library 98

M
Mahler, Gustav
    editions 104
    retouche 167, 184–185
Major Orchestra Librarians' Association (MOLA) 8, 12, 15, 18, 64, 66, 70, 82, 85–86, 128, 130, 145, 147, 161
Manning, Lucy. *Orchestral "Pops" Music* 96
Masconomet High School (Topsfield, MA) 39
McGill University (Montreal, Quebec, Canada) 16, 18
mechanical licensing. *See* performing rights–recording (mechanical licensing)
mentorship 18, 64, 65–71
Menuhin, Yehudi 157, 183
Metropolitan Opera (New York, NY) 6, 94, 102, 130
Meyer, Dirk. *Chamber Orchestra and Ensemble Repertoire: A Catalog of Modern Music* 96

Milwaukee Symphony Orchestra (Milwaukee, WI) 83
Minnesota Orchestra (Minneapolis, MN) 65, 68
MOLA. *See* Major Orchestra Librarians' Association (MOLA)
Monteux, Pierre 182
Mozart, Wolfgang 58
 editions 103–104
 retouche 167, 175–176
music copying 41, 59, 94, 142, 161–165
 hiring a professional copyist 164
music dealers 48–51, 95, 99, 105
music editing 24–27, 45, 140–143, 166–186. *See also* proofreading
music engraving. *See* computer applications–music notation
Music Information Centres 102, 118–119. *See also* International Association of Music Information Centres (IAMIC)
music notation 47, 140–142, 161–163, 174
 parts 163–164
 scores 162–163
music preparation 7, 10–11, 24–26, 33, 41, 59, 63, 77, 81–83, 86, 92, 116, 141, 163
 pops music 114–116
Music Publishers Association (MPA) 85, 122, 123, 126
 Directory of publisher imprints 101

N

National Symphony Orchestra (Washington, D.C.) 12, 75
New England Conservatory (Boston, MA) 22
New World Symphony (Miami, FL)
 library fellowship program 6
New York Philharmonic (New York, NY) 60, 64, 144
Nieweg, Clinton F. 10. *See also* Orchestra Library Information (OLI) Yahoo! group

O

offstage parts 7–8

opera 105, 129, 140
 advance planning 89–90
 galas 7, 90
 retouche 175–181
 transliteration 90
opera librarian 6–12, 16
Orchestra Library Information (OLI) Yahoo! group 70, 99
Orchestral Music Online 95–96, 100. *See also* Daniels, David
Orchestra Management Solutions (OMS) 134
Orchestra Planning and Administration System (OPAS) 69–70, 101, 134, 160
orchestration 4, 9, 20, 24, 43, 53, 57–58, 62, 70, 73, 82, 113–114, 116–117, 134–136
outreach 84–86, 154. *See also* public relations

P

performance librarian. *See also* personal characteristics
 as musician 59, 63, 84
 auditions and interviews 2, 61–64
 qualifications 37–38, 57–60
performing rights 8, 13–15, 17, 64, 99, 120. *See also* copyright
 broadcasting 17, 49, 55, 125
 concert performance (small rights) 125, 129
 grand rights 8, 15, 55, 90, 125, 129–130
 licensing 2, 8, 15, 45, 54, 64, 120–130
 recording (mechanical licensing) 17, 49, 126–127
performing rights organizations (PROs) 54, 74, 118, 125, 129–130. *See also* American Society of Composers, Authors and Publishers (ASCAP); *See also* Broadcast Music, Inc. (BMI); *See also* Society of Composers, Authors and Music Publishers of Canada (SOCAN); *See also* Society of European Stage Authors and Composers (SESAC)

personal characteristics 17, 37–38, 43, 46, 59, 69–70
    attention to detail 8, 33, 43, 75, 86
    knowledge of repertoire 5, 8, 17, 29, 44, 62, 89
    work values 76–77
Petrucci Music Library. *See* International Music Score Library Project (IMSLP)
Philadelphia Orchestra (Philadelphia, PA) 10, 102, 144
photocopier 38, 131–132
pops orchestra 113–117
    advance planning 90–91, 114
    checklist 115
    reference materials 96, 116
P R D A M Pd T Ex (proofreading system) 107–108, 111
premiere performances 17, 40, 47, 112, 142, 183
preparation. *See* advance planning; *See* music preparation
preservation of music materials 4, 150–153, 154
processing music 17, 21, 73
proofreading 107–112
    proofreader's markings 109–119
public relations 74, 154–160. *See also* outreach
    library website 159
publishers 13–15, 18, 21, 24, 49–51, 52–55, 64, 82, 99, 100, 105, 112, 122–125, 129, 141. *See also* rental librarian
    ballet publishers 30–31
    jazz publishers 35

R

Ravel, Maurice 97, 140
    retouche 182
record keeping 4–5, 24, 43, 45, 69, 74, 77, 117, 136, 142, 147
reference materials 4–5, 8, 15, 29–30, 62, 64, 66, 77, 78, 82, 95–97, 101–102, 116
    copyright and licensing 128, 130
    jazz 35–36
    preservation 153
    websites 9, 21, 30–31, 52, 85–97, 99–102, 116
rehearsal procedures 6–7, 17, 26–27, 117
Rehrig, William H., *The Heritage Encyclopedia of Band Music* 102
rental librarian 13–15, 52–55
rental music 3, 14, 48–49, 52–55, 135–136
    fees 53, 129–130
repertoire research 44–45, 50, 52, 62, 95–102, 103–106, 116, 119
reprint editions 8, 98–99. 103–105
retouche 166–186
Robbins, Lou 144
Rossini, Gioachino
    editions 105
    retouche 180–181

S

San Diego Symphony 132
San Francisco Ballet (San Francisco, CA) 23
San Francisco Symphony (San Francisco, CA) 144, 149
Schoenberg, Arnold 183
school librarian 37–39. *See also* college and conservatory librarian
    responsibilities 38–39
Schumann, Robert
    editions 104
    retouche 170–172
score reading 57–59
scoring. *See* orchestration
Seattle Symphony (Seattle, WA) 154–160
shelf arrangement 4
Shostakovich, Dmitri 172
Society of Composers, Authors and Music Publishers of Canada (SOCAN) 54, 129
Society of European Stage Authors and Composers (SESAC) 125, 129
stage band. *See* jazz ensemble

stage band parts (opera) 7
Stravinsky, Igor 25, 154, 157, 185
studio librarian. *See* film and studio librarian
supplies 11, 63
   for tours 147
   music folders 146
   music storage 3–4
   travel cases 146–147
synchronization. *See* performing rights–broadcasting
Szell, George 170, 173

T

Tafoya, John 65
Taynton, Jessie 144
Tchaikovsky, Piotr Ilyich 25
   retouche 185–186
terminology 25, 58, 63
tours 2–3, 23–24, 64, 144–
   preparation 3
   supplies 147
   travel cases 146–147
transliteration 90, 108

U

United States Army Field Band and Soldiers' Chorus (Fort George Meade, MD) 2
United States Marine Band (Washington, D.C.) 44–46, 128, 153
United States Military Academy Band (West Point, NY) 165
University of Washington (Seattle, WA) 155–156

V

vocal music 49, 91
   retouche 182
   vocal scores 8, 16, 48, 89–90, 97

W

Wagner, Richard 105, 174
   retouche 175–180
Weill, Kurt 48
WorldCat.org 95

Y

Yaffé, John, and David Daniels. *Arias, Ensembles & Choruses: An Excerpt Finder for Orchestras* 97
young persons concerts
   advance planning 91